A DICTIONARY OF BORGES

A DICTIONARY OF BORGES

Evelyn Fishburn & Psiche Hughes

Forewords by Mario Vargas Llosa
& Anthony Burgess

Duckworth

First published in 1990 by
Gerald Duckworth & Co. Ltd.
The Old Piano Factory
43 Gloucester Crescent, London NW1 7DY

ISBN 0 7156 2154 8

British Library Cataloguing in Publication Data

Fishburn, Evelyn
  A dictionary of Borges.
  1. Fiction in Spanish. Argentinian writers. Borges,
Jorge Luis, 1899–1986. Critical studies
  I. Title II. Hughes, Psiche
  863

  ISBN 0–7156–2154–8

Photoset in North Wales by
Derek Doyle & Associates, Mold, Clwyd.
Printed in Great Britain by
Redwood Press Ltd, Melksham.

Contents

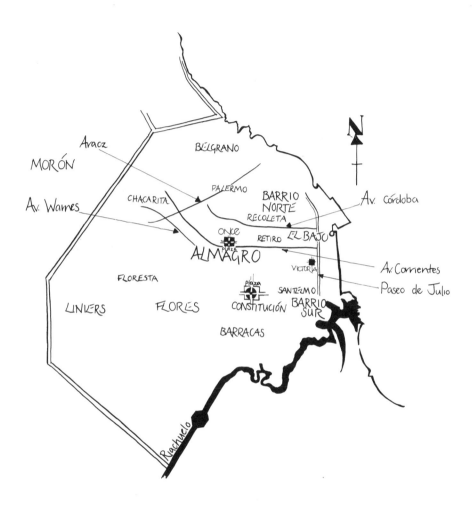

Buenos Aires

For F.J.F. & P.H.

Foreword by Mario Vargas Llosa

This is a book that would have been to Borges's taste. Although he used to pride himself on never having read anything that was written about his life or his work, I am sure he would have read it from beginning to end. This is because it is a book of imaginative erudition, or erudite fantasy, an unusual combination which he used with greater originality than anyone else, so that the genre, though of the greatest antiquity, seems now almost to have been invented by him. Like the strange sect of 'Tlön, Uqbar, Orbis Tertius' which wished secretly to interpolate a fictitious universe into the real one, Borges too, throughout his life as a writer, sought to distil beings, titles and events which his fantasy had forged into the history and literature of reality. Now they are part of them, as consistent and truthful as those which existed in objective time and real life.

With true erudition, this dictionary organises, classifies, defines, collates the thousand and one creatures of Borges's imagination, constructing a map, in the minutest detail, of its geographies and constellations. It is an entertaining manual for exploring the vastness and cohesion of the Borgesian *oeuvre*, an excellent guide to prevent us from getting lost in the labyrinth and to ensure that we always find the way out.

M.V.L.

Foreword by Anthony Burgess

I had a strong personal affection for Jorge Luis Borges. This, I think, was reciprocated and reinforced by the fact that we both had the same surname. At a party in the Argentine Embassy in Washington DC, when he was dogged by spies listening for words of disaffection, he and I spoke in Anglo-Saxon. This baffled completely the polyglot agents of a repressive state; it was very Borgesian. His life and his work tended to overlap: his work was magic and he had the face of a magician. His blindness only made him see more. Compared with the blockbusting novelists of our age, Borges must seem to have written practically nothing. But his *ficciones*, delicate, enigmatic, metaphysical, represent some of the most exquisite probing into the reality that twentieth-century literature has seen. He has created a whole world, and this dictionary serves to indicate how large this world is: we need a gazetteer to find our way round it. It is primarily an intellectual world, and it is built on the oldest of all intellectual dichotomies – the clash between nominalism and idealism. If we are nominalists, we have to say that only particulars are real, and that the universals are no more than words. A nominalist fiction-writer would have to have separate words for all the tigers, oranges, dishwashers and prostitutes in the world, but such a situation could never be handled. Fiction-writers have to use generalities, and this makes them, in the philosophical sense of the term, idealists. Borges is all too aware of his idealism, and a good deal of his work is a slap in the face of the nominalists. Thus when he constructs the Great Library of Babel, it has to be coextensive with the universe, since it contains every possible book, and the books are made, regardless of meaning, out of every possible combination of letters of the alphabet. Take also the character with total recall who wants to write but cannot, since to create logarithms for memories is beyond any man's power. To write his autobiography would require another life.

These are some of the metaphysical tricks that Borges plays. The eponym of *Doctor Brodie's Report* meets a tribe whose language has no words for artefacts. They call a hut a tree and they would have to call a book 'tree' too. Then there is the imaginary planet called Tlön which seems to have been designed by Bishop Berkeley: there is no space or time in it, only succession, and the language has no nouns, since speakers have no conception of matter independent of their perceptions. Evidently such tricks could not be played in a *ficción* the length of *Ulysses* or

Middlemarch, and Borges's limitation of form is, by an anomaly, an index of the width of his speculative power. His short stories are not the product of short-windedness, in the manner of the composer Anton Webern, but examples of a wholly original genre whose bulk and resonance depend, by that anomaly again, on an elected brevity.

The range of the *ficciones*, as of the poems, is wide enough not merely to justify the making of a lexicographical guide to them but to render it a necessity. Borges knew the world of the pampas and had read *Martín Fierro*, but he was a librarian by profession, unashamedly bookish, and had read more widely than any of his contemporaries, even his senior James Joyce. The reading he did nourished his fiction, and some of it was very abstruse. We need a dictionary to get the logarithms of it, and this is the dictionary we need. I welcome it.

The last time I saw Borges was in 1982, when we were both guests of the city of Dublin at the Joyce centennial celebrations. He gave a little talk about Joyce's importance after a banquet which was, in the Irish manner, highly bibulous, and most of its guests, who did not know who the hell he was, talked throughout his discourse. That, we may say, was the response of the great philistine world. Borges remains a taste to be cultivated, a name known and even feared but not destined to be popular. But he was no hermetic man. I drank Irish whiskey with him in the rowdy bar of the Ormonde Hotel and he said: 'What a beautiful word is mist.' I forbore to say that in German it meant manure. He would have reconciled the disparities without trouble and, if his writing days had not been done, made a *ficción* out of it. He was all magic.

Let us not pretend that Borges, for all his personal approachability, was ever easy to approach as a writer. Even when we think that we fully understand, we are often led astray by our failure to identify a reference, an allusion, a carefully planted ambiguity. That is where this dictionary comes in. We have needed it for a long time, and new readers of the master as well as old will bless its compilers. It is also, apart from its value as an aid, compulsively readable in itself. The blind Borges would have loved to have had it read out to him. That is, alas, one chance our lexicographers have missed. But they certainly help the rest of us.

A.B.

Abbreviations

English

Fict.	*Fictions*. London: Harrap, 1967
Lab.	*Labyrinths*. Harmondsworth: Penguin, 1970
Aleph	*The Aleph and Other Stories*. London: Picador, 1973
Brodie	*Doctor Brodie's Report*. Harmondsworth: Penguin, 1972

American

Lab.	*Labyrinths*. New York: New Directions, 1962
Ficc.	*Ficciones*. New York: Grove Press, 1962
Aleph	*The Aleph and Other Stories*. New York: Dutton, 1978
Brodie	*Doctor Brodie's Report*. New York: Dutton, 1978

Spanish

Ficc.	*Ficciones*. Buenos Aires: Emecé, 1956
Aleph	*El Aleph*. Buenos Aires: Emecé, 1957
Brodie	*El informe de Brodie*. Buenos Aires: Emecé, 1970

Within the entries other works by Borges are referred to; their titles are abbreviated as follows:

English and American

Other Inq.	*Other Inquisitions*. Austin: Texas U. Press, 1964
Imaginary Beings	*The Book of Imaginary Beings*. New York: Dutton, 1969
Infamy	*Universal History of Infamy*. Harmondsworth: Penguin, 1970
Sel. Poems	*Selected Poems*. London: Allen Lane, 1972
Introd. Eng. Lit.	*Introduction to English Literature*. London: Robson Books, 1974

Spanish

Inq.	*Inquisiciones.* Buenos Aires: Proa, 1925
Esperanza	*El tamaño de mi esperanza.* Buenos Aires: Proa, 1926
Ev. Carr.	*Evaristo Carriego.* Buenos Aires: Emecé 1954
Etern.	*Historia de la eternidad.* Buenos Aires: Emecé, 1956
Disc.	*Discusión.* Buenos Aires: Emecé, 1954
Hac.	*El hacedor.* Buenos Aires: Emecé, 1957
O.P.	*Obra poética* (1923-1964). Buenos Aires: Emecé, 1964
Leop. Lug.	*Leopoldo Lugones* (con Betina Edelberg). Buenos Aires: Pleamar, 1965
Cuentos breves	Cuentos breves y extraordinarios (con A. Bioy Casares). Buenos Aires: Rueda, 1967
Oro Tigre	*El oro de los tigres.* Buenos Aires: Emecé, 1972
Pról.	*Prólogos. Con un prólogo de prólogos.* Buenos Aires: Torre Agüero Editor, 1975
25 Agosto	*Veinticinco Agosto 1983 y otros cuentos de Jorge Luis Borges.* Madrid: Ediciones Siruela, 1977
Lit. germ.	*Literaturas germánicas medievales* (con María Esther Vázquez). Buenos Aires: Emecé, 1978
Siete noches	*Siete noches. Conferencias.* Buenos Aires: Fondo de Cultura Económica, 1980
Ens. dantescos	*Nueve ensayos dantescos.* Madrid: Espasa Calpe, 1982
Borges mem.	*Borges el memorioso.* Mexico: Fondo de Cultura Económica, 1982

Introduction

'He was dissuaded from this by two considerations: his awareness that the task was interminable, his awarenes that it was useless.'
J.L. Borges, 'Funes the Memorious'

'One may envision some decades hence a Borges encyclopaedia ...the work of a group of people devoted to the annihilation of the external universe and its replacement with a universe made by a human being, with its own inevitable logic and order. That human being will in time recede as a physical being and achieve the status of an idea. Then those future generations of scholars will forget the existence of English or Argentine or Latin literatures. The world will be Borges.'
D. Balderston, *The Literary Universe of Jorge Luis Borges*

The work of Jorge Luis Borges is intensely erudite, and its wealth of allusions may at times baffle and even discourage readers. The main purpose of this *Dictionary* is to explain these allusions, both for the general reader, by providing comprehensive information to make the text more immediately accessible, and for the specialist. The references, real and imaginary, with which Borges's fiction is interwoven form an echoing subtext, supporting and enriching the surface plots of his stories. Rarely gratuitous or merely ornamental, they reveal not only deliberate choice, but a remarkable degree of appositeness: in almost every case the allusion can be seen either to go with the grain of the story or to stand in parodic confrontation with it.

The *Dictionary*, which was undertaken after consulting Borges and with his encouragement, is concerned primarily with the stories that comprise the original collections published as *Ficciones* (1942), *El Aleph* (1949) and *El informe de Brodie* (1970). References are to the English and American versions and also to the Spanish originals, except in a few cases where the allusion occurs only in the Spanish text. Below each entry are page references in the following order: first to the English, secondly to the American (in brackets), and finally to the Spanish (in italics). Only the first page in any one story is recorded; but points of specific contextual relevance are indicated in the main body of the entry, where the references are to the English and American editions only. No page reference is given for generic entries, such as Buenos Aires.

Borges's often old-fashioned spelling of names has been adopted, though in most cases there is some cross-reference to modern spelling.

1

Introduction

The references explained include names of, or allusions to, personal or fictional characters, places, titles, quotations, and philosophical and religious movements. As well as factual information, the entries inevitably involve a certain amount of critical interpretation, but no attempt has been made to impose 'solutions' – the idea is to offer a range of the possible meanings that are suggested through the interaction of each allusion with the overall structure of the text. For example, the entry on Spinoza gives some basic information on his life and work, but highlights those aspects considered most relevant to the stories in which his name appears: his attempt to construct a complete coherent system of metaphysiscs is emphasised in connection with 'Tlön, Uqbar, Orbis Tertius', just as his geometrical method of philosophical exposition is crucial to the plot of 'Death and the Compass'.

The explanation of well-known names, such as Shakespeare, is limited to the particular connotations in Borges's usage; allusions considered more recondite are covered more fully. Given the tenuous dividing line between real and fictional names, the same format of surname followed by Christian name has been adopted for both.

Place names in Buenos Aires and in the area surrounding the River Plate basin are illustrated in the two maps provided.

In writing this Dictionary we have had frequent recourse to the obvious encyclopaedias and other works of reference which Borges might have consulted. A list of these would be overlong and appear ostentatious but perhaps the 11th edition of the Encyclopaedia Britannica should be singled out for special indebtedness. Similarly, all the major critical works on Borges have been consulted, but we should like to mention two which have been constant companions: M. Bervellier's *Le cosmopolitisme de Jorge Luis Borges*, Paris 1973, for help with allusions in Borges's complete oeuvre, and E. Rodríguez Monegal's *Jorge Luis Borges: A Literary Biography*, New York 1978, for biographical and anecdotal information. D. Balderston's *The Literary Universe of Jorge Luis Borges*, an exhaustive index to all of Borges's writings, was unfortunately not published until after most of our groundwork had been completed.

To all those colleagues and friends for whom we always had a question, our warmest thanks. Since they make up most of the people we know, it is impossible for them to be named individually, nor can we list the many scholars all over the world who have generously replied to our numerous recondite inquiries, but our deepest appreciation goes to them. We should like, however, to express our particular gratitude to Maurizio Adriani, Ronald Christ, John King, Jim Grant and David Wiggins. Needless to say, a work such as this is a magnet for errors; the responsibility for them rests solely with us.

E.F. & P.H.

Dictionary

Abbasids (Abbasida)

An Islamic dynasty that lasted from 750 to 1258; its eighth Caliph was
*Al-Mu'tasim Ibn Harun (794-842). In 762 the Caliph Mansur
transferred the capital from Damascus to Baghdad, a move which
marked the rise of Arab over Persian influence in Islam.
  Aleph 35 (50) *Ficc.* 41

Abdalmalik

The ruling family in eleventh-century Muslim Spain.
  Lab. 183 (151) *Aleph* 95

Abdurrahman (fl. 750-788)

Abd ar-Rahman I, known as 'the Immigrant', was the first Umayyad
Caliph in Spain. Forced to flee from Damascus when the Abbasids
overthrew the Umayyad Caliphate, he made his way to Spain, where he
deposed the Muslim ruler, proclaimed himself Emir and established an
independent Umayyad Emirate. He established his capital in *Cordoba,
and began the construction of its great Mosque. Lab. 186 (154):
Abdurrahman is said to have written verses full of nostalgia for his native
land. The traditional classical style he adopted persisted in the poetry of
*Al-Andalus.
  Lab. 186 (154) *Aleph* 99

Abensida (also **Ibn Sida**) (d. 1066)

An Arab philologist and man of letters remembered for his *Kitab-al-
Mukham*. There is some similarity between him and Borges: he was
blind, and studied with his father, who was also blind. See *Mohkam.
  Lab. 181 (149) *Aleph* 93

Aboukir Bay

The scene of the battle of the Nile (1-2 August 1798), in which the English

fleet under Nelson defeated the French.
   Aleph 76 (120) *Aleph* 128

Abramowicz, Maurice

A Jewish lawyer, writer and poet whom Borges met in the College of
Geneva in 1914 and with whom he formed a lifelong friendship. During
his stay in Spain, Borges frequently wrote to Abramowicz on literary
matters. Borges once told the authors that he had written 'The Unworthy
Friend' as a memento of Abramowicz and an expression of his feelings of
unworthiness towards him. Lab. 128 (98): the sarcastic remark
attributed by Borges to Abramowicz is obviously apocryphal.
   Lab. 128 (98) *Ficc*. 173

Abu-Bashar Mata (*c*.870-940)

A Syrian translator of *Aristotle whose work, according to *Renan, was
read by *Averroes.
   Lab. 181 (149) *Aleph* 92

Abulcasim Al-Ashari

Perhaps an allusion to Aboul-Hosein Ibn Djohein who, according to
*Renan, reproached *Averroes for straying from his faith.
   Lab. 182 (150) *Aleph* 93

Abulfeda (1273-1331)

The name commonly given to the Arab geographer and historian Abu
al-Fida. Abulfeda's two major works, *History of Mankind* and *Location of
the Countries*, were much used by orientalists in the eighteenth and
nineteenth centuries.
   Aleph 194 (161) *Aleph* 110

Academica priora

Otherwise known as the *Lucullus*, after its main speaker. The first draft
of the *Academica* was in two books. It was later recast in four, of which we
possess part of the first (*Academica posteriora*) and the *Lucullus*. In it
Cicero examines the question of the certainty of knowledge, supplying
Latin terminology for Greek philosophical ideas. He tends to favour the
Stoics, blaming the Epicureans for many failings, not least 'their neglect
of literary style'. Lab. 152 (121): two passages in the *Academica priora*
concern the possibility that people and events may be repeated across the
universe. In the first Lucullus opposes Catulus' theory that 'in this world
there exists a second Catulus, or indeed in countless other worlds there

4

exist countless copies of him' (ch. 17, para. 5). In the second passage, alluded to in the story, Cicero mocks Lucullus' idea that 'just as we are at this moment close to Bauli ... so there are countless persons in exactly similar places with our names, our honours, our achievements, our minds, our shapes, our ages, discussing the same subject' (ch. 40, para. 125).

Lab. 152 (121) *Aleph* 37

Acevedo Díaz, Eduardo (1882-1959)

An Argentine writer and jurist. In 1941 he won the Premio Nacional for his novel *Cancha Larga*; Borges's own entry, *The Garden of Forking Paths*, won second prize. Aleph 22 (29): in the English version the allusion is changed to 'our national hero General *San Martín', thus missing the irony of the autobiographical detail.

Aleph 22 (29) *Aleph* 167

Achilles (Aquiles)

In the *Iliad*, the bravest and strongest of the Greek heroes who fought in the Trojan war. Achilles was the son of the sea nymph Thetis, one of the Nereids, and endowed with superhuman qualities. See *Contest with the tortoise.

Lab. 64 (38), 148 (118) *Ficc.* 47 *Aleph* 25

Adam (Adán)

In the Biblical account, the first man. The story of Adam's creation is related twice in Genesis: first, as part of the general creation of the world, in 1:26-31, and later in more detail at 2:7: 'And the Lord God formed man of the dust of the ground and breathed into his nostrils the breath of life; and man became a living soul.' Lab. 75 (48): 'red Adam' can be explained by its Hebrew etymology, in which Adam means both man and red. Gnostic theories linking the creation of Adam by demiurges with the creation of an homunculus – a being who is soul-less until instructed in certain rites – has roots in *Cabbalistic interpretations of the creation of Adam. Lab. 74 (47): the description of the wizard who 'uttered lawful syllables of a powerful name and slept' before achieving his dream is an allusion to Cabbalistic belief in the creative power brought by knowledge of the secret combination of God's name. J. Alazraki, in 'Borges and the Kabbalah', *TriQuarterly*, 1972, points to certain parallels between the act of creation in 'The Circular Ruins' and the Cabbalistic account of the creation of Adam where, by permutation of the numbers corresponding to the letters of Adam and YHWY (see *Tetragrammaton), the creation of Adam is identified with that of God himself.

Lab. 75 (48) *Ficc.* 63

Adrogué

A city in the southern outskirts of *Buenos Aires (now part of Greater Buenos Aires) in which Borges and his family spent vacations of which he had nostalgic memories. In *Adrogué* (1977), Borges wrote: 'En cualquier lugar del mundo en que me encuentre, cuando siento el olor de los eucaliptos, estoy en Adrogué' ('Wherever I may be in the world, when I sense the smell of eucalyptus I am in Adrogué'). Lab. 43 (18): the Adrogué hotel probably refers to the now-demolished 'Las Delicias', where 'Tlön, Uqbar, Orbis Tertius' was written. *Triste-le-Roy also stands for this hotel (see Aleph 173 (268)). Other stories, such as 'Streetcorner Man' and 'The Intruder', are connected with this nostalgic city.
   Lab. 30 (6) *Ficc.* 17, Aleph 20 (27), Brodie 38 (45) *Brodie* 101

Aeneid (Eneida)

The Roman national epic written by *Virgil: it narrates the wanderings of the Trojan prince Aeneas after the destruction of *Troy and his arrival in Latium. Virgil's intention was to show the divine origins of Rome and of the Emperor Augustus as a descendant of Aeneas, the son of Venus. Lab. 138 (108): the line 'naked on the unknown sand' refers to the words spoken by Aeneas in anguish at the death of his friend the helmsman Palinurus: *'nudus in ignota, Palinure, iacebis arena'* (5.871). Softened by the prayers of Venus, Neptune had at last agreed to allow the progress of the Trojan fleet and had promised a calm sea. But a victim was required: Palinurus was tempted into sleep and thrown into the water, later to be washed up on the shores of Italy.
   Lab. 71 (44) *Ficc.* 56

Age of Innocence (Edad de la Ignorancia)

In *Islam, the time before the Muslim era known as Jalil.
   Lab. 195 (162) *Aleph* 111

Agrippa, Cornelius (Cornelio Agrippa)

Heinrich Cornelius Agrippa von Nettesheim (1486-1535), a German author of Latin texts on magic and the occult who fought against the condemnation of witchcraft. He was Professor at the University of Dôle and Pavia. Persecuted by the Inquisition, he was imprisoned for a time in Brussels. His writings, based on an explanation of the world in terms of *Pythagoras' numerology and a *Cabbalistic interpretation of the Hebrew alphabet, aim to demonstrate that God is best reached through magic.
   Lab. 145 (115) *Aleph* 21

Aguja de navegar cultos (1631)

A short satirical work by *Quevedo attacking linguistic preciosity. It consists of: a 'recipe' for writing 'Soledades' (a poem of extreme artificiality by Quevedo's rival, Luís de Góngora) in one day; a parody of a romance by another contemporary, Juan Pérez de Montalbán, describing the mouth of his beloved in the affected style of the period; and a poem on twilight, full of exaggerated metaphors and classical allusions. It concludes in self-parody by invoking 'God's mercy' on the 'Castilian language' and by wishing that the air polluted by so much arcane verse be cleared once and for all.
Lab. 63 (37) *Ficc.* 47

'Ah, bear in mind this garden was enchanted!'

A line from a romantic ode to Helen of Troy by Edgar Allan *Poe first published in 1831. The poet describes his vision of an enchanted garden in which Helen appeared to him in the still, perfumed air, under the full moon of a July night. As he enters the garden, everything disappears and he and his beloved are left alone. Finally, Helen also fades, only her eyes remaining to guide him through life.
Lab. 67 (41) *Ficc.* 51

Ahab

Captain Ahab, the central character in Herman Melville's novel *Moby Dick* (1851) who loses his leg in the vengeful pursuit of a white whale. Lab. 192 (159) alludes to an incident in chapter 36 that typifies Ahab's relentless quest: he nails an ounce of Spanish gold to the mast, with the words, 'Whosoever of ye raises me a white-headed whale with wrinkled brow and a crooked jaw, whosoever of ye raises me that white-headed whale, with three holes punctured in his starboard fluke, look ye, whosoever of ye raises me that same white whale, he shall have his gold ounce, my boys.'
Lab. 192 (159) *Aleph* 106

Aita, Antonio (1891-?)

An Argentine writer and critic, secretary of the Argentine PEN Club, who sought to disseminate interest in Latin American literaure. Aleph 22 (29): the reference to his winning of the First National Prize for literature is fictitious. He did, however, win a literary prize in Belgium.
Aleph 22 (29) *Aleph* 167

Akbar (1542-1605)

An Indian emperor of *Mongol descent who expanded his territories and reorganised their administration. Though himself a Muslim, Akbar opened the civil service to Hindus and encouraged members of different religions to discuss their beliefs. He also patronised the arts.
   Aleph 84 (132) *Aleph* 146

Al-Andalus

The Arabic word for Andalusia, probably derived from al-Andlish, Arabic for 'the Vandals'. The name al-Andalus was used only for Spain's Muslim territory, which fluctuated according to the vicissitudes of the Reconquest. During the Middle Ages it applied to almost the whole of the Iberian peninsula, but the application was progressively confined to areas still under Arab control, so that eventually it referred only to the small principality of Granada, the last Arab stronghold in the peninsula.
   Lab. 182 (150) *Aleph* 93

Al-Bokhari (El Bojarí)

A fictitious name, reminiscent of Muhammad Ben Ismail Al-Bukhari (810-870), a compiler of Arabic traditions.
   Aleph 73 (115) *Aleph* 123

Al-Mu'tasim (Almotásim)

Ibn Harun, the eighth Caliph of the *Abbasid dynasty, who reigned from 833 to 842. The son of a Turkoman slave, he had a vast number of Turkish slaves himself, whom he used as soldiers and officers. Eventually they overthrew their Abbasid masters. Aleph 35 (51): in a footnote to the *Thousand and One Nights* (1885, vol. 9, 232) Sir Richard *Burton writes that Al-Mu'tasim was 'the son of Al-Rashid by Ma'arid, a slave concubine of foreign origin. He was brave and of high spirit, but destitute of education; and his personal strength was such that he could break a man's elbow between his fingers. He imitated the apparatus of Persian kings; and he was called the "Octonary" because he was the eighth Abbasid; the eighth in descent from Abbas; the eighth son of Al-Rashid; he began his reign in A.H. 218; lived 48 years; was born under Scorpio (the eighth Zodiacal sign); was victorious in eight expeditions; slew eight important foes and left eight male and female children.'
   Aleph 31 (45) *Ficc.* 35

Alanus de Insulis (also Alain de Lille) (1128-1202)

A French theologian and poet, whose extensive learning won him the title

8

Doctor Universalis. He combined mysticism with rationality. Assuming that the principles of faith were axiomatic, he sought to refute heterodoxy on rational grounds. In a discussion of metaphors of the Universe, Borges quotes Alanus' famous formula: 'God is an intelligible sphere, whose centre is everywhere and whose circumference is nowhere' (Other Inq.7).

Aleph 19 (26) *Aleph* 164

Albert see *Liddell Hart

Aldiger

A name of Teutonic origin translated into Italian as Aldighiero (later Alighiero). Lab. 161 (129): *Dante's great-great-grandfather, the warrior Cacciaguida, had married a woman from the Aldighieri family, as he explains to the poet in the *Divine Comedy: 'My wife came from the vale of Po; / whence was derived the surname thou dost bear' (*Paradiso*, Canto XV, 137/8).

Lab. 160 (129) *Aleph* 49

Alem, Leandro Nicebro (1842-1896)

An eminent political figure in Argentina, leader of the 1880s reform movement against the power and corruption of the ruling oligarchy, and founder of what was to become the Radical Party. The party was formed largely by the sons of immigrants and supported by the rising middle classes. Its aim was to achieve greater participation in government, which represented solely the interests of the landowning families. Brodie 48 (57): one of the main aims of the Radicals was to establish popular suffrage, free from government corruption. Alem was the political and intellectual mentor of the young Radicals. See *Revolution of 1890.

Brodie 48 (57) *Brodie* 44

Aleph

The first letter of the Hebrew alphabet, with a numerical value of one. Aleph 11 (15): though silent and used mainly to indicate vowel punctuation, the aleph in *Cabbalistic belief is considered the foremost Hebrew letter, a symbol of all the other letters and thus, by extension, of the universe itself. One of the many interpretations of the Aleph is that its symmetrical shape symbolises the concept that everything in the lower world is a reflection of its archetypal form in the world above. In mathematics it indicates a higher power of infinity than integer numbers or numbers that are on a straight line. This allows for the concept of a plurality of alephs, or infinities. See *Cabbala, *Mengenlehre.

Lab. 55 (30) *Ficc.* 67, Aleph 11 (15) *Aleph* 151

Alexander of Macedon (Alejandro de Macedonia) (356-323 BC)

Alexander the Great, the son of Philip II of Macedon, from whom he inherited his military genius, and of Olympias, an Epirote princess, from whom he inherited his mysticism and impetuosity. His tutor was *Aristotle. One of history's greatest generals, Alexander conquered most of the civilised world and was responsible for the hellenisation of the non-Greek world as far as India. Lab. 108 (78): it is difficult to trace with certainty the allusion to 'the crystal sphere which the Persians attributed to Alexander'. After his death, Alexander's fame was enhanced by a collection of fantastic medieval legends known as the *Romance of Alexander*. In one version, *L'Histoire du noble et vaillant Alexandre le Grand* (1569), there is the following passage: 'Having reached the ends of the earth and conquered all the nations, Alexander aspired to the dominion of the air. For this he obtained a *magic glass cage* [our italics] which enabled him to fly through the clouds and, with the help of an enchantress who knew the language of birds, achieved their submission.' But the allusion is probably to the universal mirror said to have been fashioned by Alexander (*Iskander) in the Persian version of the legend. Aleph 56: throughout his life Alexander had a passion for *Homer. According to *Plutarch, on campaign he always slept with his sword and the *Iliad* under his pillow. See *Charles XII.

Lab. 108 (78) Ficc. 146, Aleph 56 (83) *Aleph* 55.

Alexander of Aphrodisias (Alejandro de Afrodisia) (160-220)

A Greek commentator on *Aristotle, one of the main sources of Greek culture available to *Averroes.

Lab. 181 (149) *Aleph* 92

Alexandria (Alejandría)

The principal port of *Egypt, founded by *Alexander the Great in 332/1 BC. Lab. 136 (106) refers to the war of the Romans against Egypt whose capital Alexandria became. In 30 BC Octavian (later Augustus) overthrew the last of the Ptolemies. The city and the rest of the country fell under Roman rule, and many rebellions were put down. Lab. 125 (95): by the second century AD Alexandria had become a focus of Hellenistic and Jewish learning. Heretical doctrines, such as those of the *Gnostics and of *Origen spread within its walls. Lab. 185 (153): the assertion that 'the only persons incapable of a sin are those who have already committed it and repented; to be free of an error...it is well to have professed it' is an allusion to *Carpocrates' interpretation of the Gnostics' libertarian attitude to sinning as a positive obligation to perform every kind of immoral act in order to curb the power of nature. For Carpocrates sinning was part of a programme that had to be completed, making amoralism the means by which freedom could be attained and making sin the way to salvation.

Lab. 125 (95) *Ficc.* 169, Lab. 136 (106) *Aleph* 8, Lab. 185 (153) *Aleph* 98

Alighieri see *Dante Alighieri

Alkmaar

A small town in northern Holland.

Aleph 20 (27) *Aleph* 165

Allaby, The Reverend

The name recalls Rector Allaby, the money-conscious rector of Crampsford in Samuel Butler's posthumously published autobiographical novel *The Way of All Flesh* (1903).

Aleph 75 (117) *Aleph* 125

Allah (Alá)

Arabic *al-ilah*, meaning God: the Moslem appellation for 'The Only God'. There are ninety-nine other names for God in *Islam, but Allah is the foremost.

Lab. 182 (150) *Aleph 93*, Aleph 58 (89) *Aleph* 135

Allahabad (Alahabad)

One of the oldest towns in India, regarded as sacred by the Hindus. Today it is an important town in the state of Uttar Pradesh. Aleph 32 (46): there is no record of a *Hindustan Review* having been published there; perhaps the reference is to *The Hindustani* which was published in Urdu.

Aleph 32 (46) *Ficc.* 36

Almafuerte (1854-1917)

The pseudonym of Pedro Bonifacio Palacio, an Argentine author and journalist who became a cult figure. In his youth Borges admired Almafuerte and was moved by his messianic tone, saying that almost all Argentinians of his generation learned to appreciate the full aesthetic function of language through the 'suffering' and the 'extasis' of Almafuerte (*Ev. Carr.* 39). Though Almafuerte is now somewhat neglected, Borges listed him in his Prologue to the *Anthology of Argentinian Poetry* (1941) as one of the most important Argentinian poets. Borges also wrote a preface to the collection of Almafuerte's prose and poetry published in 1962, in which he summarised the book he would have liked to have written about Almafuerte, reaffirming his admiration for his 'stoicism and inexplicable poetic power'.

Lab. 128 (98) *Ficc*. 173

Almagro

A lower-middle-class district not far from the centre of *Buenos Aires. Borges worked for nine years in the Biblioteca Miguel Cané in Almagro.

Lab. 166 (134) *Aleph* 62

Almansur Yacub (*c*.1160-1199)

Abu Yusuf Ya'qub Almansur, third Emir of the Almohad dynasty who defeated Alfonso VIII of Castile on the field of Alarcos in 1195, thus securing for the Arabs an important respite from the onslaught of the Reconquest. Considered the most enlightened of the Almohad Caliphs, Almansur surrounded himself with philosophers, physicians and poets. He encouraged *Averroes to write his commentaries on *Aristotle. Lab. 182 (150): the story is told by *Renan that the Emir liked to discuss scientific problems with Averroes. He would invite him to sit on a cushion reserved for his most intimate guests. In the familiarity of these conversations Averroes would 'abandon' himself to the point of saying to his sovereign: 'Écoute, mon frère...' ('But listen, my brother').

Lab. 182 (150) *Aleph* 93

Alvarado, Pedro de (1485-1541)

One of the Spanish conquerors of the Indies who in 1519 joined Cortes's expedition to Mexico. From his red face and blond hair he was named by the Indians *Tonatinh*, 'the sun'. In 1520 he ordered the destruction of the temple of Tenochtitlán and a ruthless massacre. In Guatemala he was responsible for the burning of the capital in 1524, after which all the Quiché tribes submitted to the Spaniards. He also went to Peru, and died under a horse while marching to the aid of an expedition in the mountains of Nochiztlán.

Lab. 203 (169) *Aleph* 115

Alvear, Carlos María (1789-1852)

An Argentine public figure and military leader. Alvear was in charge of the *criollo* revolutionary forces who in 1814 defeated the Spanish in Montevideo, replacing Spanish colonial rule with *porteño* domination. He schemed unsuccessfully with several *caudillos* of the eastern provinces against the *Unitarian government of Buenos Aires and was exiled to *Uruguay. Brodie 73 (90): during the war with Brazil Alvear was recalled and placed at the head of the Republican army, in charge of some 5,500 soldiers and some of the greatest military leaders of Argentina, such as Paz, *Lavalle and *Olavarría. In 1827 he achieved a brilliant victory at Ituzaingó, defeating the Brazilian Imperial army and bringing the war to an end. He died in the USA where he was representing *Rosas's government.

Brodie 73 (90) *Brodie* 76

Amenophis IV (also **Amenhotep**) (fl. 1379-1362 BC)

An Egyptian Pharaoh and religious reformer who introduced the monotheistic cult of Aton, the sun disc. Aton took the place of all other divinities. His worship was free of all moral codes and of the austerity demanded by former Egyptian cults. Lab. 131: Amenophis's liberal reform of religious expression did not survive him long.

Lab. 131 (101) *Ficc.* 181

American, The (of Nashville, Tennessee)

A daily paper, first issued in 1848, known as the *Nashville American*. As it ceased publication in 1910, there would not have been a reporter researching for it in 1944.

Lab. 42 (17) *Ficc.* 33

Amorim, Enrique (1900-1960)

An Uruguayan novelist related to Borges by marriage. He spent many years in *Buenos Aires and formed part of the socially committed school of writers known as the *Boedo Group. Borges considered his novel *El Paisano Aguilar* (1934) a closer description of *gaucho* life than Güiraldes's more famous *Don Segundo Sombra*. In 1934 Borges visited Amorim's home in Salto. See *Sant'Anna.

Lab. 41 (17) *Ficc.* 31

Amr

The oldest mosque in Cairo, and the first in Africa, founded in 641/2, immediately after the Muslim conquest of Egypt. Amr has been the subject of countless legends and superstitions.

Aleph 23 (30) *Aleph* 169

Amritsar

An Indian city founded in the sixteenth century, the capital of the Amritsar district in west *Punjab and the religious centre of the *Sikhs. Aleph 82 (130): the 'disturbances in a Muslim city' refer to the episode in 1919 when 379 of Gandhi's followers were killed and 1200 wounded by

British troops in Amritsar.
    Aleph 82 (130) *Aleph* 143

Analysis of Mind (1921)

A book by Bertrand *Russell examining the workings of the human mind as deduced from our experience of the physical world. Lab. 34 (10) (also Other Inq. 25): the theory that 'the past has no reality other than its present memory' is posited in chapter 9 as part of a wider discussion of the relation between memory and knowledge. In order to illustrate the difference between past sensation and present image, Russell points out that a memory-belief happens in the present, and not in the past to which the belief is said to refer. Extending his argument, he proposes that there is no logical necessity that a memory-belief be based upon a real past event, or even 'that the past should have existed at all'. His exact words at page 159 are: 'There is no logical impossibility that the world sprang into being five minutes ago, exactly as it was, with a population that "remembered" a wholly unreal past.' This statement, however, is qualified on the next page, where he asserts that he did not intend his suggestion of the non-existence of the past as a serious hypothesis but was using its logical tenability as a help in the analysis of what occurs when we remember: 'Like all sceptical hypotheses, it is logically tenable but uninteresting.'
    Lab. 34 (10) *Ficc.* 23

Anatomy of Melancholy

A treatise by Robert Burton published in 1621. Its three parts deal with the definition, causes, symptoms and properties of melancholy; its cure; and the melancholy of love and of religion. Burton argues that, though people can escape melancholy by being companionable and active, it is congenital in the human condition. In spite of its medical tone, the work addresses itself to wider issues, including contemporary politics. The overall message seems to be an ironic statement of the ineffectualness of man. The book abounds in quotations from the bible, the classics and Church literature; on this point Borges has remarked that those works which like *The Anatomy of Melancholy* are not entirely the writer's own creation, but a patchwork of references to other texts, are, paradoxically, perhaps the most personal, since 'we are the past' (*Obras completas en colaboración* 977). Lab. 78 (51): the quotation which serves as epigraph stems from the chapter 'Exercises Rectified of Body and Mind', describing the various physical and mental activities which help to overcome melancholy. Of these, study is considered the most effective. Particularly recommended are the memorising of texts, the demonstration of geometrical propositions, and algebra, 'an excellent and pleasant discipline' which allows us to envisage the whole from the part, *ex ungue *leonem*. The quotation in full reads: 'By this art you may contemplate the variation of the twenty-three letters, which may be so infinitely varied, that the words complicated and deduced thence will not be contained within the compass of the firmament; ten words may be varied 40,320 several ways.'

Lab. 78 (51) *Ficc*. 85

Ancient Mariner (1798)

A narrative poem by Samuel Taylor Coleridge (1772-1834) which tells of a haunted ship pursued by disaster and death after a mariner kills an albatross. Borges showed considerable interest in Coleridge's creative process and wrote two essays on him (Other Inq. 10,14), claiming that the same creative vision can be evolved by different artists across the centuries.

Lab. 67 (41) *Ficc*. 52

'And the Queen gave birth to a child who was called Asterion' ('Y la reina dio luz a un hijo que se llamó Asterión') see *Apollodorus

Andrade, Olegario Victor (1839-1882)

A poet born in Brazil of Argentine parentage. Andrade was a Romantic and wrote under the influence of Victor *Hugo, from whom he derived a heroic vision of man. He prophesied the future glory of the American continent. He regarded *San Martín as the hero 'par excellence'. In public life he supported *Urquiza's policy of a confederation of provinces. His death was generally mourned, and a funeral speech was delivered by the President of the Republic. In 1924 a bust of Andrade was erected in the public gardens of *Palermo, and Paul Groussac, Borges's predecessor as director of the *National Library, pronounced a magnificent oration in his memory.

Brodie 74 (91) *Brodie* 78

Andreä, Johannes Valentinus (1586-1654)

A German poet, satirist and theologian who was converted to the Lutheran Church and composed a number of interpretative and didactic works on religion, in Latin and German. Andreä wrote also under the pseudonyms Christian Rosencrutz, Menippus and Florentinus de Valentia. *De Quincey (*Collected Writings*, vol. 13, 405-10) alleged that Andreä was the anonymous author of the basic books of Rosicrucianism. According to him Andreä conceived this secret society in an attempt to reform the German people, whom he considered corrupt and evil. He envisaged a body of noble and learned men acting under the direction of a 'most enlightened one', bent on redressing public morality. To attract proselytes, he emphasised that the society was the repository of oriental mysteries and that it had already lasted for two centuries – one reason why he did not claim authorship of the texts. There are strong parallels between the story of Rosicrucianism and the imaginary society of 'Tlönistas': both can be seen as creating 'hrönir', ideal objects which are gradually embodied and become accepted and absorbed into our material world.

Lab. 29 (5) *Ficc.* 16

Andreoli, Raffaele (1823-1891)

An Italian lawyer, disbarred for his liberal views. He is best remembered for his commentaries on the *Divine Comedy*, first published in 1856, which were reprinted many times and used extensively as school texts.

Lab. 200 (167) *Aleph* 141

Anglo-American Cyclopaedia

Many pirated and mutilated editions of the ninth and tenth editions of the *Encyclopaedia Britannica* were printed in America, but none has been found with the title 'Anglo-American Cyclopaedia' or published in New York in 1917, as stated by the narrator of 'Tlön...'. The 1902 edition of the *Encyclopaedia Britannica*, of which the 'Anglo-American Cyclopaedia' is said to be a facsimile, consists of 35 volumes. Lab. 27 (35): the story's alleged vol. 46 is obviously fictitious; yet this apparently fantastic occurrence seems to reflect, in part at least, the hazardous history of real encyclopaedias. In private conversation with the present writers, Borges maintained that he owned a copy of the untraceable 'cyclopaedia'.

Lab. 27 (3) *Ficc.* 13

Annals (Anales) see *Tacitus

Anschluss

German for 'union': the term given by the Nazis to Germany's annexation of Austria in March 1938.

Lab. 119 (89) Ficc. 160

Anthology of Fantastic Literature (Antología de la literatura fantástica)

A miscellany of stories on themes related to the supernatural published by Borges in 1940 jointly with Silvina *Ocampo and A. *Bioy Casares. It included work of G.K. *Chesterton, Lewis Carroll, Edgar Allan *Poe, James *Joyce, Leon *Bloy, Rabelais, Cocteau, Wu Ch'eng En and Chuan

Tzu, and a story from the *Thousand and One Nights*. In Borges's own words, it is 'one of the books a second Noah should save from a second flood'. Lab. 39 (14): the article said to appear in this anthology is not included.

Lab. 39 (14) *Ficc.* 29

Antonio Conselheiro (also Antonio Maciel) (1828-1897)

A Brazilian religious dissident who in 1896/7 led a rebellion in Canudos in the north of the state of Bahía. The rebels were peasants, or *cabôclos*, who lived in Canudos in a system of communes, working out their own salvation. They rose against the changes introduced by the new Republican government, which they regarded as the Antichrist. Canudos was surrounded, and the siege ended with the death of all the rebels. Conselheiro's head was cut off and put on public display. The story is told by Euclides *da Cunha in his novel *Os Sertões* (1902 trans. *Revolt in the Backlands*, 1947).

Lab. 128 (98) *Ficc.* 173

Aparicio, Timoteo

A member of the Uruguayan *Blanco party who from 1870 to 1872 instituted a civil war against President Lorenzo Batlle because his party had been excluded from the government.

Brodie 40 (47) *Brodie* 103

Apocrypha (Libros Apócrifos)

Greek for 'hidden things': the name given to late Old Testament books of ambiguous status in both Jewish and Christian tradition. By the early Christians they were generally accepted, but in the fourth century the Church Fathers disagreed on whether they were 'canonical', a debate rekindled by Protestant thinkers at the Reformation. Lab. 173 (123): in the nineteenth century interest in the Apocrypha revived.

Lab. 173 (123) *Aleph* 81

Apollo (Apolo)

The Greek god of the arts, identified with the sun. His main shrine was at Delphi.

Lab. 151 (120) *Aleph* 36

Apollodorus (Apolodoro) (fl. *c*.140 BC)

An Athenian writer, author of a *Chronicle* of Greek history in iambic verse. Fragments survive of his study of *Homer's *Catalogue of ships and of texts on Greek grammar and etymology. He is also the supposed author of

17

the *Bibliotheca*, a treatise on ancient mythology which may be an abridged version of his longer study *On the Gods*, now lost. Lab. 170 (138): 'And the queen gave birth to a child who was called *Asterion' comes from the *Bibliotheca*. A rough translation of the original Greek text would be: 'who gave birth to Asterion, called the Minotaur, who had a bull's head and a man's body.'

Lab. 170 (138) *Aleph* 67

Aporia(s)

A Greek term used in philosophy to denote a difficulty, or problem, literally an 'impasse'. See *Eleatic paradoxes.

Ficc. 24

Apostle (Apóstol)

The apostle who is 'everything for everyone' is St Paul, who says (I *Corinthians 9) : 'Am I not an apostle? Am I not free?', and (I Corinthians 9:22): 'I am made all things to all men, that I might by all means save some.'

Lab. 132 (102) *Ficc.* 182

Appearance and Reality see **Francis Herbert *Bradley**

Aquileia

An ancient town in central Italy near the shores of the Adriatic, founded by the Romans in the second century BC. From its position it was a strategic base for expeditions to the north east of the Roman empire. In 12-10 BC, for example, during the wars against Pannonia, Augustus established himself for a time in Aquileia. In the third century it became an episcopal see; its bishops expounded *The Three Chapters* (a collection of writings on the divinity of Jesus). In 452 it was razed to the ground by Attila, king of the *Huns. Lab. 155 (124): the presence of the Histrionic heresy in Aquileia, obviously apocryphal, could be an allusion to Pope Virgilius' condemnation of *The Three Chapters* in 548; they were later pronounced heretical at the Council of Constantinople in 553. Aquileia eventually broke with Rome, and its bishop Macedonius took the title Patriarch in defiance of Rome. It remained schismatic until the seventh century.

Lab. 150 (119) *Aleph* 35

Arabian Gulf (Golfo Arábigo)

A reference to the Persian Gulf.

Lab. 138 (108) *Aleph* 11

Arabian Nights see **Thousand and One Nights*

Araoz

A street in Buenos Aires, in the vicinity of the penitentiary of Las Heras. Lab. 190 (157): in the 1930s it was a street of small houses inhabited by the impoverished middle class.

Lab. 190 (157) *Aleph* 105

Araucanian (Araucano)

An Indian people who originated in central Chile and spread to Argentina as far as the pampas of *Buenos Aires province, where they merged with the existing Pampa Indians. The Araucanians, who still survive in *Chile and Argentina, are mostly Mapuche, the brave people who fought against the Spanish invaders and whose leader, Lautaro, defeated Pedro de Valdavia in 1553. Persecution turned them against the colonists and their descendants, and they prevented the expansion of white colonisation. They were finally defeated in the 'Conquest of the Desert' (1879-80), when they were dispersed and their way of life was all but exterminated. In spite of the adulteration of modern life, the Araucanians retain their culture and traditional beliefs. Officially Catholic, they still worship their gods and the spirit of their ancestors, believing in power over death and the medicine of the shamans. Lab. 162 (130): Araucanian is one of the many native tongues spoken in Spanish America.

Lab. 162 (130) *Aleph* 51

Archbishop of Canterbury see *Canterbury

Arequipa

A city in southern Peru, the second largest in the country. Brodie 72: in the Wars of Independence, in August 1822, General Sucre, in command of the army of *Bolívar, arrived in Arequipa and marched to Puno. It was finally taken by Sucre's troops in January 1825, when the Spaniards surrendered Peru. Bolívar visited the city in May 1825.

Brodie 72 (89) *Brodie* 75

'Argos...This dog lying in the manure' ('Este perro tirado en el estiércol')

In the **Odyssey* Odysseus' faithful dog, who is the first to recognise him on his return to Ithaca. Lab. 143 (113): the passage describes how Odysseus had raised and trained the dog but never hunted with him before leaving for the Trojan war. Nineteen years later Argos is lying 'on the deep pile of dung' which is to be used for manure: 'Now, as he perceived that Odysseus had come close to him, / he wagged his tail, and laid back both his ears...' and died (*Odyssey* 17. 290-327).

Lab. 142/3 (112/13) *Aleph* 17/8

Ariadne (Ariadna)

In Greek mythology the daughter of Minos, king of Crete, and Pasiphaë. Ariadne falls in love with *Theseus, who has come to kill her half-brother, the *Minotaur, and helps him escape from the labyrinth. She escapes from Crete with him but he abandons her on the island of Naxos, where she dies in childbirth.

Lab. 172 (140) *Aleph* 70

Aristotle (Aristóteles) (384-322 BC)

A Greek philosopher whose comprehensive system over a range of theoretical and practical questions from metaphysics, ethics and aesthetics to politics and biology has influenced Western science for more than two thousand years. Though not a philosopher whom Borges quotes extensively, Aristotle's awareness that no one system of thought can encompass the whole of being and serve for the deduction of all truths is an underlying theme in Borges. Aristotle, a pupil of *Plato, found himself in disagreement with his master's idealism, according to which the observed world is only a reflection of the real world of ideas. Aristotle stressed the primacy of the particular or individual over the general. Thus in the *Categories* he distinguished between *primary* substances, such as particular men or horses, and *secondary* substances, such as the species or genera to which these particularities belonged. This polarity has characterised human thought through the centuries. Lab. 178 (146): when Borges, quoting an aphorism of Coleridge (Other Inq. 156), divides men into Aristotelians or Platonists, he refers to their contrasting world views. The difference between the Aristotelian concept of the particularising nature of reality and the Platonic concept of its abstract, generalising nature as manifested in language is humorously treated by Borges in 'Funes the Memorious'. A link between the discussion of the mnemonic system in Aristotle's *De Memoria* and Borges's story is suggested by R. Sorabji (*Aristotle on Memory*, London 1972, ch. 2). Developing an argument used by Plato against himself (in his *Parmenides*), Aristotle further refutes the duality of the Platonic doctrine in his famous argument of the Third Man, who provides a necessary ideal for the combination of the First Man, the archetype, and any Second Man, its visible manifestation, and who in turn will necessitate a Fourth Man, and so on, postulating an infinite regress. This theme, much used by Borges, finds its prime example in 'The Circular Ruins'. Aleph 70 (109):

20

reference to Aristotle's denial that 'it is within God's power to make what once was into something that has never been' can be found in his *Nicomachean Ethics* (1139b) where he quotes the poet Agathon in support: 'For this alone is lacking even to God, / To make undone things that have once been done.' Lab. 181 (149): Aristotle's thought was rekindled in Western Europe by the writings of his Arab commentator *Averroes and, through Aquinas, became the dominant influence in medieval theology. See *Politics, *Rhetoric, *Summa Theologiae.

Lab. 178 (146) Aleph 88, Lab. 181 (149) Aleph 92, Aleph 70 (109) *Aleph* 77

Armenia

A district south of the Caucasus and the Black Sea.
Lab. 28 (5) *Ficc*. 28

Army of the Andes (Ejército de los Andes)

The army of General *San Martín which in January 1817 crossed the Andes from Mendoza, a province in western Argentina, to Chile. Made up of two divisions, it consisted of 4,000 soldiers, 1,400 auxiliaries, 2,400 animals, 18 cannon and other artillery. After the crossing, which took eighteen days, the army defeated the Royalist forces at the battle of *Chacabuco.
Brodie 72 (89) *Brodie* 75

Arrecifes

A small town in the district of Bartolomé Mitre in *Buenos Aires province.
Brodie 54 (65) *Brodie* 17

Arianism (Arrianismo)

A heresy founded and promulgated by Arius (280-369). It was based on the denial of the divinity of Jesus, who was claimed not to be consubstantial with God but merely a reflection of him. Lab. 160 (128): the Arians converted the Visigoths, the *Lombards and the Vandals. Lab. 153 (122): several councils of the Church were held to counter Arian beliefs, such as the Council of Nicea in 325, which proclaimed the divinity of Jesus, and the Councils of *Constantinople in 381 and 553. The last of these reaffirmed the Nicene creed and pronounced anathemas against the Arians.
Lab. 153 (122) *Aleph* 39, Lab. 160 (128) *Aleph* 48

Arroyo see *Maldonado

Ars Magna Generalis see **Raymond *Lully**

Arsinoë

A city of Upper Egypt, west of the Nile, of which extensive ruins remain.
   Lab. 137 (107) *Aleph* 9

Artigas, José Gervasio (1764-1850)

A Uruguayan hero and military leader who fought against the Spaniards
by offering his services to the Junta at *Buenos Aires. Recruiting his
troops from *gauchos and outlaws, Artigas won a notable victory at Las
Piedras in 1811. He championed the *Federalists, who demanded greater
autonomy for the *Banda Oriental, against the *Unitarians, who
supported the centralised power of Buenos Aires. In the civil war against
Buenos Aires which followed in 1815, Artigas defeated the *porteño* forces
and drove them off Uruguayan soil. The result was an invasion by Brazil,
and Artigas was eventually defeated. Fleeing to Paraguay, where he was
briefly imprisoned, he was given a farm and a pension by President
Francia and died there thirty years later. See *Saavedra.
   Brodie 75 (929 *Brodie* 78

Ashkenazim

The plural of the Hebrew 'Ashkenaz', meaning 'Germany': the term
applied to the descendants of the Jews resident in medieval Germany and
France, including Polish and Russian Jews. They are distinguished from
*Sephardim, the Jews of Spain and Portugal and their descendants.
   Lab. 177 (144) *Aleph* 86

Asín Palacios, Miguel (1871-1944)

A Spanish Arabist largely responsible for the upsurge of Islamic studies
in Spain in the 1930s.
   Lab. 188 (155) *Aleph* 101

Asrar Nama

A poem by the Persian mystical poet *Farid Attar of which a recurring
motif is the entanglement of the soul in the material world. Lab. 196
(164): the 'interpolated verse' is probably fictitious, since there is no
reference to the *Zahir in the index.
   Lab. 196 (164) *Aleph* 112

Asterion

As noted in *Apollodorus' *Biblioteca*, Asterios ('starry' or 'starred') was the father of Minos. The Minotaur was also named Asterios. Lab. 170 (138): *Asterion* is the accusative case of *Asterios*. The neuter word *asterion* denoted an unknown plant, or a spider.

    Lab. 170 (138) *Aleph* 67

Augural Canto (Canto Augural)

One of several examples in 'The Aleph' of 'universal poems': that is, poems which take a global view of the universe. Others are *Drayton's *Polyolbion* and, though not specifically mentioned, the *Divine Comedy*. The title may be an allusion to Neruda's *Canto General*, in which he tells the history of America, from earliest times, before it got its name, to the present. The *Canto* was not published until 1950, a year after 'The Aleph', but Neruda began writing it in 1938 and Borges probably knew of it. Borges was critical of Neruda's denunciation of the USA in the *Canto*, because of his silence about Perón, which Borges attributed to self-interest. Earlier, Neruda had written a collection of poems entitled *Residence on Earth*. 'The Earth', the poem mentioned in the same story, may be an allusion to this.

    Aleph 13 (17) *Aleph* 154

Augustine (Agustín) (354-430)

One of the four Fathers of the Christian Church. In his youth Augustine abandoned the Christian faith, but he returned to it in 386. When he became bishop of Hippo he described his spiritual struggle in his *Confessions*. After his conversion he was fully engaged in church activities and religious controversies, denouncing the preachings of the various Christian sects which had sprung up before orthodoxy had been formalised. Dominant among these sects were the Manichaeans, who saw the world as the scene of a conflict between good and evil, and the Pelagians, who held that the sin of Adam did not affect the rest of humanity – a doctrine expounded by Augustine's pupil Coelestus, who was later tried and excommunicated. According to Augustine all human nature is sinful and divine intervention is imperative. This view dominates his moral and theological treatises, his *Letters*, the commentaries on the Gospel, and his main work *Civitas Dei* ('City of God'), which elaborates the theory of human predestination: the principle that God has established *a priori* who will be damned and who saved.

    Lab. 151 (120) *Aleph* 37

Auto(s) da fé (auto(s) de fe)

'Act of faith': a ceremony of the Spanish Inquisition in which heretics were burnt alive.
   Lab. 68 (42) *Ficc.* 53

Avellanos, José

A character in Conrad's *Nostromo*, described as 'a statesman, a poet, a man of culture, and author of *The History of Fifty Years of Misrule*'. Conrad claims to have derived the history of the fictitious Costaguana from his own character Avellanos, a claim which would not have been lost on Borges. Brodie 82 (100): Avellanos's text, as explained by Conrad in the Author's Note, was, of course, never published; the manuscript is seen later in the course of the novel 'flowing in the gutter, blown in the wind, trampled in the mud'. See *Estado Occidental, *Golfo Plácido, *Higuerota, José *Korzeniovski, *Sulaco.
   Brodie 82 (100) *Brodie* 112

Aventinus (Aventino)

The Aventine, one of the seven hills of Rome.
   Lab. 156 (125) *Aleph* 43

Averroes (1126-1198)

A celebrated Arab philosopher and physician born in Cordoba, known as 'The Commentator'. Averroes was one of the most important Islamic thinkers, renowned for his commentaries on *Aristotle, which became the principal source of Greek thought for medieval Christian and Jewish theology. He also wrote a commentary on *Plato's *Republic. His most famous book is the *Tahafut-ul-Tahafut ('Incoherence of Incoherence'). Averroes held that one universal intelligence exists for all humanity, and that the individual soul, destined to die with the body, is capable of thought only through its temporary union with it. This notion ran counter to the Islamic idea of personal immortality, and Averroes was accused of unorthodoxy. Lab. 185/6 (153/4): the discussion of Averroes's preoccupation with metaphor may be linked to a famous statement attributed to the philosopher about 'twofold truth', viz. that propositions may be theologically true and philosophically false, or vice versa; what Averroes actually taught, however, was that religious *imagery* expressed a higher philosophical truth. Lab. 182 (150): Averroes was physician to the Emir Yacub Yusuf *Almansur, at *Marrakesh, where he enjoyed a privileged position. After being attacked and dismissed, he was recalled to Marrakesh, where he died. Much of what is said about him in 'Averroes' Search' stems from *Renan's *Averroès et l'Averroïsme*.

Axes (Achas)

A 'temple of the axes' seems not to have existed in Crete, but a temple was uncovered at Haghia Triadha in southern Crete containing carvings of axes on the pedestals. A sarcophagus found in the same area shows two scenes in which an axe is worshipped. In Greek *labrys*, a word of Lydian origin, meant a double-edged axe, often related to the figure of an ox, from which the word labyrinth is thought to derive.

Lab 171 (139) *Aleph* 68

Ayacucho

A decisive battle fought on 9 December 1824 in the Peruvian Sierra, half-way between Lima and Cuzco, in which the Peruvian forces led by José Sucre defeated the royalist army of Spain. This victory finally established the independence of Peru after three centuries of Spanish colonial rule.

Brodie 72 (90) *Brodie* 76

Azevedo (also Acevedo)

Borges's family surname on his mother's side. Its Sephardic associations have suggested that Borges had Jewish ancestry, something that he has ambiguously both 'regretfully denied' and acknowledged (Emir *Rodríguez Monegal, *Jorge Luis Borges: A Literary Biography*, NY 1978, 12-13). Aleph 55 (82): Francisco Xavier Acevedo was a relative of Borges.

Lab. 109 (79) *Ficc.* 147, Aleph 60 (94)) *Aleph* 27, Aleph 55 (82) *Aleph* 54, Brodie 60 (73) *Brodie* 53

Baal (Bel)

The semitic for 'Lord': the name of many ancient near-eastern fertility gods. In *Babylon, Baal was identified with the planet Jupiter and later became one of their chief gods. Though used at times to designate the god of Israel, the name is normally associated in the Old Testament with lesser, more local gods and condemned by the Hebrew prophets. Jeremiah associates the cult with heathen practices of a violent and cruel kind. Lab. 57 (32): given the fluidity of the worship of Baal, it is difficult to establish the mysteries alluded to. The cult was based on magic, on violent and ecstatic exercises and on human sacrifice.

Lab. 57 (32) *Ficc.* 70

Baal Shem

A Hebrew word, meaning 'master of the Name'. Israel ben Eliezer (c.1700-1760) was known as Baal Shem Tov. He originated from *Podolsk and was the founder of eighteenth-century Polish *Hasidism. The title Baal Shem is based on his belief in the miraculous power of the Sacred Name, which he invoked to work miracles. Lab. 107 (77): any biography of Baal Shem would necessarily be highly fictional, since he left no writings and the little we know of him is interwoven with legend. Borges may, however, be referring to Martin *Buber's *Die Legende des Baalschem* (1908: trans. 1955).

Lab. 107 (77) *Ficc.* 145

Babel

An Assyrian word, Bab-ili, meaning 'the gate of the God', the original name of Babylon; cf. Hebrew *balal*, to 'confuse'. The story of the Tower of Babel (Genesis 11:1-9) seeks to explain the diversity of mankind. Man's presumption in building a tower to reach heaven is frustrated by God, who confounds the language of those who built it, dividing their speech. The story was probably inspired by the pyramidal temple-tower in *Babylon.

Lab. 78 (51) *Ficc.* 85

Babylon (Babilonia)

The Greek form of *Babel. An ancient city on the *Euphrates, first mentioned in a tablet of 3800 BC, famous for its astronomical and astrological practices. From 2250 BC Babylon was the capital of an extensive commercial empire periodically fighting for supremacy with the neighbouring Assyrians. After the fall of Nineveh in 606 BC Nebuchadnezzar II rebuilt the town, fortifying it with towers and a wall which joined the Tigris to the Euphrates. When the western regions of the empire rose in revolt, led by Egypt, Babylon retaliated, destroying Jerusalem and enslaving the Jews. The decay of Babylon began in 500 BC with King Belshazzar, who saw the 'writing on the wall'. It was occupied first by *Cyrus of Persia and then by *Alexander of Macedon, after whose death in 323 BC it dwindled to a group of villages. Lab. 55 (30): among the Babylonians all transactions were carried out on clay tablets, many of which survive, along with documentation of their religion, magic and astrology. A complex system of gods involved a hierarchy of priests and many liturgical rites, including the making of horoscopes. A vast legal organisation governed the life of individuals: capital punishment was applied for theft, and the judicial system was based on the Lex Talionis ('an eye for an eye').

Lab. 55 (30) *Ficc.* 67, Lab. 94 (65) *Ficc.* 126

Back to Methuselah see George Bernard *Shaw

Bacon, Francis (1561-1626)

An English courtier, jurist and philosopher, best known for his *Novum Organum* (1620) and *Essays* (1625). The *Novum Organum* sets out his plan for restructuring scientific knowledge. The *Essays* deal with family life, virtues and vices, religion, education, health, politics, friendship and beauty. Lab. 135 (105): in Essay 58, 'Of Vicissitude of Things', Bacon begins with Solomon's dictum 'There is no new thing under the sun'. He then discusses the recurring calamities in human experience – earthquakes and deluges, religious discord, wars and the fall of empires – and ends by warning us not to 'look too long upon these turning wheels of vicissitudes lest we become giddy'.
　Lab. 135 (105) *Aleph* 7

Baedeker, Karl (1801-1859)

A German publisher, famous for the guide books bearing his name.
　Lab. 112 (82) *Ficc.* 151

Bagé

A city in southern *Rio Grande do Sul in *Brazil near the border with Uruguay.
　Lab. 164 (132) *Aleph* 59

Baghdad (Bagdad)

The capital of Iraq, a city on the river Tigris. Under the *Abbasid dynasty it was a celebrated centre of Arab culture and the glory of the Moslem world, a position it later shared with *Cordoba. Many of the tales of the *Thousand and One Nights*, centred on the court of the Abbasid Caliph Harun al-Rashid (763-809), are set in Baghdad.
　Lab. 180 (148) *Aleph* 91

Bajo, El

The unhealthy low-lying swamp land by the waterfront of *Buenos Aires, always considered a rough and dangerous district. It was subject to floods and epidemics due to poor housing and associated with smuggling and prostitution. Brodie 24 (26): the English translation is simply 'the waterfront'.
　Brodie 27

Balkan state (Estado balcánico)

A state in the Balkan peninsula, extending from the Adriatic to the Black Sea. The Balkan states were once under the control of the Ottoman Empire and later fought to define their boundaries.

Lab. 102 (72) *Ficc.* 137

Banda Oriental

The name given to all Spanish possessions east of the River Uruguay. Today it is an old-fashioned name for the Republic of Uruguay. The Banda Oriental was settled by Spanish colonialists in the eighteenth century and was hated by its neighbours on either side. In 1776 it was annexed to the viceroyalty of La Plata and in 1821 to Brazil. Only in 1828, after much fighting, was it declared an independent state. It then acted as a buffer between the two contending nations and maintained the balance of power. Lab. 87 (59): the dominating role of *Buenos Aires in the Plate area during the campaigns of Independence was resented in the Banda Oriental. Hence the terms used in Uruguay to describe an inhabitant of Buenos Aires: *literato* ('highbrow'), *cajetilla* ('city slicker') and *porteño* ('dude'). See *Montevideo.

Ficc. 117

Bari

A city and port on the Adriatic in southern Italy, originally a Roman colony and later occupied by Goths, *Lombards and Byzantines. During the Middle Ages it was an important base for the Crusades.

Lab. 159 (127) *Aleph* 47

Barracas

A working-class district in southern Buenos Aires near La Boca and *Constitución and bordering the *Riachuelo.

Brodie 68 (83) *Brodie* 67

Barrès, Maurice (1862-1923)

A French writer, whose works include a text on bull-fighting, entitled *Du sang, de la volupté et de la mort*, and a biography of the Spanish painter El Greco, *Greco, ou le secret de Tolédo*.

Lab. 68 (42) *Ficc.* 53

Barrio Sur

The southern district of *Buenos Aires, the oldest and now unfashionable side of the city, in the area surrounding Plaza *Constitución. Situated at the mouth of the River Plate, it was subject to floods and epidemics causing the wealthy to leave for the higher ground of what is now known as Barrio Norte.

Lab. 190 (158) *Aleph* 105

Basilides (d. 139 AD)

An early *Gnostic from *Alexandria who integrated *Pythagorean and *Cabbalistic principles and Oriental traditions with the Christian faith. Lab. 125 (95): Basilides held that, according to Greek numeration, the sum of the numerical values of the letters composing the name Abraxas, his name for God, came to 365. Abraxas created 'Understanding' and this in turn created 'The Word'; by a successive hierarchical process the different orders of angels (365 in fact) were created. The lowest of these – to which the god of the Jews who included – created the world: an attempt by Basilides to resolve the problem of evil. To redeem creation from corruption, Abraxas sent his own son ('Understanding'), who became one with the man Jesus. Basilides rejected the doctrine of the resurrection, since the body was made of evil matter. His followers, therefore, unable to reconcile themselves to the resurrection of Jesus, were compelled to deny the physical aspects of the crucifixion. Some said that Jesus was only a phantom in the moment of death; others that Simon of Cyrene was crucified in his stead.

Lab. 81 (54) Ficc. 90, Lab. 125 (95) *Ficc.* 169

Basra

A town in southern Iraq near the Persian Gulf.

Lab. 183 (151) *Aleph* 95

'Bateau ivre, Le' (1871)

'The Drunken Boat': a poem by Rimbaud (1854-1891) written when he was 17. The poet imagines himself floating in a crewless boat across luminous seas and through fierce hurricanes. The swirling images and hallucinatory language of the poem mark it as a precursor of the French symbolist movement.

Lab. 67 (41) *Ficc.* 52

Baton Rouge

The capital of Louisiana, situated on the Mississippi near New Orleans.

Lab. 40 (15) *Ficc.* 30

Baudelaire, Charles (1821-1867)

A French poet, an admirer of Edgar Allan *Poe, much of whose work he translated. Baudelaire is best known for his collection *Les Fleurs du mal*, in which morbid and occasionally crude touches of realism are combined with exuberant imagery and lyric grace.

Lab. 67 (40) *Ficc.* 51

Bayonne

A French town in the Basses Pyrenées, famous for its thirteenth-century cathedral.

Lab. 66 (39) *Ficc.* 50

'Beatus ille ...'

'Happy is he...' the first words of a poem by Horace (*Epodes* 2) in praise of country life: 'Happy is he who, far from business cares, like the pristine race of mortals, works his ancestral acres with his oxen, from all money-lending free.'

Brodie 35 (39) *Brodie* 95

Belgrano

A wealthy residential suburb in *Buenos Aires, whose cosmopolitan population included many English inhabitants.

Aleph 15 (19) *Aleph* 156

Belgrano Street (Avenida Belgrano)

A street in the vicinity of *Barrio Sur, some three blocks from *Chile and *Tacuarí.

Lab. 192 (159) *Aleph* 107.

Belisarius (Belisario) (c.505-565)

Justinian's general, one of the greatest military leaders of the eastern Roman Empire. Lab. 191 (158): refers to the apocryphal story that in old age Belisarius went blind and was reduced to begging his bread from door to door.

Lab. 191 (158) *Aleph* 106

Bello, Andrés (1781-1865)

A Chilean politician, poet and grammarian, considered a master of the Spanish language. In his *Gramática de la lengua castellaña* (1847) Bello systematised Spanish grammar according to common usage rather than Latin rules. The work is still influential. A Neoclassicist, Bello engaged in a protracted polemic against *Sarmiento's Romanticism and introduced *Locke, *Berkeley and Mill to South America. Lab. 89 (61): examples of Bello's proposed spelling changes may be found in Borges's quotation from Sarmiento's *Recuerdos de provincia* (*Pról.* 131).

Lab. 89 (619) *Ficc.* 120

Benares

A city in northern *India, the principal Hindu holy centre, famous for its pilgrimages.

Aleph 33 (48) *Ficc.* 38

Bengal (Bengala)

A region in north-east *India. In 1700 the British East India Company established itself in Fort William, which became its base for colonial expansion and subsequently contained the administrative headquarters of the Presidency of Bengal.

Lab. 98 (69) *Ficc.* 132 Aleph 20 (27) *Aleph* 165

Berenice

A city in southern *Egypt on the Red Sea, founded in memory of his mother by Ptolemy Philadelphus in the third century BC.

Lab. 135 (106) *Aleph* 8, Lab. 155 (124) *Aleph* 42

Bergson, Henri (1859-1941)

A French philosopher and Academician, winner of the Nobel Prize for literature in 1927, whose ideas were influential in the years leading up to World War I. Lab. 192 (159): Bergson argued against the mechanistic determinism prevalent in the late nineteenth century, and proposed a doctrine of 'vitalism' stressing the open flow of time. During his early reading of Positivist philosophy he became conscious that scientific time does not endure, and attempted to establish the notion of duration (*durée*): time apprehended by intuition – an inner, or lived, time – which he opposed to the concept of chronometric or spatial time used by science. His ideas on duration led him to oppose the Darwinian interpretation of evolution, and to propose an evolutionary theory based on *élan vital*, a vital impulse resulting in a dynamic generative process.

Lab. 192 (159) *Aleph* 107

Berkeley, General

No record exists in the British Army List of a General Berkeley serving in *Bengal during the autumn of 1923, but the choice of name is convincing. An Irish officer, James Berkeley (1839-1926), joined the British forces in 1857 and became a Major-General in the Indian Army. In 1862 he entered the political service and after serving a number of Indian princes became agent to the Governor-General at Baroda.
    Lab. 98 (69) *Ficc*. 132

Berkeley, George (1685-1753)

An Irish bishop, exponent of the idealist philosophy and author of, among other works, *The Principles of Human Knowledge*, in which he denied the independent existence of matter. The world, Berkeley maintains, is precisely as we perceive it and does not exist outside our perception: '*esse est percipi*.' Berkeley does not suggest, however, that objects jump in and out of existence, but believes that they are sustained by God's own continuous perception of them. Borges, who quoted *Hume's aphorism that Berkeley's arguments are completely irrefutable and completely unconvincing (*Disc*. 67), acknowledges his debt to Berkeley: 'What are all the nights of Scheherezade compared to one argument of Berkeley?' Lab. 39 (15): Berkeley and others planned a new university in America, and the University of California at Berkeley was later named after him.
    Lab. 32 (8) *Ficc*. 20

Bernardo de Yrigoyen

A street in central *Buenos Aires, now part of Avenida Nueve de Julio, known in earlier times as one of the *Calles Largas.
    Aleph 16 (22) *Aleph* 159

Beth

The second letter of the Hebrew alphabet, with the numerical value of two. Beth as the opening letter of the bible has been explained as reflecting the dual nature of the universe, which consists of heaven and earth. See *Sepher Yezirah.
    Lab. 55 (30) *Ficc*. 67

Bibliotheca (Biblioteca) see *Apollodorus

Bikaner (Bikanir)

An Indian city, founded in 488 in the Thor Desert in north Rajasthan. The princely state of Bikaner was loyal to the *Mongol Islamic dynasty in *Delhi which ruled over most of India from 1526 to 1857. Lab. 147 (116): the attention given by the Arabs to the study of astrology throughout the Middle and Far East makes 'professing' this science in Bikaner plausible.

Lab. 147 (116) *Aleph* 23, Aleph 33 (48) *Ficc.* 38

Bioy Casares, Adolfo (1914-)

A distinguished Argentine novelist, short-story writer and critic. His best-known novels are *La invención de Morel* (1940: trans. *Morel's Invention* 1964) and *El sueño de los héroes* (1954: trans. *The Dream of Heroes* 1987). Bioy was a close friend and co-author of Borges, and they published several satirical works under the joint pseudonyms of H. Bustos Domecq, B. Suarez Lynch and B. Lynch such as *Seis problemas para Don Isidro Parodi* (1942), a parody of detective fiction, and *Crónicas de Bustos Domecq* (1967). Bioy married Silvina *Ocampo, who was also a friend of Borges. The three together compiled an *Anthology of Fantastic Literature* (1940) and developed the theory and practice of fantastic literature in close collaboration. Lab. 43: the 'Quevedian translation' may be the translation of chapter 5 of *Browne's *Urn Burial* which Borges published together with Bioy.

Lab. 27 (3) Ficc. 13, Aleph 82 (129) *Aleph* 143

Black and Tans

A force of special constabulary operating in *Ireland towards the end of the Anglo-Irish 'Troubles' (1916-22), recruited from demobilised British soldiers. The name derived from the improvised uniform of khaki military trousers and black police tunics. It was also the name of a well-known pack of hounds in Limerick. Lab. 100 (71): the ferocity with which the Black and Tans carried out reprisals against the Irish Republican Army earned them lasting notoriety. They were associated with some of the worst atrocities of the civil war, notably the killings at Croke Park in Derry on 21 November 1920.

Lab. 100 (71) *Ficc.* 134

Blancos

A Uruguayan political party founded by the followers of *Oribe, so called because, at the battle of Carpentería against *Rivera in 1836, they wore white hatbands, while their enemies, the *Colorados, wore red. The Blanco party consisted of rich landowners who supported the *Federalist policy of *Rosas in Buenos Aires. The two-party system continued to dominate the political scene in *Uruguay for over a century. The Blancos are now known as the Nationalists and represent the conservative classes, while the Colorados, more radical, sponsor the labour forces of

*Montevideo and the new non-Spanish immigrants. See *Guerra Grande.
Brodie 40 (47) *Brodie* 76, Brodie 73 (90) *Brodie* 105

Bloom, Leopold

The seemingly mock-heroic, yet still heroic, protagonist of James *Joyce's *Ulysses*, whose peregrinations around Dublin are closely identified with the wanderings in the Mediterranean of the Homeric *Odysseus (Ulysses). Lab. 192 (159): Leopold Bloom's 'irreversible florin' is an allusion to the 'Ithaca' episode in *Ulysses* in which Bloom marks a florin with three notches on the milled edge before spending it in order to see whether it will come back to him. It does not (*Ulysses*, Harmondsworth, 617).
Lab. 192 (159) *Aleph* 106

Bloy, Léon (1846-1917)

A French writer who became a Catholic convert and proselyte. His *L'âme de Napoléon* (1912), *Journal* (1939) and published letters are characterised by mysticism. Bloy's faith rested on the concept that man is saved through suffering and love, a source of mystical inspiration. Thus enlightened, he can understand his function in the economy of the universe, just as he can the verse of a liturgical text. This idea, akin to the *Cabbalistic interpretation of creation, appealed considerably to Borges, and was quoted by him in his essays (Other Inq. 120, 127). Lab. 154 (123): the allusion to Bloy, echoing the belief that each man has a counterpart in heaven in 'inverted reflection' of his identity, is probably based on the argument of the last chapter of *L'âme de Napoléon* entitled 'The Invisible Companion'. This refers to the doctrine of the guardian angel who acompanies each person, knowing and seeing what he does not know and see, and crying whenever he sins. 'Conforming with the law of supernatural equilibrium', the relationship between man and his angel must be such that the lowest of sinners will be under the protection of a high-ranking angel, capable of bearing the weight of his sins, while the angels appointed to great men such as Napoleon, would be 'humble and timid', the 'smallest of the Blessed Messengers'.
Lab. 154 (123) *Aleph* 41

Boedo

An avenue in a poor district in south-western *Buenos Aires, the name of which gave rise in the 1920s to the 'Group of Boedo'. The members of this group were mostly of immigrant descent with Marxist or anarchist tendencies. They wrote for the people, unlike the more elitist and cosmopolitan 'Group of Florida' with which Borges was identified.
Lab. 193 (160) *Aleph* 108

Bohemia

A province of Czechoslovakia and the centre of many artistic and cultural traditions. Lab. 147 (116): professing astrology in Bohemia could be a veiled allusion to Johannes Kepler (1571-1630) who came to *Prague Observatory in 1600 and established the laws of planetary motion which later enabled *Newton to formulate his theory of gravitation. See *Clementinum.

Lab. 147 (116) *Aleph* 23

Böhme, Jacob (1575-1624)

A German Lutheran mystic, author of many theosophical works, including an allegorical explanation of the book of Genesis entitled *Mysterium Magnum*. Böhme had experienced mystical revelations from childhood, and believed that he could penetrate the mysteries of God through contemplation. Lab. 118 (88): the 'indirect Jewish sources' may refer to Böhme's use of Christian metaphors to express his intuition and close affinity to *Cabbalistic thought.

Lab. 118 (88) Ficc. 159

Bolívar, Simón (1783-1830)

A military and political leader, the liberator of northern Spanish America, regarded as South America's greatest political genius. After freeing his native Venezuela from Spanish rule in 1813, and Colombia in 1819, Bolívar was elected in 1821 President of a conglomeration of Andean countries known as Gran Colombia. In 1822 with the help of his officer, General Sucre, he defeated the Spaniards in Ecuador. He then marched on Peru, the stronghold of Spanish power, and in 1824 achieved South America's final victory over Spain at the battle of *Ayacucho. Brodie 82 (100): during his long campaign Bolívar wrote a great many letters, which were edited in twelve volumes by Vicente Lecuna (1929-1959). The letters to *San Martín concerning preparations for the meeting at *Guayaquil are both deferential and effusive. Brodie 72 (89): a letter dated 13 August 1822 is stated as the cause of the rivalry between the two scholars in 'Guayaquil': the existing letter of that date is unlikely to be the one meant. It is addressed to General Santander, and in it Bolívar declines Santander's invitation to return to Bogotá to take charge of the government. The only mention made of San Martín is of the possibility of his army's defeat, which was another reason why Bolívar had to remain in the south. A letter allegedly written by San Martín to Bolívar, on the existence of which the legend of Guayaquil appeared substantiated, was found in 1939 to be a forgery, causing a furore in the Academy of History.

Brodie 72 (89) *Brodie* 75, Brodie 81 (99)) *Brodie* 111

Bombay

The second largest city of India, whose name derives from the Portuguese Boa Bahia, meaning 'good harbour'. Aleph 31 (45): Bombay has a university and is a notable publishing centre.
   Lab. 147 (116) *Aleph* 23, Aleph 31(45) *Ficc.* 35

Bombay Gazette

Published from about 1792 to 1914, one of the few early papers to continue after the establishment of official government gazettes in 1830.
   Aleph 31 (46) *Ficc.* 36

Bombay Quarterly Review

Published 1855-8.
   Aleph 31 (46) *Ficc.* 36

Bonfanti, Mario

A pompous and pathetic character created by Borges in collaboration with *Bioy Casares under their pseudonym Bustos Domecq.
   Aleph 22 (29) *Aleph* 167

Book of the Common (Libro del Común)

The *Popol Vuh*, the national book of the Quiché Maya, which contains their mythology and history. The manuscript was found in the village of Chichicastenango, in the Quiché area, by Father Francisco Ximénez, who transcribed it and translated it into Spanish. It became known to the Spaniards as *The Book of the Council* or *The Book of the Community*. Lab. 207 (173): the expressions used by *Tzinacán to describe his mystical vision are taken more or less directly from the first two chapters of Part One which describe the creation of the world – 'The mountains appeared from the water; and instantly the mountains grew' – and of the first men, made of wood: 'And instantly the figures were made of wood. They looked like men, talked like men.' These first men, the narrative continues, behaved cruelly towards the objects and animals which surrounded them, and 'their earthen jars, plates, pots and grinding stones' turned against them, and so did the dogs which took revenge 'and destroyed their faces'. Equally, at the beginning of chapter 1 we read that only the Great Father and the Great Mother (*Qaholom and Alom, for the Quiché had a dual concept of divinity) were there, in the water, hidden under green and blue feathers. After 'the word came' they united their thoughts and 'planned the creation'.
   Lab. 207 (173) *Aleph* 120

Boole, George (1815-1864)

An English logician and mathematician. In *The Laws of Thought* Boole dealt with the methodology of deriving logical inferences. Boole was the first mathematician to associate mathematics with logic, showing how the symbols of algebra can be made to represent logical forms and syllogisms. By the use of such symbols all propositions can be reduced to universally accessible equations. If, for example, the symbols x and y signify respectively 'horned' and 'sheep', the combination xy will mean 'horned sheep'. Equally $1-x$ will indicate everything except horned things, and $(1-x)$ $(1-y)$ everything which is neither horned nor sheep. Boole's *Memoirs* were published by the Royal Society, one of whose founders, John *Wilkins, had advocated the possibility of a universal language based on a system of logical symbols.

Lab. 63 (37) *Ficc.* 47

Borges, Francisco (1833-1874)

Borges's grandfather, a colonel in the *Santa Fe garrison on the frontiers with the open pampa. In 1870, while defending the town of Paraná against an attack of *montoneros*, Francisco Borges met and later married Borges's grandmother, Frances (Fanny) Haslam. He died in action at La Verde in 1874, while fighting to suppress *Mitre's revolt (see Sel. Poems 149, 269). Lab. 161 (129): after her husband's death in 1874 Borges's English grandmother, who came from Staffordshire, was left to bring up their two sons in the alien surroundings of Paraná. Her loneliness and divided loyalties are recalled in 'Story of the Warrior and the Captive'.

Lab. 161 (129) *Aleph* 50

Bosch

A well-known private clinic in *Buenos Aires frequented by the *porteño* elite.

Lab. 196 (163) *Aleph* 112

Boston

Brodie 31(35): in Henry *James's novels Boston represents the set of moral and intellectual values, contrasted with European culture, particularly the culture of London: correct behaviour and conventional morality coupled with intellectual sterility, ignorance and sexual repression.

Brodie 31 (35) *Brodie* 89

Bousset, Wilhelm (1865-1920)

A German theologian, the founder of a school of biblical studies, whose writings include works on the early Church and *Gnosticism. Bousset highlighted the influence of Hellenistic traditions on the expansion of orthodox Christianity, claiming that many biblical passages stemmed from ancient myths of Egyptian and Babylonian origin. Lab. 153 (122): Bousset's standpoint was opposed to that of his contemporary *Harnack. This rivalry, in the context of 'The Theologians', can be perceived in the differences within the theological schools mentioned in the story.

Lab. 153 (122) *Aleph* 39

Bradley, Francis Herbert (1846-1924)

An English idealist philosopher, a follower of *Hegel and *Kant and an outspoken critic of the utilitarian and empiricist schools. Bradley's best-known work is *Appearance and Reality* (1893), an 'essay on metaphysics'. Described in the Preface as 'a critical discussion of first principles', it is an invitation to doubt all preconceptions and to ascertain how far reality can be known. Though claiming that knowledge of the Absolute is available to us, Bradley argues that our comprehension of it, based as it is on appearance, must be partial, but that this imperfect knowledge is not worthless. Appearance, even when misleading, is still a component of reality. Borges, always intrigued by epistemological problems of the limitations of the human mind, recalls Bradley's theories in two essays (Other Inq. 112-13 and 186). In a discussion of regression *ad infinitum* in relationships Borges quotes Bradley's ideas as expounded in chapter 4 of *Appearance and Reality* where Bradley denies causal relations, and indeed all types of relation, arguing that relations are realities in their own right. Thus no unitary thing can be considered a collection of its properties; rather the relatedness of its properties is a constituent of reality. Appearance, even when misleading, is still a component of reality. Fict. 68 (75) refers to Bradley's argument that 'direction' is relative to 'our' world but not necessarily an aspect of reality. For we can suppose that there are beings who have no contact with the world we experience whose lives run in a direction opposite to ours. If we could know their world, a world in which, as Borges quoting Bradley says, 'death would come before birth, the blow would follow the wound', this would appear to us irrational and inconsistent only because of our experience. But, transcending the limits of our life, we might find a reality which had 'no direction', or rather which showed 'both directions harmoniously combined in a consistent whole'. Lab. 120 (90) refers to Bradley's postulation that time, like space, is merely appearance, and that neither belongs to reality. Bradley denies the existence of time on the grounds that it is endless, whereas an end is essential to being. Like space, time is a relation between terms which can never be found, since there are no clear demarcations separating the past, the present and future. As Borges explains, 'if the now is divisible into other nows, it is no less complicated than time and, if indivisible, time is a mere relation between non-temporal things'.

Fict. 68 (75) *Ficc.* 79, Lab. 120 (90) *Ficc.* 162

Bragado

A town and river in the province of *Buenos Aires. The district of the same name, a centre of the da ry industry, lies near the river *Salado.

Brodie 18 (18) *Brodie* 131

Brahms, Johannes (1833-97)

The only composer to be mentioned in Borges's stories. See *Deutsches Requiem.

Lab. 174 (142) *Aleph* 82

Brasil, Calle

An avenue in the district of *Constitución.

Fict. 154 (169) *Fict.* 190

Brave New World (1932)

A dystopian novel by Aldous Huxley. The title comes from Shakespeare's *Tempest* (V:i:183): 'O brave new world / that has such people in it!'

Lab. 32 (7) *Ficc.* 19

Brazil (Brasil)

The largest of all Latin American countries, containing 48 per cent of South America's area and population. Aleph 54 (81): the war between Argentina and Brazil (1825-8) was fought over a dispute about the *Banda Oriental, to which both powers laid claim. A most unpopular war with all countries concerned, it was fought at great cost and resulted in the creation of *Uruguay as an independent buffer state between Argentina and Brazil. Lab. 96 (67): after the abolition of slavery in 1888, the Brazilian government encouraged immigration from Europe in order to expand the cotton and coffee plantations. The flood of immigrants reached its height in the early 1920s. The frontier areas of Brazil have long been characterised by illicit traffic with Argentina, Paraguay and Uruguay.

Lab. 96 (67) *Ficc.* 129, Aleph 22 (30) 54 (81) *Aleph* 53, 168

Breslau

The German name of Wroclaw, a city in Polish Silesia, which belonged to Germany until 1945. Lab. 176 (144): Jews have lived in and been expelled from Breslau many times since 1203. At the end of the eighteenth century they gained a foothold in the city, and Breslau was the home of many distinguished Jewish scholars. In 1939 the Jews numbered 10,309; from 1941 they were deported to concentration camps and only a few hundred survived.

  Lab. 176 (144) Aleph 85

Brighton

A middle-class seaside resort in Sussex, fashionable in the early nineteenth century under the patronage of the Prince Regent, later George IV, who built its ornate Royal Pavilion.

  Aleph 31 (45) *Ficc*. 35, Aleph 15 (20) *Aleph* 156

Britannia (Britania)

The name, probably of Iberian or Gallic origin, of the ancient Roman province of Britain. Christianity probably did not reach Britain before the middle of the third century. Lab. 153 (122): no mention has been found of a diocese of Britain during the sixth century. Reference to the inversion of crucifixes, though fictitious, may be an oblique allusion to the doctrine of the British lay monk Pelagius who in the fifth century questioned original sin and was charged with heresy. His followers developed his theories, denying that Christ had to die for human redemption or act as an intermediary between man and his salvation.

  Lab. 153 (122) *Aleph* 39

British Council (Consejo Británico)

An independent organisation founded in 1934, with a royal charter, for the promotion of British culture. It now operates in eighty countries.

  Aleph 82 (129) *Aleph* 143

Brodie, David

The fictional Scottish Protestant missionary who visits the *Yahoos. Brodie has associations not only with Swift, but with the Spanish Dominican missionary Bartolomé de las Casas (1474-1566). Brodie's appeal to the generosity of his king not to ignore the destiny of that 'barbarous nation' resembles Las Casas's plea to Charles V to stop his Spanish subjects exploiting the Indians. Borges alludes elsewhere to this incident, commenting, ironically, on Las Casas's suggestion that the

Indians 'languishing' in the 'hellish' gold mines of the Antilles be replaced by black slaves to 'languish' in the same mines (see *Infamy* 19).
Brodie 91 (111) *Brodie* 139

Browne, Sir Thomas (1605-1682)

An English author and physician. Browne was a student of Platonism, the belief that the world is the imperfect reflection of a perfect system in which all things have a purpose and are worthy of observation. His style abounds in quaint expressions, latinate words and neologisms. His *Religio Medici*, the expression of a mind at once credulous and sceptical, was regarded by his contemporaries as a bundle of contradictions, and it was put on the Papal Index. A Spanish translation was published in fifty instalments in *Sur*. Lab. 43 (18): the idiosyncratic quality of Browne's writing is clearly revealed in *Urn Burial*, considered the most imaginative and elegant of his books. Lab. 154 (123): the remark about the Histrionic gospels must surely be apocryphal.
Lab. 43 (18) *Ficc.* 34, Lab. 154 (123) *Aleph* 40

Browning, Robert (1812-1889)

An English poet and dramatist who dwells on the personality and problems of man, upholding spiritual values and human conduct based on the committed pursuit of an ideal. Browning's most famous work, considered by Borges his greatest, is *The Ring and the Book*, which was published in four volumes between 1868 and 1869. It describes the events of a seventeenth-century murder trial in Rome. Lab. 102 (72): though the assertion that Fergus *Kilpatrick's name illustrates Browning's verses cannot be confirmed, Browning was interested in themes related to patriotism, especially in his early work (e.g. 'The Italian in England' and 'The Patriot'). He was also interested in the psychology and redeeming features of wicked men (e.g. *Mr.Sludge the Medium*, discussed by G.K.*Chesterton in his *Robert Browning*, which may have been known to Borges). In Browning's works the passage that may be most relevant to the story of Fergus Kilpatrick is the end of *Sordello* (1840). Sordello, who has been a supporter of the progressive party, the Guelphs, is offered the leadership of the repressive party, the Ghibellines. He eventually rejects the offer and dies of his own conflicting feelings.
Lab. 102 (72) *Ficc.* 137

Buber, Martin (1878-1965)

A German philosopher, Zionist and translator of the bible, author of an extensive study of the sect of the *Hasidim. When his programme to propagate Jewish culture and organise educational courses for Jews was stopped by the Nazis, Buber took refuge in Palestine, where he worked once more in adult education and advocated communal living in kibbutzim. Lab. 131 (102): in his famous work *I and Thou* (1937) Buber used the word 'pathetic' (translated as 'with cosmic pathos') to describe the experience of man awakening to the realisation of his alienation in the dual system of a world in which there are only two partners: man and what confronts him. It was perhaps in this sense that early Zionist leaders, of whom Buber was one, declared that the Jews would remain a 'pathetic people' until they had a homeland of their own.

Lab. 131 (102) *Ficc.* 182

Buddhism (Budismo)

A philosophical/religious system founded by Siddharta, or Gautama, known as the Buddha, and practised through most of South Asia. The essence of Buddhism, enunciated in the 'Four Truths', involves a process of purification, which is the result of progressive detachment from sensual desire, intellectual activity, emotional involvement and, finally, any sense of satisfaction or even serenity. This process, achieved over the course of multiple lives through reincarnations ('Samsara'), leads to supreme indifference, and then to a stage in which even the activity of contemplation is transcended. A total nullification ('Karma') of the traces of the life cycles, which do not end with individual deaths, is achieved. Perfect enlightment follows, leading to supernatural consciousness and, finally, the indescribable condition of 'Nirvana'. Lab. 48 (23): Stephen Albert's composure and his imperturbable acceptance of death can be seen as manifestations of a Buddhist attitude to existence. Lab. 131 (101): concerning the different names of Buddhist monks, members of some of the many schools of Buddhism do take a new name once they enter 'refuge' and, at various stages of their spiritual life, adopt new names according to the degree of enlightenment they have achieved. The 'refuge' names are normally composite, such as 'Ocean of Teaching' or 'Glorious Banner' etc.

Lab. 49 (24) *Ficc.* 105, Lab 131 (101) *Ficc.* 181

Buen Orden

The old name of the street *Bernardo de Yrigoyen.

Brodie 75 (92) *Brodie* 79/80

Buenos Aires

Buenos Aires originated in 1536 as a small settlement near the mouth of a meandering stream now known as *Riachuelo. Attacked by belligerent Indian tribes, the settlement was too weak to last. In 1580 Juan de Garay sailed down the river Paraná from Asunción with greater resources and established another settlement, north of the original, around the area of today's Plaza de Mayo (see Plaza *Victoria). A church, whose foundations lie beneath the present cathedral, a municipal chamber or *cabildo* and a jail were built, and the city was expanded in the form of a grid of squares, or *manzanas*, surrounding the central square. The Crown of Castile's purpose in encouraging this settlement in an area devoid of silver was to control the mouth of the estuary: its rivers provided the easiest route between the rich mining areas of the north and a port on the Atlantic and hence to Spain. Even after the silver mines became exhausted, the city grew in importance. The port proved convenient for the reception of European goods, and the fertile surrounding lands of the pampas were ideally suited for the export of agricultural products. Attention was focused on Buenos Aires, not only by Spain, but by other expansionist European countries, particularly England, and it attracted one of the largest immigrations of the nineteenth century. At first most of the population lived in the south. The patrician families inhabited the area surrounding Plaza de Mayo, in *Barrio Sur and *San Telmo, and the poor lived in primitive tenement buildings, or *conventillos*, nearby and by the river mouth in unsanitary areas such as *Bajo, *Barracas and Boca. This was the old, colonial Buenos Aires which Borges often recalls. It was not, however, the Buenos Aires into which he was born. By 1899, the year of his birth, the thrust of the city had developed northwards, away from floods and epidemics, to higher terrain. Borges was born, as he says, 'in the very heart of the city', in Barrio Norte, but his family soon moved to *Palermo, where the 'shabby but genteel' lived cheek by jowl with the seedier elements of the population, the *compadritos* or hoodlums of so many of Borges's stories. In addition to Palermo, northern Buenos Aires is divided into the following sections, all of which are mentioned by Borges. Barrio Norte, the wealthiest part, contains the palatial homes of the landed and commercial oligarchy. In its ostentation and cosmopolitanism it contrasts with the older, more patrician and restrained Barrio Sur, now decayed and dilapidated. The area near the port, on the northern side, was known for its brothels and drinking bars. It extended as far as the *Maldonado, a small stream dividing the city from its outskirts, a rough area in which many of the stories in *Doctor Brodie's Report* are set. Beyond the Maldonado is *Belgrano, also a mixed area, with some rough enclaves, but mainly cosmopolitan, professional and suburban. West of the centre are the districts of Plaza del *Once and Villa Crespo, which became small commercial business centres, bustling with immigrants. Further out are the lower-middle-class areas of *Flores and *Floresta. For the historical development of Buenos Aires in relation to the rest of the country, see *Federalism and *Unitarianism. Borges's attachment to Buenos Aires is deep-rooted. He left the city in 1914 and spent the war years in Europe. When he returned it became an inspiration for his work, particularly his poetry. 'It was more than a homecoming; it was a rediscovery,' he wrote in 'Autobiographical Essay'. Works such as *Fervor de Buenos Aires*, his first poetry collection, the monograph dedicated to the *porteño* poet Evaristo Carriego and the many stories set in Buenos Aires recalling either the city of his youth or the city's legendary past bear witness to Borges's nostalgia. See map.

Bulaq (also Bulak)

Once a suburb of *Cairo, now part of the city, renowned for its museum of Egyptology.
   Lab. 146 (116) *Aleph* 22

Bulwer Lytton, Edward George, Baron Lytton (1803-1873)

An English novelist, author of *The Last Days of Pompeii*, whose work reflects the influence of Byron and the Gothic novel. Bulwer Lytton's grandiloquent style and exaggerated characters were mercilessly attacked by some of his contemporaries and his reputation has declined considerably in the course of the twentieth century.
   Fict. 70 (77) *Ficc.* 82

Burton, Sir Richard (1821-1890)

An eminent British scholar and explorer who, disguised as a Muslim, was the first European to penetrate the secret cities of Mecca and Medina. Burton was a man of many parts: poet, ethnologist, linguist and translator of Arabian erotica. His version of the *Thousand and One Nights* is unsurpassed. Borges discusses it at some length in his essay on the translators, summarising Burton's aims as: (a) to increase his reputation as an Arabist, (b) to improve on *Lane's translation, which he regarded as prosaic and bland and which he 'corrected' by expanding the erotic incidents, and (c) to interest nineteenth-century British gentlemen in Arab letters of the thirteenth century. According to Borges the last aim was incompatible with the first, given the directness of the original text and the scepticism and scholarly preferences of contemporary readership, but Burton overcame this not only by swelling the text with idiosyncratic notes, but by falsifying it with the 'richness of his English' (*Etern.* 108-19). Aleph 22 (30): Burton's diplomatic career took him in 1864 to *Santos, where he spent four years as Consul and wrote a book on the highlands of Brazil. See *Parliament of Birds*.
   Lab. 187 (155) *Aleph* 101, Aleph 22 (30) *Aleph* 168

Cabbala (or Cabala)

From the Hebrew *Kabbal*, meaning 'to receive': 'the received', or traditional, lore. This general term is applied in Judaeo-Christianity to a body of religious knowledge and experience which seeks to provide a means of approaching God directly. The Cabbala is largely concerned with postulating cosmological systems: that is to say, with theories of the creation, maintenance and destiny of the world and the interrelation of its components. It includes a description of the role of man and other living creatures, the behaviour of the heavenly hosts and the interaction of these with the Godhead. As a method of mystical and poetical exposition of the Scriptures, the Cabbala adopts an immanent approach to the Universe, believing in the hidden existence of godliness behind and within every material object. Thus in Cabbalistic thought the visible world is likened to a veil or curtain which esoteric interpretations are able to lift, revealing a more direct vision of the true mysteries of God and his creation. Since, according to the Jewish account of creation, language preceded the act of creation ('And God said, "Let there be light"; and there was light'), there followed a belief in the magical properties of Hebrew, the language employed by God. In Hebrew each of the 22 letters has its equivalent numerical value, and an important Cabbalistic method of exegesis is *Gematria*, or the interpretation of the Scriptures based upon numerical calculations and combinations of the Hebrew letters. This method did not exclude belief in the magic and creative properties of the Hebrew letters which, if deciphered, might reveal not only the ineffable presence of God, but also his mysterious power of creation. A guide to the different Cabbalistic theories can be found in the *Zohar, the holy book of Cabbalism. Borges was attracted to any idea which postulated the unreality of the visible world; what fascinated him particularly about the Cabbala was the idea of a systematic combinatorial method of mystical revelation (see 'Una vindicación de la cábala', *Disc.* 55-60). See *Pentateuch.

Lab. 39 (15) *Ficc.* 30, Lab. 107 (77) *Ficc.* 145

Cabrera Street

A street in the centre of *Buenos Aires, near *Palermo, in what used to be a rough neighbourhood.

Brodie 47 (56) *Brodie* 43

Caesar (Cesar)

The cognomen of Caius Julius Caesar and hence the title given to Roman emperors. Lab. 136 (106): the Caesar referred to is probably *Diocletian. See *Alexandria.

Lab. 136 (106) *Aleph* 8, Lab. 142 (112) *Aleph* 17

Cagancha

A battle in 1839 between the Uruguayans, led by Fructuoso Rivera, and the invading *Federalist forces of Juan Manuel *Rosas under the command of *Urquiza. Urquiza was defeated and his forces were

temporarily pushed back into *Entre Ríos.
    Aleph 69 (107) *Aleph* 75

Cain

The first murderer, the son of Adam and Eve, who killed his brother Abel out of jealousy and was cursed by God (Genesis 4:8-10).
    Brodie 56 (67) *Brodie* 20

Cainites (Cainitas)

A heretical *Gnostic sect mentioned by Irenaeus,.Epiphanius of Salamis and other Christian writers. Their name was derived from the cult of Cain whom they acclaimed for withstanding the God of the Old Testament, regarded by them as the cause of evil in the world. The Cainites possessed an apocryphal *Gospel of Judas* and believed that *Judas, being in contact with the 'Truth', was aware of providence and brought about Jesus's betrayal because he knew in advance that it had to happen. The Cainites stressed the importance of evil in perpetual contest with good for supremacy in the universe, and held a dualistic creed not unlike the system of the *Gnostics.
    Lab. 153 (122) *Aleph* 40

Cairo

The capital of Egypt, situated on the right bank of the Nile about twelve miles from the apex of its delta. Founded by the Arabs in 641-2, it is famous for its mosques, of which *Amr is the oldest.
    Lab. 180 (148) *Aleph* 91, Aleph 23 (30) *Aleph* 169

Calcutta (Calcuta)

The largest city in India, and the capital of West *Bengal. Calcutta was the capital of India under the British between 1833 and 1912.
    Aleph 33 (48) *Ficc*. 38

Calcutta Englishman

The London supplement of *The Englishman Extraordinary*, published in Calcutta 17 March 1838 – 13 April 1839.
    Aleph 32 ((46) *Ficc*. 36

Calcutta Review

A quarterly review published by the University of Calcutta, 1846-1945.
    Aleph 31 (46) *Ficc*. 36

Calles Largas

The streets Rivadavia and Montes de Oca in *Barracas and *Constitución, an old part of *Buenos Aires, once patrician, now run down. See *Bernardo de Yrigoyen.
Brodie 76 (92) *Brodie* 80

Calpurnia

The third wife of *Julius Caesar, whom he married in 59 BC.
Lab. 103 (73) *Ficc*. 138

Calvinism

A religious movement initiated by the French theologian and reformist John Calvin (1509-1564). Calvin established a strict theocratic regime in *Geneva, assuming wide-ranging powers over the private life of its citizens; infringements led to excommunication and exile. Calvinism was in direct opposition to Rome. Hence the distaste with which the presumably traditionally Roman Catholic narrator in Lab. 62 (36) alluded to it; but it also differed from other Protestant movements by its extreme position on predestination. Calvinism held that after the Fall, itself determined by God, everything that man wills and does is sin. There are only two paths to follow, concupiscence or grace, but man has no power over which to adopt, the choice having been predestined by God.
Lab. 62 (36) *Ficc*. 45

Cambaceres de Alvear, Mariana

A fictitious name composed of the surname of a prominent Argentine novelist, Eugenio Cambaceres (1843-1888), and Elvira de Alvear, with whom Borges was said to have been in love while working at a municipal library similar to the Lafinur Library mentioned in Aleph 13 (18) (see Monegal, *Jorge Luis Borges: A Literary Biography*, NY 1978, 308-9).
Aleph 15 (19) *Aleph* 156

Cancha Rayada

The site of a battle in Chile fought on 19 March 1818, when the army of *San Martín was defeated by the Royalist forces. San Martín managed to save most of his men, but lost nearly all his military equipment. For a brief period the independence of Chile, which had seemed secure after the victory of *Chacabuco, was uncertain, but it was finally assured on 5 April 1818 with the triumph at Maipú.
Brodie 72 (89) *Brodie* 75

Cannabière, La

One of the busiest streets of Marseilles, running from the old port to the central Boulevard de la Madeleine.
Lab. 65 (39) *Ficc.* 49

Canterbury

A city in Kent, the see of the Primate of All England. Lab. 187 (155): the archbishop of Canterbury referred to is St Anselm (*c*.1033-1109), one of the foremost scholastic thinkers. In what has come to be known as the Ontological Argument, Anselm sought to prove the existence of God on purely logical grounds, reasoning that if, as we must, we mean by God 'that than which nothing greater can be conceived', we cannot conceive of this entity unless it exists: what exists in external reality must be greater than what exists in the mind: thus God must exist not only inside the mind but also outside, in the 'real' world. The argument was shown to be circular by Aquinas and *Kant, since existence cannot be regarded as predicate.
Lab. 187 (155) *Aleph* 101

Canto, Estela (1919-)

A novelist with whom Borges had an emotional relationship at the time of writing 'The Aleph'. See Beatriz *Viterbo.
Aleph 11 (title page) *Aleph* 169

Canton

The largest city of southern China, situated at the delta of inland rivers flowing into the South China Sea. After contact with Hindu and Arab traders in the tenth century it grew vastly in size and became the first Chinese port to be visited regularly by European merchants.
Lab. 184 (151) *Aleph* 96

Canudos see *Antonio Conselheiro

Capanga

A pejorative term used in the River Plate to designate a bodyguard, or bully's henchman.
Lab. 30 (6) *Ficc.* 18

Capella, Martianus see *Satyricon

Capital

The name commonly given to Buenos Aires, the capital of the Argentine Republic. Its inhabitants are known as *porteños*, or people of the port.
Brodie 20

Caraguatá

A tributary of the *Tacuarembó river in north-west *Uruguay.
Lab. 96 (67) *Ficc.* 129

Cardoso marshes (Laguna de Cardoso)

A region in the northern province of *Buenos Aires. See Eusebio *Laprida.
Aleph 55 (83) *Aleph* 55

Carlyle, Thomas (1795-1881)

A Scottish historian and essayist, at first much admired by Borges, for whom he epitomised literature (Other Inq. 13). Borges later rejected Carlyle's cult of heroism, condemning him as the inventor of the idea of the Teutonic race and the direct precursor of the Nazis. Carlyle's *Sartor Resartus* (The Taylor Re-patched), is an apocryphal biography of a Dr Teufelsdröckh (Devil's Dirt), said to contain many autobiographical details. Carlyle quotes from Teufelsdröckh's mystical writings as if they existed, adding his own commentaries. Borges used similar devices, notably in 'The Approach to Almotasim' and 'Pierre Menard, author of Don Quixote'. Brodie 25 (26): Carlyle's thesis that men need heroes occurs throughout his writings but particularly in *On Heroes, Hero-Worship and the Heroic in History* (1841: translated by Borges) and *Past and Present* (1843). See *Pról.* 32-9.
Brodie 25 (26) *Brodie* 26

Carmen

The main character of an opera by Bizet, which was first produced in 1875, with a libretto by Meilhac and Halévy based on a novel by Prosper Mérimée. Its melodramatic plot of love and death, gypsies, soldiers and toreadors creates what seems a typically Spanish ambience.
Lab. 68 (42) *Ficc.* 53

Carpathians (Cárpatos)

A mountain range in eastern Europe. Lab. 106 (76): a 'war in the Carpathians' cannot be precisely located. The area is closely associated with Jewish pogroms and has a tenuous historical connection with

*Hasidism, *Baal Shem Tov having gone into retreat there for a period.
Lab. 106 (76) *Ficc.* 144

Carpocrates

A second-century Neoplatonist from *Alexandria, the founder of a heretical sect which believed in the dualism of good and evil, denied the divinity of Christ and held that the soul is imprisoned in the body from which it strives to be free. Lab. 155 (124): Carpocrates believed that a man could be redeemed only after he had undergone experiences of all kinds and committed every possible deed, good and bad. Carpocrates himself seems to have led a simple life, but his followers were often accused of gross indulgence and superstition.
Lab. 125 (95), 155 (124) *Ficc.* 169 *Aleph* 41

Carriego, Evaristo (1883-1912)

A popular poet, story-writer and playwright whose principal theme was his own *barrio* *Palermo. At his early death, from pneumonia, he had published only one volume of poetry, *Misas herejes* (1908), his work being known mainly through informal readings in neighbourhood cafés. In his poetry Carriego creates the myth of the *porteño* suburb, describing the starkness of life in the *barrio* in a spirit that owes much to Modernism and Baudelairian decadence. Carriego was a friend of Borges's father and visited their house every Sunday; Borges claims to have been greatly influenced as a child by their literary discussions. Brodie 66 (81): like the narrator of 'Juan *Muraña', Borges wrote a literary biography of Carriego, which was published in 1930.
Brodie 66 (81) *Brodie* 65

Cartagena

The capital of a department in northern Colombia, a seaport on the Caribbean. Brodie 82 (100): Cartagena proclaimed its independence from Spain in 1811 and was reoccupied four years later. It did not become free until 1821, under the presidency of *Bolívar.
Brodie 36 (39) *Brodie* 95, Brodie 82 (100) *Brodie* 112

Cartaphilus, Joseph

A fictional character in 'The Immortal'. His name alludes to the legend of the Wandering Jew, which first appeared in a thirteenth-century chronicle by Roger Wendover. According to Wendover, a certain Cartaphilus (believed to be St Joseph of Arimathaea), taunted Jesus on his way to the Cross and was told by him that he would have to wait on earth until he returned. Cartaphilus lived to a hundred and then reverted to thirty, at which age he was destined to remain until the end of the world. Lab. 135 (105): the legend of the Jew condemned to wander about the world until Christ's second coming has been told in several versions and was a popular subject in the eighteenth and nineteenth centuries. Through these reworkings the legend shares with the *Odyssey the fate of 'immortality' (see 'Las versiones homéricas' in *Disc.*).

Lab. 135 (105) *Aleph* 7

Carthage (Cartago)

A city in North Africa sacked by the Romans in 146 BC after the Third Punic War. Lab. 153 (122): after the second century Carthage became an important centre of Christianity, counting among its bishops two of the Church fathers, Tertullian and Cyprian. Between 251 and 553 it was the seat of several ecclesiastical councils. Brodie 83 (101): Carthage is of special interest to Jews on account of its inhabitants' Phoenician origin. Its early form of government recalls that of the Hebrew judges, and there are similarities in religious practices. The history of Carthage has interested Jewish historians since *Josephus, who sought to establish the antiquity of the Jews by reference to the foundation of Carthage, adducing a document stating that the Temple was built 143 years and 8 months before the Tyrians founded Carthage.

Lab. 153 (122) *Aleph* 39, Brodie 83 (101) *Brodie* 113

Caseros

A street in southern *Buenos Aires, near Plaza *Constitución. Aleph 17 (23): that a firm of lawyers has offices there, rather than in the vicinity of Tribunales (the Law Courts), implies that it is relatively obscure. In the English translation this interpretation is made explicit by the added phrase 'the unlikely address'.

Aleph 17 (23) *Aleph* 160

Catalogue of ships (Catálogo de las naves)

The detailed description of the Greek armaments in book 2 of *Homer's *Iliad*.

Lab. 148 (117) *Aleph* 24

Catriel, Cipriano (d. 1874)

An Indian chieftain, who fought against the Indians on the side of the Argentine national government, leading his 800 men into battle against the invading Chilean Indians under their *cacique* Calfucurá. Some years later he fought on the side of the revolutionary forces. He was taken captive and handed over to loyalist Indians, who stabbed him to death.

Fict. 152 (167) *Ficc*. 187

Cavalieri, Francesco Bonaventura (1598-1647)

An Italian mathematician, a disciple of Galileo, whose work in geometry was fundamental to the development of integral calculus. Lab. 86 (58): Cavalieri expounded his geometry of indivisibles in *A Certain Method for the Development of a New Geometry of Continuous Indivisibility* (1635), a work that provoked much criticism at the time.

Lab. 86 (58) *Ficc*. 95

Celestial archetype (Arquetipo celestial)

A term used in Platonism for an ideal 'form' existing outside the sensible world whose individual physical manifestations are but reflections. See *Republic*.

Lab. 59 (34) *Ficc*. 73

Céline, Louis Ferdinand (1894-1961)

A French writer, best known for his provocative novel *Journey to the End of Night* (1934) which portrays French life during and after World War I. Its profane tone and obscenity were regarded as offensive. A supporter of fascist doctrines, Céline also wrote an anti-semitic work entitled *Bagatelles pour un massacre*.

Lab. 71 (44) *Ficc*. 57

Celtic literature (Letras célticas)

Literature written in *Gaelic and the ancient languages of Wales, Ireland and Brittany. Lab. 103: this literature includes many elements of the culture of the *Druids, such as their belief in the transmigration of souls. The two cycles of Irish epics, composed originally in the seventh and eighth centuries and transcribed in the tenth century, are part of the tradition. Lab. 97 (68): the epic poems mentioned refer to the cycle of Ulster and the Fenian cycle, the most important documents of Irish mythology, written in a mixture of prose and poetry. The first, relating to the first century BC, contains the famous *Táin-bó-Cuailinge* describing the war between Ulster and *Connaught which was started by the disappearance of the black bull of Cuailinge. Then, at the court of Medh, the Queen of Connaught, the bull defeated the white-horned bull of Connaught and returned triumphantly to Ulster. In the Fenian cycle, concerning events in *Munster and Leinster in the third century, the legend of Finn tells how Finn gained his knowledge from eating the flesh of a salmon.

Lab. 103 (73) *Ficc*. 139

Centennial (Centenario)

Celebrations of the centenary of the Declaration of Independence in the River Plate Provinces in 1810.
    Brodie 67 (83) *Brodie* 67

Cepeda

A site north west of *Buenos Aires where the Confederation forces under *Urquiza defeated the *porteño* Mitre on 23 October 1859, forcing the province of Buenos Aires to abandon its autonomy and become part of the Argentine Confederation.
    Brodie 73 (90) *Brodie* 77

Cerro Largo

A department in north-east *Uruguay near the frontier with *Brazil.
    Brodie 38 (45) *Brodie* 101

Cervantes Saavedra, Miguel de (1547-1616)

Spain's most celebrated writer, the author of *Don *Quixote*. Cervantes was born in Alcalá de Henares and probably studied at Salamanca. He enlisted in 1570, was wounded at the battle of *Lepanto and served in Corfú and Tunis. In 1575 he was captured by pirates and was not ransomed until 1580. He became Commissioner of Provisions for the Armada in Andalusia and later a tax collector. Imprisoned in 1597 for alleged malpractices, he lived in obscurity until, in 1605, he achieved fame as the author of *Don Quixote*, Part I. In 1606 he followed the court to Madrid, where many of his later poems and stories, including his *Novelas Ejemplares* (*Exemplary Novels), were written. Before his death he took the robe of the Franciscan Tertiaries. Borges claims that the appeal of *Don Quixote* is based chiefly on Cervantes's ability to introduce fantasy in an apparently realistic narrative. Cervantes, says Borges, has given us a poetic image of seventeenth-century Spain, and though his style of writing does not allow him to introduce supernatural elements he manages to suggest the supernatural in a more subtle, and therefore more effective, way (Other Inq. 43/4).
    Lab. 66 (40) *Ficc.* 50

Cesarea

A Roman port in Palestine, the seat of Herod the Great and the site of a Roman massacre of the Jews in 66 AD. In 231 it became the home of *Origen. By the fourth century it was a centre of Christianity and later a crusaders' stronghold, destroyed by the Muslims in 1291. Lab. 153 (122):

the present writers have found no information relevant to 'the image of the Lord' being 'replaced by a mirror'.

Lab. 153 (122) *Aleph* 39

Chacabuco

The sight of a battle fought on 12 February 1817, sixty miles north of Santiago, where *San Martín, commanding the *Army of the Andes, defeated the Royal forces led by Francisco Marcó del Pont, the Governor of Chile. San Martín then acquired a base on the Pacific, from which he later fought for Peru.

Brodie 18 (18) *Brodie* 131 Brodie 72 (89) *Brodie* 75

Chacarita

A district of Buenos Aires with a cemetery of the same name. The cemetery, less imposing than 'La Recoleta', where the élite Argentine families (including Borges's) have their mausolea, was opened during the *Yellow Fever epidemic of 1871. Brodie 49 (58): the name is omitted in the English translation.

Aleph 20 (27) *Aleph* 166 *Brodie* 46

Chacra, La

An agricultural monthly published in Argentina since November 1930. Brodie 18 (18): the English translation has 'Farm Journal'.

Brodie 131

Chaiz de Bazra

Probably Khalil of *Basra (d. *c*.791), a distinguished Arab grammarian, author of an influential study of the rhythmical structures of Arab poetry.

Lab. 183 (151) *Aleph* 95

Chanut, Hector Pierre (*c*.1604-1667)

A French diplomat, ambassador to Sweden and counsellor to Queen Christina. Chanut had a fluent knowledge of Hebrew, classical and modern languages, law, science and philosophy. He was a friend of *Descartes, whom he introduced to the queen and with whom he remained in correspondence. Lab. 149 (118): the epistle referred to, in *Lettres sur la morale*, is Descartes's letter to Chanut dated 1 November 1646 describing what savage people think of monkeys: 'They imagine that monkeys could talk, if they so wished, but refrain from doing so for fear of being obliged to work' (cf. Lab. 142 (112)).

Lab. 149 (118) *Aleph* 26

Characteristica universalis

'Universal characteristic': the subject of numerous articles, memoranda and letters of *Leibniz dating from all periods of his working life, including for example 'Elementa characteristicae universalis' (April 1679) in *Opuscules et fragments inédits de Leibniz* (Paris 1903). Lab. 63 (37): the project, anticipated by *Wilkins, *Dalgarno and *Descartes, stemmed from the idea of bringing mathematical methods to bear on every kind of intellectual problem. The universal characteristic was to have been at once an international language, a scientific notation, an instrument of discovery and a method of proof. Leibniz hoped that, by the development of such a characteristic supplanting the symbols of natural language, even moral and metaphysical questions could be worked out 'in much the same way as in geometry and analysis'.

Lab. 63 (37) *Ficc*. 46

Charles I (Carlos Primero) (1600-1649)

King of England, Scotland and Ireland from 1625, who came into conflict with the Commons over divine right. Defeated in the Civil War, he was executed in 1649. Eye-witnesses of his execution paid tribute to his demeanour on the scaffold: for example Andrew Marvell, who wrote, 'He nothing common did or mean / Upon that memorable scene' ('Upon Cromwell's Return from Ireland'). Borges described the execution in a poem entitled 'A Morning in 1649'. Its poignancy lies in the irony of the final verse. Fearlessly approaching death, the king greets the crowds with the same smile with which he had responded in previous years to their ovations: 'Lightly he nods his head / And smiles. He has done it so many times' (Sel. Poems 237).

Brodie 17 (17) *Brodie* 130

Charles XII (Carlos XII) (1682-1718)

A king of Sweden, known as 'The Alexander of the North', who led his country in military campaigns for eighteen years, defending it from its northern neighbours. He was an enlightened and reforming ruler. Aleph 56 (83): Charles XII admired the historian Quintus Curtius' biography of Alexander and carried a copy with him on all his campaigns. Once, when asked to compromise on a military matter, he was heard to say: *'Memini me Alexandrum, non mercatorem'* ('I remember that I am Alexander, not a merchant'). Borges wrote a poem entitled 'Carlos XII' (Sel. Poems 183).

Aleph 56 (83) *Aleph* 55

Charon (Caronte)

In Greek mythology the divinity charged with transporting the dead across the river Styx. Lab. 191 (158): Charon's fee was an obol, which was placed in the mouth of the dead at burial.

Lab. 191 (158) *Aleph* 106

Chesterton, Gilbert Keith (1874-1936)

An English critic and novelist, best known today for five collections of short stories featuring the detective Father Brown. Chesterton was attracted to Catholicism early in life and most of his work is inspired by a deep mystical awareness – an astonishment, as Borges has put it, at the paradox of Christianity's attraction and its boundless improbabilities. Lab. 102 (72): Chesterton's constant perception of the uncanny and mysterious, which he illustrates in terms of detective plots, and the elegance and felicity of his reasoning, were qualities much admired by Borges, who claimed to have learnt from Chesterton how to reduce an argument to a geometrical diagram and the idea that the criminal is the creative artist while the detective is only the critic. Though he first proposes a supernatural explanation for his mysteries, Chesterton always returns for the solution to the rational world. Borges, however, who also exploits the tension of the detective plot to illustrate the concatenation of human events and the anxiety of man's metaphysical search, offers no such comfort.

Lab. 102 (72) *Ficc*. 137 Aleph 31 (45) *Ficc*. 35

Chile

Chile obtained its independence from Spanish colonial rule with the help of General *San Martín who, in 1817, crossed the Andes with an army supplied and equipped by the Argentine government (see *Army of the Andes). Chile in turn joined forces with San Martín in a military and naval effort to defeat the Spanish army in Peru. Brodie 24 (26): this reference is omitted from the English version.

Brodie 26

Chile (Street)

A street in the southern part of *Buenos Aires, intersecting with *Tacuarí some ten blocks from Plaza *Constitución. Brodie 83 (101): the autobiographical links between the narrator of 'Guayaquil' and Borges are emphasised in a roundabout way. The narrator lives in a street called Chile, Borges lived in a street called Maipú and both names are associated in the Argentine mind, since *San Martín's great victory in *Chile was the battle of *Maipú.

Lab. 191 (158) *Aleph* 106, Brodie 83 (101) *Brodie* 114

China see *Germany, *Lost Encyclopaedia, *Luminous Dynasty, *Mongols, *Sin

Christie, Agatha (1890-1976)

An English writer of detective stories with an upper-middle-class background. Her first successful book was *Murder at the Vicarage* (1930). The intriguing complexity of Agatha Christie's plots, often determined by a highly specific closed world (an island, a ship, an hotel) in which murderer, victim and detective are confined, and her ability to hold suspense and create a final twist are the hallmarks of her work. Her most memorable characters are the eccentric Belgian detective Hercule Poirot and the elderly spinster Miss Marple whose acumen exceeds that of many police inspectors.

Fict. 66 (73) *Ficc.* 77

Church, Richard William (1815-1890)

An English clergyman and writer, Dean of St Paul's from 1871 to 1890. Church was the author of two monographs in the 'English Men of Letters' series, on *Bacon and *Spenser.

Aleph 36 (51) *Ficc.* 42

Cicero, Marcus Tullius (106-43 BC)

A Roman orator, statesman and philosopher whose elegance of language has been a model of Latinity through the ages. Cicero's moral integrity and patriotism in defence of the republic permeate his forensic and political speeches, and his bulky surviving *Letters* have made him the best-known figure of the ancient world. During the year of his consulship (63 BC) he unmasked Catiline's conspiracy, but when he opposed the triumvirate planned by *Julius Caesar, *Pompey and Crassus he was forced into exile. On his return, reconciled to the triumvirate, he was made governor of Cilicia. When Caesar broke with Pompey, Cicero joined Pompey's forces; he did not, however, take part in the plot to assassinate Caesar. He also opposed the second triumvirate established by Octavian (Augustus) and wrote his *Philippics* against Mark Antony in 44-43 BC; after being hounded by Anthony and his vengeful wife Fulvia, he was executed. Cicero is also remembered as the author of treatises popularising Greek philosophy, including the *Academica priora and posteriora* in which he opposes Stoic and Epicurean views.

Lab. 152 (121) *Aleph* 37

Cimitière marin, Le

A long meditative poem in decasyllables on the theme of death by Paul
*Valéry, first published in *NRF* (no. 81) in June 1920 and later, with
slight variations, in August 1920. The cemetery referred to is that of Sète,
where the author was eventually buried. Lab. 64 (38): the 'transposition'
of the poem 'into alexandrines' may be a humorous allusion to the 'Essai
de traduction en vers français' by a certain Colonel Godchot, translator of
Virgil and director of the literary periodical *Ma Revue*. To Godchot's
attack on the innovative language and style of his poem, Valéry
mockingly responded by thanking him for a translation which clarified
the text, adding that it could not have been too obscure if he had been able
to paraphrase it. Colonel Godchot was gratified, nevertheless, and both
versions of the poem appeared together in *Ma Revue* in July 1930. On the
other hand, Borges may have remembered that Valéry himself was not
averse to transposing poems into a different metre and had proposed to
change the versification of *Baudelaire's 'Invitation au Voyage' by
lengthening the heptasyllable following each couplet of pentasyllables
into an octosyllable (see Jean Provost, *Baudelaire*, Paris 1953, 329).

Lab. 64 (38) *Ficc.* 47

City of bronze (Ciudad de bronce)

A tale from the *Thousand and One Nights*, whose theme is the universal
triumph of death. Viewed by Amir Musa from the top of a mountain, the
city appears to have no human beings in it, only bronze statues and
vampires. Bronze columns, tombs, domes and sepulchral inscriptions are
the dominant images, and the narrative concludes with the lament: 'Why
is man born if he must die?' In an annotation to his translation of the
Thousand and One Nights, *Lane explains that the city's image was
associated in the Arab mind with that of temples, statues and tombs in
Egypt. Lab. 146 (116): the story of the city of bronze follows that of
*Sinbad the Sailor.

Lab. 146 (116) *Aleph* 23

Civitas Dei

'The City of God': St *Augustine's main theological work. Written
between 413 and 425, it consists of 22 books in which Christianity is
presented as a growing civic system in the face of the decaying Roman
Empire. Lab. 150: with reference to the belief that events recur 'at the
centuries' end', Borges has observed that several chapters of book 12 of
Civitas Dei try to refute the theory of cyclical time (see *Eternidad* 81). The
controversial passage which was read as if propounding, rather than
refuting, this theory occurs at the end of chapter 14, where Augustine
refers to Solomon's observation that 'there is no new thing under the sun'

(Ecclesiastes 1:10). Augustine, however, explains that these words do not mean, as has been said, that *Plato will come back 'at long but fixed intervals' to teach 'in the same city, in the same Academy and to the same students'. Such a doctrine would be totally against the Christian faith, for once 'Christ dies for our sins...he dieth no more'. The chapter ends with a quotation from the Psalms condemning outright anyone who believes in cyclical return: 'The wicked walk in a circle' (12:8). Lab. 151 (120): the reference to Augustine's statement that 'Jesus is the straight path' paraphrases another passage in the same chapter in which he condemns the 'false, circuitous ways' of 'treacherous and false teachers' and invites Christians not to stray from the right path but to follow the true doctrine (bk. 12, ch. 14, para. 1).

Lab. 150 (119) *Aleph* 37

Clausewitz, Carl von (1780-1831)

A German military historian whose theories on military strategy were highly influential, especially in the Prussian army. Clausewitz entered the Tsar's service in 1812 when Napoleon invaded Russia, and distinguished himself both for his courage and for the advice he gave the Russians on the retreat from Moscow which led to the defeat of the French. Lab. 100 (70): most of the military theories expounded in his book *On War* (which appeared in English in 1873) are based on the campaigns of Frederick the Great and Napoleon. 'War is nothing but the continuation of political intercourse with the admixture of different means.'

Lab. 100 (70) *Ficc.* 134

Clementine Library (Clementinum)

A sixteenth-century baroque building in *Prague, formerly a Jesuit college but now part of the university, renowned for its magnificent library. Kepler used the tower for his astronomical observations.

Lab. 122 (92) *Ficc.* 164

Coat of Many Colours see Nahum *Cordovero

Cochin (Kochín)

A nation state formerly in the presidency of Madras in south-west India. Today the Jewish community is divided into three groups – White Jews, Black Jews and Freedmen – who are influenced by the caste system of the area and do not intermarry.

Aleph 34 (50) *Ficc.* 40

Collins, Wilkie (1824-1889)

An English novelist, known as the father of the detective story for his mastery of suspense and involved plots. Collins's fame was established by *The Woman in White* (1860), an intricate work employing for the first time the technique of each character telling the story from his point of view.
Aleph 31 (45) *Ficc*. 35

Colorados

One of the two traditional political parties in *Uruguay, opposed to the *Blancos. The Colorados, originally the followers of Fructuoso Rivera, were so called from the red bands they used to distinguish them from their enemies at the battle of Carpentería (1836). Colorado policy was to encourage social and economic innovation, and to improve the status of Italian and Central European immigrants relative to that of Spanish immigrants. *Brodie* 16: in Argentina Rosas's followers were also known as 'Colorados', but in this context the name is a pun on the protagonists' red hair, as the translation makes clear.
Brodie 40 (47) *Brodie* 105, *Brodie* 16

Commentaries (Comentarios) see *Julius Caesar

Compadrito

An Argentine term usually applied to a city swaggerer, a boaster, a show-off; also a low-lifer, a ruffian, a trouble-maker. Fict. 158 (173): the English reference is 'tough'.
Ficc. 194

Concepción

Lab. 192 (159) refers to an imposing church in Buenos Aires in *Barrio Sur, in the proximity of Plaza *Constitución. Aleph 15 (19): there are several parishes of this name in *Buenos Aires, but the one referred to is probably that of the church mentioned above.
Lab. 192 (159) *Aleph* 107, Aleph 15 (19) *Aleph* 156

Condorcet, Jean Antoine Nicolas de Caritat, Marquis de (1743-1794)

A French philosopher and mathematician, a supporter of Voltaire and the Enlightenment. During the Revolution Condorcet became an active member of the Girondist faction. He was imprisoned on 7 April 1794 and found dead the next day. Condorcet wrote various essays on probability, but his most interesting work is his *Sketch for a Historical Picture of the Progress of the Human Mind* (translated into English in 1955). Lab. 103: Condorcet's sketch develops the theory that humanity has reached the ninth stage in its sociological progress, starting from a condition of total savagery and moving towards complete enlightenment which will be fully achieved in the tenth stage. Condorcet specifies that throughout these stages certain characteristics will reappear.

Lab. 103 (73) *Ficc.* 138/9

Confessions of a Thug see Philip Meadows *Taylor

Confucius (Confucio) (*c*.550-478 BC)

A celebrated Chinese philosopher and moral teacher. Confucianism is a secular faith based on lofty ideals of goodness, justice, filial devotion and other virtues derived from the contemplation of man in society. Anyone who lives according to Confucian principles is carrying out the will of God and contributing to social harmony. The editing of the *Lî Kî*, or Book of Rites, has been mistakenly attributed to Confucius.

Lab. 190 (157) *Aleph* 104

Connaught (also Connacht)

A province in the west of *Ireland which includes the five counties of Galway, Leitrim, Mayo, Roscommon and Sligo. Connaught was an ancient kingdom which, as told in the Irish epics (see *Celtic literature), was for long at war with the kingdom of Ulster. In June 1920 it was the scene of a rebellion against the *Black and Tans. Fourteen of the protesters were sentenced to death by court martial, but thirteen were reprieved.

Lab. 97 (68) *Ficc.* 130

Conque, La

A literary review published in Paris from March 1891 to January 1892, also known as *Anthologie des plus jeunes poètes*. Lab. 63 (37): the issues of March and October 1899 must be fictitious.

Lab. 63 (37) *Ficc.* 46

Conrad, Joseph see José *Korzeniovski

Constantinople (Constantinopla)

The former capital of the Byzantine and Ottoman Empires, now Istanbul.

Lab. 153 (122): in 553 Constantinople was the seat of a second Council which, among other dogmas, declared the divinity of Jesus and pronounced anathemas against all who opposed this creed. See *Arianism.

Lab. 153 (122) *Aleph* 39

Constitución, Plaza

Fict. 156 (171): the main terminal of the *Southern Railways, now known as Ferrocarril Nacional General Roca. Aleph 11 (159): also a bustling square on the southern side of *Buenos Aires (*Barrio Sur) which used to be the older, more traditional part of the city. The *criollo* élite once lived in the vicinity of Constitución, but after the *Yellow Fever epidemic of 1871 they gradually moved to the higher northern areas. Its connotation in 'The Aleph' may be intended as ironic, for at the time of the story Constitución had become a somewhat dilapidated neighbourhood, inhabited largely by poorer families.

Fict. 154 (169) *Ficc.* 189, Aleph 11 (15) *Aleph* 151

'Contempsit caros dum nos amat ille parentes'

'While loving us, he despised his dear parents', the Latin epitaph inscribed by the people of *Ravenna on the tomb of *Droctulft. The epitaph is quoted in full by *Paul the Deacon in his *Acts of the Lombards* (3.19) and by Benedetto *Croce in *La Poesia*. See *'Terribilis visu facies...'

Lab. 160 (127) *Aleph* 49

Contest with the tortoise (Certamen con la tortuga)

The second of Zeno's paradoxes, illustrating the illusion of movement. Achilles gives the tortoise a start but cannot overtake it. For when he reaches the point from which the tortoise began the tortoise will have moved on, and when he gets to where the tortoise has moved on to it will have moved on once more and so on *ad infinitum*. This paradox has intrigued philosophers from *Descartes to *Russell. Borges wrote an essay on the subject (see *Disc.* 149, Other Inq. 109) and alluded to it more than once in his fiction (see Lab. 64 (38), 177 (86)). See *'Ne craignez point, Monsieur, la tortue'.

Lab. 59 (38) *Ficc.* 73

Cordoba

A city on the river *Guadalquivir in southern Spain. From the seventh to the twelfth century it was the capital of the caliphate in Spain and the most important centre of Moslem culture in the West. In power and prestige it rivalled, and eventually surpassed, *Baghdad and Damascus.

Contemporary Arab writers praised the city's splendour, its magnificent palaces, mansions, gardens and fountains, its 700 mosques and 900 public baths and, above all, its splendid *mezquita*, the largest mosque in western Islam, 'a dream of light, grace and colour'. In the great days of the caliphate Cordoba epitomised Islam's conception of a life to come in a heaven of 'gardens with lofty apartments, beneath which the rivers flow'. Lab. 180 (148): *Averroes was born in Cordoba, and spent much of his life there as physician and *qadi* (judge).

Lab. 180 (148) *Aleph* 91

Cordoba, Calle

One of the main thoroughfares of northern *Buenos Aires, containing the Biblioteca de la Municipalidad.

Fict. 152 (167) *Ficc.* 187

Cordovero, Nahum

A fictional character with biblical and historical associations. Nahum, which in Hebrew means 'comfort' or 'source of comfort', is one of the twelve minor prophets of the Old Testament. Cordovero (Moses ben Jacob), who lived in Safed, a centre of Cabbalism in the seventeenth century, was held to be the greatest theoretician of Jewish mysticism (see G. Scholem, *Major Trends in Jewish Mysticism*, NY 1961, 252). His teachings, which exerted a marked influence on his contemporary Isaac *Luria, dealt with questions of immortality and the transmigration of souls. Lab. 149 (118): *A Coat of Many Colours*, the title of Nahum Cordovero's fictional text, refers to the long-sleeved coat given by Jacob to Joseph, his favourite son (Gen. 37:3). Its some hundred pages suggest that it is itself a *cento* (*cien*), a work made up of quotations and fragments of other works.

Lab. 149 (118) *Aleph* 25

Corinthians (Corintios)

Two epistles by St *Paul addressed to the Christians in Corinth. In the first, written in *Ephesus in 57, Paul emphasises the unity of all Christians in Christ and answers questions on specific points of behaviour. All the following quotations are taken from I Corinthians. Lab. 128 (98): 'He that glorieth, let him glory in the Lord' is the concluding verse of the first chapter. Particular relevance to Judas's abasement may be found in the preceding passages: 'God has chosen the foolish things of this world to confound the wise'(1:27) and 'that no flesh should glory in his presence'(1:29). Lab. 154 (123): 'For we now see through a glass darkly': the 'perversion' of taking this famous apocalyptic quotation as proof that 'everything we see is false' is explained by its context. Now our heavenly vision is limited and obscured, whereas 'when that which is perfect is come' it will be complete. Aleph 54/5 (82): 'All things to all men.' This quotation, used to summarise different readers' attitudes to Martín *Fierro, has a more didactic meaning in its own context. The complete verse reads: 'To the weak became I as weak, that I might gain the weak: I am made all things to all men, that I might by all means save some'(9:22). The same verse is alluded to as a definition of the *Apostle in Lab. 132 (102).

Lab. 128 (98) *Ficc.* 172, Lab. 154 (123) *Aleph* 41, Aleph 54/5 (82) *Aleph* 53

Coronel

Avenida Coronel Díaz: a street in the centre of *Buenos Aires, near *Palermo, which used to be one of the few paved roads in the area.

Brodie 67 (82) *Brodie* 67

Corrientes

A fertile province in north-eastern Argentina, bordering Paraguay and *Brazil. After 1814 Corrientes supported *Federalism in the struggle against centralised government. Brodie 32 (36): ladies in Corrientes would have had a rudimentary knowledge of *Guaraní, in order to communicate with their Indian maids from the nearby provinces of Misiones, or from Paraguay.

Brodie 32 (36) *Brodie* 91

Corrientes

An important thoroughfare in the centre of *Buenos Aires. See *Talcahuano.

Brodie 32 (36) *Brodie* 91

Corybantes (Coribantes)

Attendants of Cybele, the Asiatic goddess known as the 'Great Mother', in whose honour they performed orgiastic rites. These wild dances were thought to be good for mental illnesses.

Lab. 143 (113) *Aleph* 18

Cosmas

A sixth-century merchant and traveller born in Alexandria. After sailing to Africa and the Far East (for which he became known as Indicopleustes, or 'Indian sailor'), Cosmas retreated to a monastery and composed the *Topographia Christiana* (Christian Topography), with the purpose of denying the heathen hypothesis of the shape of the earth and proving the factual truth of biblical definitions of the universe. According to Cosmas, the earth is rectangular, its inhabited part surrounded by the ocean, beyond which lies the Garden of Eden.

Lab. 153 (122) *Aleph* 39

Costa Brava

A small town in the district of Ramallo, a province of Buenos Aires, not to be confused with the island of the same name in the *Paraná River, scene of various battles, including a naval defeat of Garibaldi.

Brodie 55 (66) *Brodie* 17

Cowley, Abraham (1618-1667)

An English poet, contemporary with Milton, whose verse marks the transition between the Metaphysical and Augustan poets. His Pindaric Odes established the form of the English ode. His *Epic of King David* (1656) embodies the principles of the neo-classical couplet.

Fict. 66 (73) *Ficc.* 77

Crete (Creta)

A Greek island in the south Aegean. Aleph 79 (123): the famous labyrinth of Crete was constructed by Daedalus for the *Minotaur.

Aleph 79 (123) *Aleph* 131

Criollo

From the Portuguese *crioulo*, 'nursling', a term originally applied to 'whites' born of European parentage. With increasing miscegenation, however, it was given to natives of mixed blood. The word has wide applications, from the high-ranking local élite, the leaders of the Independence Movement, to the native *mestizo* masses, often with pejorative connotations. As R.B. Scobie observes, 'In the nineteenth century, *criollo* became synonymous with shiftiness and laziness' (*Buenos Aires from Plaza to Suburb*, Oxford 1974, 219).

Croce, Benedetto (1866-1952)

An Italian idealist philosopher and humanist who was strongly opposed to Fascism, author of *Philosophy of the Spirit* and several treatises discussing the principles of art criticism and defining his own aesthetic system. The most significant aspect of his philosophy is the total dissociation of the work of art from any pre-existing concept, whether of the artist or of the observer. The work of art exists independently in the mind of its creator, even before being realised through its medium. The artist knows his creation only when he has completed it, and the observer of the work of art will enjoy its aesthetic values only when he recaptures and re-expresses the artist's intention. Borges refers to Croce in his essays, challenging his condemnation of allegories. For Croce allegory is 'a kind of...cryptography', in so far as it encodes two ideas in one image. To this Borges answers by agreeing, with *Chesterton, on the inadequacy of language to express reality; allegory is another form of communication offering a means by which we can attempt to utter the ineffable (Other Inq. 49/50, 154/5). Lab. 159 (127): *La Poesia*, one of Croce's miscellaneous philosophical treatises, first published as a collection in 1910 under the title *Saggi Filosofici* (Philosophical Essays), is an introduction to the history of literature and to critical theory. See *'Terribilis visu facies...'

Lab. 159 (127) *Aleph* 47

Cross (Cruz)

An ancient mystical symbol indicating originally the four cardinal points of the earth and so signifying life. It has also been seen as a phallic image and an emblem of immortality. In the history of Christianity it is associated with the passion and death of Christ and has become a symbol of reparation and redemption.

Lab. 150 (119) *Aleph* 35, Brodie 22 (22) *Brodie* 136

Cruz, Tadeo Isidoro

Sergeant Cruz, a character in the poem *Martín *Fierro*, who so admires the outlaw Fierro's bravery when he fights alone against him and his posse of fellow-policemen that he cries out: 'Cruz no consiente/ Que se cometa el delito/ De matar ansí un valiente!' ('Cruz will not permit the crime of slaughtering such a brave man'). Cruz crosses to Fierro's side and shares his fate. His friendship with Fierro is considered one of the supreme examples of brotherly love in *gaucho* literature. Cruz is traditionally seen as Fierro's 'double', a more prosaic version of the legendary *gaucho* whose history of injustice and persecution he had shared before being forced to work on the side of the government. *Martínez Estrada has an interesting interpretation of the incident that serves as a basis for 'The Life of Tadeo Isidoro Cruz': the moment Cruz joins Martín Fierro he destroys his independence and spontaneity, depriving him of any spiritual life and turning him into 'su sombra envejecida' ('his ageing shadow').

Aleph 54 (81) *Aleph* 54

Cuareim

A river forming part of the boundary between Uruguay and Brazil.

Cuchilla Negra

A hill range on the borders of Brazil and Uruguay.
Lab. 41 (16) *Ficc.* 31

Cynics (Cínicos)

A philosophical school founded by Diogenes in the second half of the
fourth century BC. The name, derived from *kuôn*, a dog, was given to its
members to indicate their harsh and aggressive behaviour. Their main
tenet, though not formally expressed, was an adherence to certain moral
principles aiming at a return to 'natural' living, without the conventions
and comforts that go with a position in society. Simplicity and poverty
made for independence and self-sufficiency but entailed a life of
promiscuity and lack of shame.
Brodie 92 (113) *Brodie* 141

Cyrus III (Ciro) (*c*.590-529 BC)

Cyrus the Great, the founder of the Persian Empire, the son of Cambyses.
Cyrus was a wise ruler revered by the Persians who, according to
Herodotus, called him the father of his people. The first of a dynasty, he
has inspired a legend in which he is seen to exemplify all the qualities
expected of a monarch. When *Babylon fell to him in 539, Cyrus was
generous and tolerant towards its inhabitants, honouring their gods and
supporting local customs. He also permitted the Jewish exiles in Babylon
to return to their own country and rebuild the Temple in Jerusalem, as
recorded in the First Book of Ezra. Lab. 91 (63): *Pliny (7.88) says that
Cyrus knew every soldier serving in his army by name. See *Smerdis.
Lab. 91 (63) *Ficc.* 122

D'Annunzio, Gabriele (1864-1938)

An Italian poet, novelist and playwright. D'Annunzio's poetry,
characterised by sensual language and neo-classical imagery, shows the
influence of the Symbolist movement in Italy. D'Annunzio was an
admirer of *Nietzsche and exemplified the concept of the 'Superman' and
the Dionysiac interpretation of human destiny. Lab. 64 (38): he was an
eccentric and a showman with a fondness for extravagant language.
Lab. 64 (38) *Ficc.* 48

Da Cunha, Euclides (Euclydes) (1866-1909)

A Brazilian writer, author of *Os sertões* (1902: trans. *Revolt in the*

Backlands 1947), a fictionalised account of the uprising at *Canudos, in the northern state of Bahía. The rebellion, which took a fanatical tinge, began as an act of defiance against the system of taxation and other centralising measures imposed by the new republican government. Da Cunha participated in the fourth of the expeditions (1896-7) sent to put down the rebels. Steeped in the positive rationalism of the time, he did not at first understand the movement's mystical dimension. But, as events developed, the spirit and bravery of the local peasants, or *cabôclos*, who preferred death to defeat, soon commanded his admiration. See *Antonio Conselheiro.

Lab. 128 (98) *Ficc.* 173

Dahlmann

A fictitious name, which may allude to the Danish historian Friedrich Christoph Dahlmann (1785-1860). Borges quotes a passage from *Carlyle's introduction to *Early Kings of Norway* (1875) which mentions Dahlmann (*Lit. germ.* 169).

Fict. 152 (167) *Ficc.* 187

Dalgarno, George (c.1626-1687)

A Scottish philologist who devoted himself to the creation of a universal language and worked on perfecting a 'dactylogy', or language for the deaf and dumb, based on a universally acceptable ideographic system which seeks to express ideas through signs.

Lab. 39 (15) *Ficc.* 29

Damiani, Pier (1007-1072)

An Italian ecclesiastic, whose writings are recorded in *Migne's *Patrology*. Damiani was prominent in the eleventh-century reform movement for his attack on simony, his advocacy of celibacy of the clergy and his introduction of severe disciplinary practices, including self-flagellation. From his hermitage near Gubbio, Damiani distinguished himself on a political level by his support of Pope Alexander II in the schism against Honorius IV, and for persuading the Emperor Henry IV of Germany not to divorce his wife Bertha. Aleph 70 (109): in his theological treatise *De Divina Omnipotentia* (1067), Damiani addresses himself to the question of whether God is able to undo the past. The argument springs from a statement by St Jerome, quoted in the first chapter, that virginity cannot be restored once it is lost through intercourse. Damiani's answer is that God can make a woman a virgin again if she so dedicates herself to the spiritual life as to wipe out the memory of her previous actions. Equally God chose to destroy in the flood the men he had once created, for their evil removed them utterly from the sole source of being: though men may survive their bad actions, the negative part of their life is non-existent and can therefore be obliterated. Borges's reference to Canto XXI of *Dante's *Paradiso is to lines 124-5 in which Damiani refers to a confusion of identity after his death, when he was taken for another 'Pietro', who also founded a monastery near Ravenna and was known as *Peccatore*, the Sinner, on account of his public life before retiring into the Church.

Aleph 70 (109) *Aleph* 77

Daneri, Carlos Argentino

In 'The Aleph', a fictional character whose surname may be a contraction of, and a parodic allusion to, *Dante Alighieri, the poet whose presence underlies the story. Like the Florentine master, Daneri had a vision of the whole of the universe which he sought to encompass in his poem. See Beatriz *Viterbo, *Augural Canto.

Aleph 12 (15) *Aleph* 151

Dante Alighieri (1265-1321)

Italy's foremost poet, born in Florence, where he held several political offices as a member of the Bianchi faction. When Charles de Valois, brother of the King of France, was called into the city by the Pope in 1302 and a new government was constituted under the Neri, Dante was exiled, never to return. He is best known for his *Vita Nuova* (1294), inspired by his love for Beatrice Portinari, and his *Divine Comedy*, published between 1310 and 1320. The Divine Comedy consists of a hundred cantos describing the poet's mystical journey through *Hell and Purgatory to Heaven and salvation. Many mythological and historical figures illustrate the three kingdoms and are placed according to their deserts, following the principles of Christian theology and its system of punishment and retribution. Although Dante's sense of justice never fails, his opinions of his contemporaries and his civic experiences are given full rein. Lab. 125 (95): the 'fiery grave' to which Dante would have condemned Nils *Runeberg is a reference to Cantos IX, X and XI of Hell which describe the circles of the heretics. Lab. 200 (168): the last circle in Hell is the one in which traitors are punished. For Lab. 201 (168) see *Ugolino, *Ruggieri.

Lab. 125 (95) *Ficc.* 169, Lab 201 (168) *Aleph* 141, Lab. 161 (129) *Aleph* 49

Danube (Danubio)

The second largest river in Europe after the Volga, rich in historical and political associations. Lab. 173 (141): the crossing of the Danube in 1916 probably refers to the German counter-attack after the Brusilov offensives and the Russian attempt to regain lost territories.

Lab. 150 (119) *Aleph* 35, Lab. 159 (128) *Aleph* 48, Lab. 173 (141) *Aleph* 81

Dardania

The name given by the Romans to the territory now corresponding to southern Serbia, derived from its first inhabitants, the Dardani, an Illyrian tribe first mentioned in the *Iliad* (2.819, 15.425). Under Constantine Dardania became part of the Roman province of Illyria, and its inhabitants were converted to Christianity.

Lab. 153 (122) *Aleph* 40

Daudet, Alphonse (1840-1897)

A French humorist, author of *Les Aventures prodigieuses de Tartarin de Tarascon* (1872) whose protagonist personifies the good-natured bombastic hero. Famous in his home town for his exploits in the chase, Tartarin is sent to hunt the great lions of the Atlas. Once in Algiers, he first shoots a *bourricot* (little donkey) in a carrot field, which he assumes to be the desert, and eventually kills an old blind lion, whose remains he sends back to Tarascon. The novel concludes with his triumphant return to relate his exploits to ecstatic crowds. Its success led to a sequel, *Tartarin sur les Alpes* (1885).

Lab. 65 (39) *Ficc.* 49

Daughters of the Republic (Damas de la Patria)

Argentine society ladies, daughters of the patrician women who, during the wars of Independence, gave their jewels to help *San Martín cross the Andes.

Brodie 79 (95) *Brodie* 84

David (d. *c*.970 BC)

The second king of Israel, first king of the Judaean dynasty. Lab. 179 (146): the incident mentioned alludes to the sequel to the story of Uriah the Hittite, whom David sent to the front line so that he could marry his wife Bathsheba with whom he had committed adultery. The prophet Nathan tells David a parable of a rich man with many flocks who took a poor man's only ewe lamb to offer it to a visitor at his table. When David heard the story 'his anger was greatly kindled against the man', whereupon he was told: 'Thou art the man' (II Samuel 12:7). Brodie 83 (101) alludes to the description of David dancing, as he brought the Covenant into Zion: 'And David danced before the Lord with all his might...'(II Samuel 6:14).

Dayman

A river crossed by *Saravia on his way to the battle of *Masoller.
Aleph 67 (105) *Aleph* 73

De Cusa, Nicolas (1400-1464)

A German cardinal, scientist and philosopher, influential in Renaissance thought for the doctrine of human knowledge expounded in *Of Learned Ignorance* (1440). Arguing that the essential nature of God, from whom everything flows and returns was unknowable, De Cusa concluded that all human knowledge was simply 'learned ignorance'. His philosophy was humanistic, with pantheistic tendencies. His cosmology, anticipating Copernicus, held that the earth moves round the sun. Aleph 74 (116) refers to De Cusa's preoccupation with straight lines which, according to him, were segments of a large circle.
Aleph 74 (116) *Aleph* 124

De Principiis

The most important dogmatic work of *Origen (c.185-c.254). The original Greek text is mostly lost, and what remains is a Latin translation by Rufinus. The first three books are on the nature of God, the fall of the soul, anthropology and ethics; the fourth explains the divinity of the Scriptures. The text expounds the four main points in which Origen departed from orthodoxy: namely, the pre-existence of the human soul, the pre-existence of the human soul of Christ, the resurrection of the body into a purely ethereal being, and the final redemption of all men, and devils, through Christ's mediation. Lab. 151 (121): the passage comes from book 2 in which Origen professes the unceasing variety of all spiritual and physical events, arguing against those who assert that worlds 'will come into existence which are not dissimilar to each other' so that 'it will come to pass that Adam and Eve will do the same thing...there will be ...the same deluge...Judas will also a second time betray the Lord...Paul...will keep the garments of those who stoned Stephen...' (ch.3, sect.4).
Lab. 151 (121) *Aleph* 37

De Quincey, Thomas (1785-1859)

An English essayist, remembered chiefly for *Confessions of an English Opium Eater* (1821). De Quincey exerted a strong influence on Borges's fiction (see Christ, *The Narrow Act*, NY 1969). Though Borges never wrote specifically on De Quincey, he acknowledged his 'vast debt' to him

(Other Inq. 89) and often quoted from his collected *Writings*, generally citing the 1889/90 David Masson edition. Lab. 29 (5) refers to De Quincey's statement that the Lutheran pastor Johannes Valentinus *Andreä (1586-1654) was the author of an anonymous text from which the community of the *Rosae Crucis (Rosicrucians) derived (vol. 12, 405/10). Lab. 149 (118): the 'interpolation' mentioned refers to the description of the City of the Immortals inspired by De Quincey's account of a set of plates by Piranesi. These plates, illustrating the visions of De Quincey's delirium, present images of 'gothic halls' and stairs which reach 'an abrupt termination, without any balustrade, and allowing no step onwards to him who should reach the extremity' (vol. 5, 439). The plate called 'The Gothic Arch' from the *Carceri* set may be particularly relevant. For Lab. 126 (96) see *'Not one but all things...'

Lab. 29 (5) *Ficc*. 16, Lab. 126 (96) *Ficc*. 170, Lab. 149 (118) *Aleph* 26

De Rerum Natura

'On the Nature of Things': a didactic and philosophical poem in six books by the Roman poet Lucretius (*c*.95-55 BC) in which the universe is explained, from an Epicurean point of view, as the result of the chance encounter of atoms rather than the intervention of the gods. Lab. 174 (142): the *Faust-like traits found in *De Rerum Natura* refer to its challenge to religion, liberating man from the fear of death.

Lab. 174 (142) *Aleph* 83

De Vedia, Agustín (1843-1910)

An influential Argentine journalist born in Montevideo.
Lab. 93 (64) *Ficc*. 124

De Viris Illustribus see Charles *Lhomond

Decline and Fall see Edward *Gibbon

Delhi

The capital of the state of Delhi, which borders on the *Punjab. The old town is enclosed by stone walls, built in the seventeenth century, whose towers were made into bastions by the British in 1810. Aleph 84 (132): in 1857 Delhi was besieged by rebels for five months during the Indian *Mutiny. John Nicholson (1821-1857), an Irish soldier who had served in the *Bengal Army and fought in Kashmir and the *Punjab during the second Anglo-Sikh war, raised the siege; he died of wounds soon after.

Aleph 84 (132) *Aleph* 146

Demosthenes (Demóstenes) (384-322 BC)

The most celebrated ancient Greek orator, whose speeches against Philip of Macedon roused the Athenians to fight for the freedom of Greece. A proposal that a golden crown be awarded to Demosthenes for public services was contested by his rival Aeschines, whose speeches had facilitated Philip's entry into central Greece and the consequent capitulation of Athens. Later, while Philip's son Alexander was absent from Greece, Demosthenes attacked Aeschines in his oration *On the Crown*; to discredit him he described how as a boy Aeschines had helped his mother in her ritual initiations. From this passage Borges derives the reference to the *Orphic mysteries in Lab. 155 (123). Despite the success of *On the Crown*, Demosthenes' life continued full of strife. He was sentenced to death and committed suicide. The rivalry between Demosthenes and Aeschines is consistent with the theme of rivalry in 'The Theologians'.

Lab. 155 (123) *Aleph* 41

Denmark (Dinamarca)

Borges was an admirer of old Danish sagas: witness his comments on the *Gesta Danorum*, a work in sixteen volumes by the twelfth-century Danish historian Saxo Grammaticus. Brodie 53 (64): in his discussion of this book, Borges remarks on the cruelty and intrepid horsemanship displayed by the Danes in their conquest of Ireland (*Lit. germ.*, 190).

Brodie 53 (64) *Brodie* 16

Der Golem see Gustav *Meyrink

Descartes, René (1596-1650)

A celebrated French philosopher, regarded as the father of modern philosophy, whose method, enunciated in his *Discours de la méthode* (1637), is based on the principle that no statement is valid until proved to be so. Starting from a condition of total doubt, Descartes arrives at the initial proposition that, in order to doubt, one has to think and therefore to exist: '*dubito, ergo cogito, ergo sum.*' His methodological principle is that anything which we 'perceive clearly and distinctly' must exist. Since we think of God, the perfect being, he must exist, for such an idea could not originate from our imperfect nature unless it had been implanted there by God. Moreover the very nature of perfection involves, among other attributes, that of existence, which proves the existence of God: the Ontological Argument. Being perfection, God cannot deceive us; therefore we must believe any phenomenon true to which our consciousness testifies with clarity and distinctness: this implies that the world also exists. Descartes believed in the dualism of spirit and substance which he held to be reconcilable only through the influence of God. Lab. 63 (37): Descartes made a notable contribution to geometry, showing how geometrical problems could be resolved in algebraic terms. He proposed that this same method could be used to set out all existing knowledge systematically, in universally understandable symbols, which would lead to a universal language, a project that interested many other philosophers, such as *Wilkins and *Leibniz. See *Characteristica Universalis, Pierre *Chanut.

Lab. 63 (37) *Fict.* 46, Lab. 149 (118) *Aleph* 26

Deutsches Requiem

Literally 'requiem in German', also understood as 'requiem *for* Germany': a choral work by *Brahms composed upon the death of his mother and first performed in Vienna in 1867. In spite of its devotional and liturgical associations, it dwells upon problems of individual human destiny without mention of Christ.

Lab. 173 (141) *Aleph* 81

Dewey, Christopher

A possible allusion to John Dewey (1859-1952), a leading pragmatist philosopher and exponent of 'instrumentalism'. This theory qualifies the traditional notion of 'truth', suggesting that propositions are to be judged not by whether what they describe is true but by their effectiveness. Aleph 84 (132): instrumentalism could be illustrated by the tale told by the 'old man' to the narrator, whose value lies not in the truth of its content but in its effectiveness in delaying the investigation until justice is done. At the beginning of the final paragraph, when the tale has achieved its purpose, the whole event comes to an abrupt end and the narrator feels dismissed, as if he 'no longer existed' (Aleph 86 (135)).

Aleph 82 (129) *Aleph* 143

Diana

The Roman goddess of hunting, chastity, the moon and childbirth, identified with the Greek Artemis, twin sister of *Apollo. Lab. 113 (83): the Greek statue of Diana the Huntress in the Louvre is commonly regarded as a companion piece to the Vatican's Apollo Belvedere. Both statues were much copied as ornamental figures in Neoclassical formal gardens.

Lab. 113 (83) *Ficc.* 153, Lab. 151 (120) *Aleph* 36

Dichtung der Zeit see *Soergel

Diocletian, Gaius Aurelius Valerius (Diocleciano) (245-313)

Roman emperor from 284 until his abdication in 305. In 286 he reorganised the administration of the vast empire by sharing his power with Maximian, a colleague at arms, and in 293 with two assistants. The empire was divided into four parts, each controlled by one of its four Caesars who were united by religious bonds and later by ties of marriage. Lab. 135 (106): Diocletian was in charge of Thrace, Asia and *Egypt. In 296 he led his army to quell the rebellion of Achilleus in Egypt, and was exceptionally ruthless in the accomplishment of this task.
   Lab. 135 (106) *Aleph* 7

Diophantus (Diofanto) (fl. 250)

A Greek mathematician who introduced symbolism into Greek algebra. His chief work is the *Arithmetica*, which was translated and commented on by the Arabs. See *Fermat.
   Aleph 73 (115) *Aleph* 123

Divine Comedy (Divina Comedia)

An allegorical work by the Italian poet *Dante Alighieri which aims at systematising medieval theology in a universal poem. Consisting of three parts known as *canticas*, it describes Dante's spiritual journey through *Hell and Purgatory before he reaches the celestial sight of Beatrice, the woman he had loved since childhood, and the mystical revelation of God in Paradise. The system of punishment and retribution on which Dante's vision rests permits him to present a multiplicity of characters, both mythological and historical, placed in the three realms – Hell, Purgatory and Paradise – according to their deserts. Borges had a long-standing interest in Dante's poem and published a collection of essays on it (*Ens. dantescos*, Madrid 1982), claiming in the prologue that not a single word in the *Divine Comedy* is unjustified. For Lab. 201 (167) see *Ugolino. See Beatriz *Viterbo, *Hell, *Paradiso*, *Ruggieri.
   Lab. 201 (167) *Aleph* 141

Docetism (Docetas)

A heresy embraced by some early *Gnostics who thought of Christ's body as appearance and not reality.
   Lab. 127 (97) *Fict.* 171

Doctor Universalis see *Alanus de Insulis

Don Segundo Sombra

A novel by the Argentine Ricardo Güiraldes, published in 1926 to exalt the *gaucho way of life at a time when it was giving way to the needs of an industrial, export-oriented economy. *Don Segundo Sombra* is a nostalgic portrayal of a *gaucho* with the virtues of an idealised archetype: courage, honesty, self-control and a sense of responsibility. Though romanticised at times, Don Segundo remains the symbol of an age and a society removed from the corrupting influence of an urban environment. As Borges points out, the final lines of the story describing the hero riding into the distance symbolise the disappearance of the golden age of the pampas (*Ev. Carr.* 128). Brodie 18 (18): the novel narrates episodes in the education of Don Segundo's pupil, including many *costumbrista* elements concerning the life and customs of the *troperos*, the pampas herdsmen. This is why the book is said not to appeal to the *Gutres, who themselves had first-hand experience of this kind of life. *Aleph* 157: the reference to 'nuestro ya laureado' (our praised) Don Segundo Sombra is omitted in the English translation.

Aleph 157, Brodie 18 (18) *Brodie* 131

Donne see John William *Dunne

Drayton, Michael (1563-1631)

An English poet, favoured at the court of Elizabeth I, reputedly a friend of Shakespeare and Ben Jonson, who fought against the Armada. Drayton's vast output covered religious, historical, satirical and topographical themes. His most famous work is the great topographical poem on England *Polyolbion* (Greek: 'having many blessings'), completed in 1622. Though Drayton had resolved to create a poem which would celebrate everything of topographical or antiquarian interest in Britain as a whole, he found the task a 'Herculean toil' and confined himself in the end to England. See *Augural Canto*.

Aleph 19 (17) *Aleph* 156

Dresden see *Novalis

Drieu la Rochelle, Pierre (1893-1945)

A French novelist, short-story writer, journalist and essayist, editor for a time of the *Nouvelle Revue Francaise*. He visited Argentina in 1933, when he met Borges and became one of the first critics to recognise his genius. On his return to France he declared: 'Borges vaut le voyage' ('Borges is worth the journey').

Droctulft

A member of the *Lombard army which descended into Italy in the sixth century, as recorded by *Paul the Deacon in his *Acts of the Lombards*. Droctulft, captured and held prisoner in *Ravenna, went over to the enemy in revenge for his leader's failure to come to his rescue.
  Lab. 159 (127) *Aleph* 47

Druids (Druidas)

The title given by the ancient Celts of Gaul and Britain to the learned men who presided over religious ceremonies, judged legal disputes and recited the verses that form the bulk of *Celtic literature. Lab. 103 (73): in *Caesar's *Commentaries*, perhaps the best source of information we possess on the Druids, they are said to believe in the transmigration of souls (*De Bello Gallico* 4. 18).
  Lab. 103 (73) *Ficc.* 139

Du Cange, Charles du Fresne (1610-1688)

A learned French philologist and historian, author of *A Glossary of Medieval and Low Latin* and *A Glossary of Medieval and Low Greek*. Well-documented from original texts, they focus on the historical aspects of the two languages and the relation between their classical and medieval forms.
  Lab. 133 (103) *Fict.* 184

Dungarven

An Irish coastal district in the county of Waterford, *Munster, containing the remains of a castle built by King John. The castle, annexed to the Crown by Henry VIII, had a long history of aggression, culminating in its sack by Cromwell in 1649. In 1846, during the Great Famine, Dungarven was the scene of a riot against the export of grain.
  Lab. 97(68) *Ficc.* 130

Dunne, John William (1875-1949)

An Irish popular philosopher, known for his theories of 'serial time', 'time regression' and precognition which influenced J.B. Priestley. Dunne claimed that the arguments of his best-known book, *An Experiment with Time*, were 'considerably easier to understand than are the rules of contract bridge' and of 'considerably more importance to mankind'. In the course of his own reasoning he arrived, much to his own surprise, at a formulation of the first scientific argument for human immortality. Borges has speculated at length on this book, with particular reference to chapters 21 and 22 in which 'a clear view of the nature of time regress' is illustrated by examples and by a series of diagrams. Though fascinated by Dunne's concept of 'hypothetic times' and by his postulation of a future which already exists, Borges cannot but be amused by the 'inextricable' quality of his diagrams and politely hints at the fallacies of his argument (*Other Inq.* 19-20). Fict. 68 (75): the English version confuses Dunne with the Elizabethan poet John Donne.

Fict. 68 (75) *Ficc.* 79

Dupin, C. Auguste

The detective hero of *Poe's 'The Murder in the Rue Morgue', 'The Purloined Letter' and 'The Mystery of Marie Roget' who, by identifying with the mind of his opponent, manages to outwit him. Dupin is characterised as the analyst who, combining reason and intuition, glories in the solving of enigmas almost as a spiritual pursuit. Poe conceived of him as 'a poet who brings to commonplace reality the discriminating eye of the artist, but who weighs his evidence as a logician and is able to extrapolate from the raw materials of the *real* world the *ideal* solution'.

Lab. 106 (76) *Ficc.* 143

Dürer, Albrecht (Durero) (1471-1528)

A German painter, engraver and illustrator, whose treatment of the human figure combines the hallucinatory imagery of German late Gothic with the idealised vision of the Italian Renaissance. Brodie 33 (37): Dürer is here called a heretic because his representational painting can be said to break the Third Commandment: 'Thou shalt not make unto thee any graven image or any likeness...' (Exodus 20:4).

Brodie 33 (37) *Brodie* 92

Durtain, Luc (1881-1959)

The pseudonym of André Nepveu, a French writer whose literary aim was 'the conquest of the world through images and visions'. Luc Durtain was a member of 'L'Abbaye', an artistic society founded in 1906, which sought to unite writers and painters in an atmosphere of intellectual comradeship, away from the constraints of society.

Lab. 63 (37) *Ficc.* 47

Eald (also Alt)

A fictional name, referring perhaps to the novelist Roberto Arlt who grew up in the rough working-class and *compadrito* areas west of *Buenos

Aires, such as Villa Luro, in which so many of the short stories in *Doctor Brodie's Report* are set. Roberto Arlt is mentioned in the preface.
Brodie 29 (31) *Brodie* 33

Eclogue (Égloga) see *Virgil

Ecuador, Calle

A street in *Buenos Aires running from *Once to Barrio Norte.
Fict. 153 (168) *Ficc.* 188

Egypt (Egipto)

A country in north Africa whose culture has profoundly influenced the growth of western civilisation. Its fertility and prosperity are due to the yearly flooding of the Nile, whose origin was a mystery both to the ancient Egyptians and to the Greeks because, unlike other rivers known to them, it flowed from south to north. Its Egyptian name was *Ar* or *Aur* meaning black (the colour of its mud). Lab. 147/8 (117): the reference to Egypt as the river Nile stems from the *Odyssey* (4.355,385) where the same word *Aigyptos* in the feminine gender designates the country but in the masculine designates the river (rivers in Greek were always masculine). Lab. 131 (101): the 'monuments of Egypt' inscribed with hieroglyphs are the first written documents in the world, the earliest dating to 3350 BC. By 250 AD the Greek alphabet with six added letters had replaced the hieroglyphs; the last known hieroglyphs were carved in 394. For Lab. 135 (106) see *Diocletian.
Lab. 94 (66) *Ficc.* 127, Lab. 131 (101) *Ficc.* 181, Lab. 135 (106) *Aleph* 8, Lab. 153 (123) *Aleph* 39, Lab. 170 (138) *Aleph* 67

El Alamein

The name applied to several military operations in North Africa in World War II, but more specifically to the decisive British battle under Montgomery on 4 November 1942 which resulted in Germany's retreat.
Lab. 178 (145) *Aleph* 87

Eleatic paradoxes (Aporías eleáticas)

A term derived from the school of philosophy founded in the fifth century BC by *Parmenides of Elea, whose favourite pupil was Zeno. Opposing Heraclitus, and foreshadowing the idealism of *Berkeley, the Eleatics argued against belief in the reality of motion and the plurality of things which would involve changes in the state of 'being'. They held that 'being' was necessarily one and unchanged, while individual things and movement were an illusion. Their teaching methods were based on a system of paradoxes or proofs 'ad absurdum', such as the flying arrow which passes through a series of points in which it is static and the race between Achilles and the tortoise to which Borges frequently refers. See *Aporias, *Contest with the tortoise.

Lab. 35 (11) *Ficc*. 24

Elijah (Elías)

Judaism's greatest prophet, regarded as the champion of monotheism and the protector of its moral law from the corrupt worship of *Baal. Lab. 129 (99) refers to the episode on Mount Horeb when Elijah, called by God, covered his face: 'And it was so, when Elijah heard it, that he wrapped his face in his mantle, and went out and stood in the entering of the cave' (I Kings 19:13).

Lab. 129 (99) *Ficc*. 175

Eliot, Thomas Stearns (1888-1965)

An English poet and critic, born in USA. Eliot was the author of 'The Waste Land' (1922), an allegorical poem expressing man's need for salvation, and *Four Quartets* (1936-42), a series of poems evincing a preoccupation, shared by Borges, with time, individuality and the place of man in history. Lab. 149 (118) refers to Eliot's allusive vocabulary and deliberate anachronisms introduced 'to forge an appearance of eternity' (*Disc*. 122). Aleph 36 (51): Eliot's work as a literary critic was equally important. Borges admired his criticism of the Elizabethans and shared his classical approach. Borges's seminal essay 'Kafka and his Precursors' (Other Inq. 106), in which he argues that a writer influences not only the future but also the past, is based on ideas expressed by Eliot in 'Tradition and Individual Talent'.

Lab. 149 (118) *Aleph* 26, Aleph 36 (51) *Ficc*. 42

Ellus Lampridius (Ello Lampridio) see *Heliogabalus

Elphin

A port in County *Roscommon, *Connaught, some eighty miles north west of *Dublin; the diocese is said to have been founded by St Patrick. The area is famous for its caves and ancient burial grounds traditionally associated with the kings of Connaught.

Lab. 99 (70) *Ficc*. 134

Elysian Plains (Llanura elísea)

In Greek mythology the destination of heroes to whom the Gods had granted immortality.
  Lab. 136 (106) *Aleph* 9

Emerson, Ralph Waldo (1803-1882)

An American poet and essayist who travelled to Europe in 1847-8, where he met *Carlyle. He became one of the major exponents of the New England 'Transcendental School'. The philosophy of the movement, which had strong mystical and religious undertones, operated on him as a liberating force. It was based on the superiority of insight over logic, the unity of nature and the innate goodness of man. Many of Emerson's poems and essays elaborate the ideology of transcendentalism, as do the articles which he contributed to *The Dial* which he founded in 1840 as an organ of the movement. Aleph 66 (103): 'The Past', which first appeared in the collection *May-Day and Other Pieces* (1867), begins with the lines: 'The debt is paid, / The verdict said', a statement that no power can alter what has been, for reality is irrevocable: 'Not the Gods can shake the past, nor the devil can finish what is packed / Alter or mend eternal Fact.' Aleph 69 (107): the dry remark of the character Patricio Gannon that Spanish literature is so boring that 'it makes Emerson quite superfluous' does not reflect Borges's own opinion. Borges dedicated a poem to Emerson, declaring how vitally present Emerson's name remained to him and attributing to Emerson a nostalgia for a life 'not lived' which reflects Borges's own regrets (Sel. Poems, 189).
  Aleph 66 (103), 69 (107) *Aleph* 71, 75

En Soph

Hebrew for 'endless': a *Cabbalistic term designating the impersonal and ineffable nature of God before his manifestation in the creation of the world. The negative emphasis of the term (*en*, 'nothing'; *sof*, 'end') seeks to convey the idea that God, as he existed before Creation, was unknowable to man, who was unable to express his existence. Any actual name would imply a limitation on the concept of God and therefore be an impossibility; the negative signifies a refusal to impose any boundaries upon the designation of God. This concept of a hidden God, 'that which is not conceivable by thinking', was a factor leading to the heretical belief in a duality between the impersonal and unfathomable God and the personal Demiurge of Creation which lay at the root of *Gnosticism.
  Aleph 22 (29) *Aleph* 168

Encyclopaedia Britannica

Borges, attracted to the claim that encyclopaedias embrace the totality of human knowledge, as the word implies, owned a set of the eleventh edition of the *Encyclopaedia Britannica* in 29 volumes (1910-11), the last edition to have been published in Britain. The tenth edition (1902-3), said in 'Tlön, Uqbar, Orbis Tertius' to be the original of the piratical *Anglo-American Cyclopaedia*, is a reprint of the 24 volumes of the ninth edition plus 11 supplementary volumes, one containing new maps and one a comprehensive index to the whole work. The 20 volumes mentioned as circulating in the USA in about 1824 are probably the sixth edition of 1823. In 1824 these were reprinted with six supplementary volumes.

Lab. 27 (3) *Ficc.* 13

England (Inglaterra)

Borges had strong personal ties with England through his paternal grandmother, and he often expressed his admiration for the English language and English literature.

Lab. 30 (6) *Ficc.* 17, Lab 46 (19) *Ficc.* 98

Enneads (Enéadas) see *Plotinus

Entre Ríos (Entrerriano)

A province in eastern Argentina on the border with *Uruguay. Because of its strategic position near *Buenos Aires and across the river from Uruguay, Entre Ríos has played an important part in the history of both countries. During the years of *Federalism it was ruled by *Urquiza, the *caudillo* who first invaded Uruguay under the orders of *Rosas but later led the uprising that brought about Rosas's defeat. Entre Ríos played a seminal part in the eventual unification of the provinces. Aleph 66 (103): Entre Ríos was often involved in Uruguayan battles, and it is realistic to suppose that its men would probably have fought in the revolution of Aparicio *Saravia. See *India Muerta.

Aleph 66 (103) *Aleph* 71

Ephesus (Efeso)

One of the largest cities of Greek origin in the Roman world, the capital of the Roman province of Asia. The temple of *Diana at Ephesus was one of the 'seven wonders of the world'. Lab. 176 (144): St *Paul lived and preached in Ephesus for three years (Acts 18 and 19); subsequently the city was the scene of many acts of Christian persecution. Lab. 191 (158) refers to the seven sleepers of Ephesus: according to Christian legend seven noble Christian youths who took refuge in a cave during the Decian persecution (c. AD 250) and were walled in. They fell asleep for 187 years, awakening at the time of Theodosius II, when Christianity had become the established religion. The coin referred to was tendered by one of the sleepers at a baker's shop, arousing suspicion because it was of the time of Decius. The youth was accused of hoarding hidden treasure but proved his innocence by leading the authorities to the cave, where the other six recently awakened sleepers were waiting for him 'beaming with a holy radiance'. The youths proclaimed to the emperor that 'God had wrought this wonder to confirm his faith in the resurrection of the dead'; after which they died.

Lab. 157 (126) *Aleph* 45, Lab. 176 (144) *Aleph* 84

Epictetus (Epícteto) (c.55-135)

A Stoic philosopher and moralist. Epictetus left no written work, but his teachings were recorded by his pupil, the historian Flavius Arrianus (Arrian). He preached a gospel of inner freedom attainable by contentment and forbearance and a sense of detachment from all that lies beyond one's reach.

Lab. 192 (159) *Aleph* 107

Epistle to the Hebrews (Epístola a los Hebreos)

An Epistle traditionally attributed to St *Paul, though its authorship is now disputed. It seeks to demonstrate the superiority of Christianity to Judaism. Lab. 152 (121): in chapter 9 the repeated yearly sacrifices of the high priest in accordance with the Old Covenant are contrasted with Christ's atonement which is eternal: 'So Christ was once offered to bear the sins of many; and unto them that look for him shall he appear a second time without sin unto salvation' (9:28).

Lab. 152 (121) *Aleph* 38

Erdkunde see Karl *Ritter

Erfjord

A fictional character who appears in several stories: in Lab. 39 (14) as Gunnar Erfjord, one of the inventors of Tlön; in Lab. 128 (98) as Erik Erfjord, a Danish Hebraicist; and in Lab. 153 (122) simply as Erfjord, a Christian theologist.

Lab. 39 (14) *Ficc.* 29, Lab. 128 (98) *Ficc.* 174, Lab. 153 (122) *Aleph* 40

Erzerum (also **Erzurum**)

A province in north-eastern Turkey and the name of its capital, an important trading centre and fortress. The region is crossed by caravan routes.

Lab. 28 (5) *Ficc*. 15

Essays see Francis *Bacon

Estado Occidental

The 'occidental province' of the imaginary state of Costaguana in which Conrad set his novel *Nostromo* (1917). The province was the stronghold of the Blanco Party, to which the President-Dictator of the country belonged. See *Avellanos, *Golfo Plácido, *Higuerota, José *Korzeniovski, *Sulaco.

Brodie 81 (99) *Brodie* 111

Euclid (fl. *c*.323-285 BC)

A Greek mathematician from Alexandria who systematised contemporary mathematical knowledge. His treatise on geometry, *The Elements*, has remained the pre-eminent elementary geometry textbook for two thousand years. Such was Euclid's influence that until the beginning of the twentieth century geometry was referred to in British schools simply as 'Euclid'. Brodie 23 (25): the reference is to Spinoza's use of geometry in the exposition of his philosophical ideas. See *More geometrico.

Brodie 23 (25) *Brodie* 25

Euphorbus (**Euforbo**)

A Trojan hero who, when he was killed by Menelaus, then dedicated his shield in the temple of Hera in Argos (*Iliad* 17.45ff). Lab. 55 (30): to prove his theory of metempsychosis, or reincarnation, *Pythagoras, who claimed to have been Euphorbus in a previous life, took down the shield from the temple wall and pointed to the name inscribed on the back (Horace, *Odes* 1.28.11). Lab. 152 (121): no record has been found of a heretic called Euphorbus burnt at the stake. In the light of Pythagoras' statement, the name could have been deliberately chosen to reinforce the concept of people and events returning through time, as believed by 'the heretics of the wheel'.

Lab. 55 (30) *Ficc*. 67, Lab. 152 (121) *Aleph* 38

Euphrates (Eufrates)

The largest river of Western Asia.
Lab. 60 (34) *Ficc.* 73

Ex ungue leonem

'You can judge a lion from its claw': a Latin phrase meaning that from the sample you can judge the whole.
Lab. 31 (7) *Ficc.* 19

Exemplary Novels (Novelas ejemplares)

Twelve moral tales on various themes by *Cervantes published in 1613.
Lab. 67 (41) *Ficc.* 52

Ezeiza

Argentina's main international airport, near *Buenos Aires.
Brodie 123

Ezekiel (Ezequiel)

The book of Ezekiel is the most mystical of the Old Testament books of prophecy. Ezekiel was deported by *Nebuchadnezzar from *Jerusalem to *Babylon in 597, where he prophesied the redemption of the Jewish people from captivity. He preached the universality of God, insisting that the divine presence was confined neither to the Temple nor to Jerusalem. More than any other of the prophets, Ezekiel makes vivid use of symbolism; vision and ecstasy are his hallmarks. Aleph 19 (26) refers to 'the vision of the four wheels' which is taken from Ezekiel 1:5-11, a passage remarkable in that it does not seek to describe God directly but is a metaphor of the unfathomable appearance of his likeness. This powerful image later became the basis of a form of Jewish mysticism (Merkabah) concerned with speculations on the appearance of God on the Throne, and was also used in Christian iconography.
Aleph 19 (26) *Aleph* 164

Faerie Queene, The

The foremost English epic poem of the Renaissance, written by Edmund Spenser (1552-1599) in heroic or 'spenserian' stanzas (rhyming pattern: ababbcbcc). The poem is highly allegorical, in the tradition of Ariosto and Tasso, though based upon English legend. It is set in the land of Fairie (England) ruled by its queen *Gloriana (Elizabeth) and tells of the adventures of six of her knights, each representing a different virtue.

Spenser uses the example of the mythical world of romance to illustrate the political and ecclesiastical conflict between Protestant England and Catholic Spain. A serious ethical intention underlies the poem, the conceits of the knights' adventures exemplifying a moral quest in which the individual, faced by the mysteries of life, chooses the principal Christian virtues of valour, temperance, friendship, love, justice and courtesy. Aleph 36 (51): comparison between the mystical quest in 'The Approach to Almotásim' and *The Faerie Queene* is well-founded: it has been said that 'enjoyment of the poem's sensuous surface is itself to undergo an experience, an ascent in vision with the protagonist' (A. Kent Hieatt). Aleph 22 (30): in book 3 (2. 19) the story is told of a mirror made by Merlin for King Ryence which gives him the power to see all. It is in the form of a glass orb, shaped like the world, and enables the viewer to look into the hearts of men and foresee the intentions of his enemies and the treachery of his friends.

Aleph 36 (51) *Ficc.* 42, Aleph 22 (30) *Aleph* 168

Fafnir

In the Old Norse Volsungsaga mythology the giant who killed his father in order to take possession of a treasure of gold, transforming himself into a dragon. Fafnir in turn was killed by *Sigurd. See *Fáfnismál*.

Aleph 193 (160) *Aleph* 109

Fáfnismál

'The Lay of *Fafnir', one of the Volsung sagas recounted in the Norse *Eddas*. *Sigurd is persuaded by Regin, his guardian and Fafnir's brother, to slay the dragon Fafnir in order to steal his treasure of gold. He goes to Gnitaheidr to lie in wait for Fafnir, whose custom it is to go there in search of water. Fafnir arrives and, realising that he is about to be killed, prophesies his slayer's death: 'The glistening gold, and the glow-red hoard / the rings thy bane will be.' He warns Sigurd that Regin, who 'betrayed me, will betray thee too, / and will be the bane of us both'. Sigurd responds by killing Fafnir and cutting off Regin's head; he also eats Fafnir's heart and drinks the blood of both his victims. Yet the prophecy proves strangely true: Sigurd himself is killed, as are all who subsequently own the gold.

Lab. 194 (160) *Aleph* 109

Famille rose (Familia rosa)

A form of eighteenth-century Chinese porcelain.

Lab. 49 (24) Ficc. 104

Faucigny Lucinge, Princess of

An Argentine friend of Borges, née Lidia Lloveras, who married Prince Faucigny Lucinge and went to live in Paris. Salvador Dali in his *Diary of a Genius* refers to her death with regret, together with the death of aesthetic movements such as surrealism and existentialism.

Lab. 40 (16) *Ficc.* 31

Faust (c.1488-1541)

A wandering conjuror and charlatan who was said to have sold his soul to the devil in exchange for knowledge and power. Faust, as a concept, has undergone various forms: as magician, pursuer of all knowledge and experience, prototype of Romantic introspection, and symbol of German dynamism epitomised by the *Third Reich. See *Goethe, *Spengler.

Lab. 174 (142) *Aleph* 82

Federalism

After the Wars of Independence (1810-24) the two major opposing parties in Argentina were the Federalists and the *Unitarians, whose differences plunged the country into civil war for nearly six decades. Federalism stood for the autonomy and equality of all the provinces and their traditional Hispanic and *criollo* values, as opposed to the growing ascendancy of cosmopolitan *Buenos Aires. Its leaders were self-elected *caudillos* with a popular following among the local *gauchos, the most notable being Facundo in the interior (see *Sarmiento) and *Rosas in the littoral. This division reflected a difference in economic policy within Federalism itself, the isolated interior wishing to preserve its outmoded factories, while the littoral wished to pursue the more Unitarian policy of an export-oriented international economy, selling off its agricultural produce in return for cheap manufactured goods from Europe. The Federalists wished to restrict the high revenues that such a policy would produce to the littoral, while the Unitarians proposed to share them with the rest of the nation. The last important Federalist leader, Rosas, gradually disposed of all opposition until he became dictator: Unitarian policies were thus achieved under a Federalist banner. Rosas was brought down in 1852 by one of his generals, *Urquiza, but the constitution remained Federalist in name and Unitarian in character. Between 1852 and 1880 the struggle continued between the newly formed Federation of Provinces and the province of Buenos Aires, which remained outside it. In many ways it was a struggle between the old *criollo* values of the patrician families and the cosmopolitan values of the new land-owning and commercial bourgeoisie. This struggle underpins many of the stories in *Doctor Brodie's Report*.

Fenton

A town in the Potteries district of north-west *Staffordshire.
  Lab. 46 (21) *Ficc.* 99

Farid (also Ferid), Al-din Abu Talib Muhammad Ben Ibrahim Attar (c.1145-1229)

One of the greatest Muslim mystical poets, born in *Nishapur, the famous centre of Sufi mysticism. As his name indicates (*attar* is Persian for 'scent') he probably dealt in perfumes or drugs, but the details of his life remain obscure. He is said to have received 'the call' from a passing Sufi beggar who challenged him to renounce his worldly goods and lead a life of poverty and contentment, after which the beggar dropped dead before him. Inspired to become a mystic, Attar set out on travels through the Middle East and central Asia and eventually returned to his native town, where he was killed during the *Mongol invasion of *c.* 1220. Margaret *Smith, relating the legendary account of his death, describes how, when he was taken captive by a Mongol, another Mongol offered a ransom of a thousand pieces of silver to save his life. His captor was on the verge of accepting, but Attar advised him that he was worth much more. Later a third Mongol arrived offering a ransom of a sack of straw, whereupon Attar said, 'Take it, that's what I'm worth.' His captor, furious, beheaded him. Aleph 36 (52): there appear to be no references relating this legend to that of *Tule's soldiers. Attar's mystical doctrine may be summarised as follows: God contains everything and yet transcends all things. He is the One in whom all is lost, and also the One in whom all is found. He is Being, Will, the source and goal towards which all things move. Man is separated from God; his soul, divine in origin but tied to the material body like a bird within a cage, is constantly striving to return to his source and become reunited with the divine. The ascent is difficult, and only love can tear aside the veil that hangs between man and the unknowable God. The quest, therefore, not only emanates from man's soul but is reciprocal, needing the grace and help of God for union to be attained.
  Aleph 31 (45) *Ficc.* 35

Fermat, Pierre de (1601-1665)

A distinguished French mathematician, in his day second only to René *Descartes, some of whose ideas he disputed. Fermat was considered by some the discoverer of differential calculus and is credited as the founder of the modern theory of numbers. Aleph 73 (115): the story is told that, while reading an edition of the *Arithmetica* of *Diophantus, Fermat discovered an important theory of higher mathematics which he noted on the margin of his copy but did not bother to set out fully. It has never been reconstructed. Fermat was reluctant to give demonstrations of his results, and it was often left to others to provide the proofs of his theories.

Aleph 73 (115) *Aleph* 123

Fierro, Martín

The eponymous hero of José Hernández's narrative poem *El gaucho Martín Fierro* (pt.1 1872, pt.2 1879), considered by many to be Argentina's national poem. Written to expose the government's corruption and abuse of the **gauchos*, the poem tells of the maltreatment suffered by Martín Fierro, a fate he shares with all the other characters. In Argentine tradition the mythified Martín Fierro has become the exemplar of national values of physical and moral courage. This, however, is not borne out by the actions of the poem. As Borges pointed out in *El 'Martín Fierro'*, the *gaucho*, who becomes an outlaw, is shown to be lazy, forever lamenting his fate, cowardly in battle, a deserter who will seek revenge for his misfortunes by wantonly killing a negro and beating up his female companion. But, as Borges also pointed out, Martín Fierro's greatness is aesthetic and not moral: it lies not in his actions but in the tone of his lament, his evocation of past happiness, his awareness of suffering and his acceptance of the vicissitudes of destiny as part of the human condition. Aleph 57 (85) refers to Martín Fierro's desertion from the army in pt.1, canto vi. The incidents alluded to in Aleph 56 (84), which are based on the poem, can be found as follows: pt.1, canto vi: Martín Fierro's desertion; pt.1, canto vii: the killing of a negro; pt.1, canto viii: the second killing (no mention of the district of **Rojas*); pt.1, canto ix (specifically ll.1624-6): the fight against **Cruz* and the troop of police and Cruz's eventual defection to his side. Fict. 146 (161): the episode alluded to in 'The End' is the *payada*, or song contest, between Martín Fierro and *el moreno*, who was the brother of the murdered negro. In the *payada* the *gauchos* discuss metaphysical themes, but towards the end *el moreno* reveals his identity, and his desire for revenge is made clear. In keeping with the more conciliatory tone of pt.2 a fight is prevented between the two contestants, each going his own way. 'The End' is a gloss on this episode, the fight that might have taken place.

Aleph 57 (85) *Aleph* 57, Fict. 146 (162) *Ficc.* 180, Fict. 152 (167) *Ficc.* 187

Firdusi (also Firdawasi) (c.941-1020)

The name by which the Persian poet Abul Kasim Mansu is commonly known. Firdusi was the author of the *Book of Kings (Shahnamah)*, the Persian national epic which recounts the history and legends of Persia until the fall of the Sassanid empire. According to tradition, Mahmud of Ghazni, the Sultan to whom the *Shahnamah* was dedicated, promised to pay Firdusi a piece of gold for every verse. When he sent silver instead,

Firdusi was so offended by the deceit that he gave it away to his attendants. The Sultan repented and sent the promised gold pieces, but it was too late: the messenger arrived in time to meet the poet's funeral train.

Lab. 192 (159) *Aleph* 106

FitzGerald, Edward (1809-1883)

An English poet and translator, most famous for his version of the *Rubaiyat* of Omar Khayam, first published anonymously by *Quaritch in 1859. FitzGerald maintained that to be readable a translation must be a paraphrase and wrote: 'It is an amusement to me to take what liberty I like with these Persians, who as I think are not poets enough to frighten me from such excursions, and who really do want a little care to shape them.' Aleph 36 (51): FitzGerald's translation of the *Mantig al-Tayr*, or *Parliament of Birds*, is extremely free. The original is a lengthy poem, which FitzGerald condenses into a few pages, selecting particularly apologues, or little stories with obvious morals. See 'The Enigma of Edward FitzGerald', Other Inq. 75.

Aleph 36 (51) *Ficc.* 43

Flaubert, Gustave (1821-1880)

A French novelist best remembered for *Madame Bovary* (1857), the story of a provincial doctor's wife constrained by the social and intellectual codes of the bourgeoisie. Fict. 66 (73): Flaubert, like Henry *James, is renowned for the painstaking documentation of his novels and the care with which he sought stylistic perfection. Borges, arguing against what he terms 'the vanity of perfection', points out that, paradoxically, the totally correct or perfect text, such as Flaubert was at pains to achieve because he thought it unassailable, is, by the very nature of its perfection, the most precarious and the least able to withstand the changes to which language is subject. But he adds that Flaubert was happily saved from the excesses of his doctrine (*Disc.* 47). Lab. 124 (94): the 'wearing cacophonies' said to have alarmed Flaubert is an ironic allusion to Flaubert's belief in the pre-established harmony between the 'mot juste' and its sound. Lab. 190 (157): Flaubert's search for the 'Absolute' has already been hinted at in the two previous references in terms of his search for perfection, not only of form, but of corresponding sound. Borges discusses these and other aspects of Flaubert's work in two essays in *Disc.* In 'Vindicación de *Bouvard et Pécuchet*' – about Flaubert's unfinished novel which was to conclude with a 'Dictionnaire des Idées Reçues' (Dictionary of Platitudes) – Borges sees the efforts of the unimaginative scribes of the title as an ironic reflection of Flaubert's failure and his own to interpret the universe. In 'Flaubert y su destino ejemplar' Borges remarks upon the irony that Flaubert, who wanted to be totally absent from his novels, placing his characters at the forefront of the text, has survived not simply through them as their creator, but personally, as the author of the 'impersonal' narrative technique (illustrated in his work and discussed in his correspondence) which so markedly influenced the development of the modern novel.

Lab. 124 (94) *Ficc.* 167, Fict. 66 (73) *Ficc.* 78, Lab. 190 (157) *Aleph* 104

*Flores

In the nineteenth century, a village outside *Buenos Aires, 100 feet above sea level and much sought after by the wealthy as a weekend and summer retreat. During the *Yellow fever epidemic of 1871, when it was overrun by people fleeing the city, it grew in size and importance. Today it forms part of greater Buenos Aires.

Brodie 65 (77) *Brodie* 60

Floresta

A district of Buenos Aires to the west of Flores where, at the turn of the century, workers were encouraged to settle rather than in the insanitary, overcrowded port area.

Brodie 45 (54) *Brodie* 40

Fludd, Robert (1574-1637)

An English physician and mystical philosopher, who combined medicine with faith-healing. As a philosopher Fludd was attracted to *Cabbalistic thought and argued for the identity of physical and spiritual truth. His system, which may be termed 'materialist pantheism', held that the universe and all things created proceed from God and return to him. The universe consists of three worlds – the archetypal (God), the macrocosm (the world), and the microcosm (man) – which interrelate and act sympathetically on each other. Fludd was involved with the secret society of the *Rosae Crucis (Rosicrucians) and was thought by *De Quincey to have been influential in the resurgence of Freemasonry.

Lab. 107 (77) *Ficc.* 145, Lab. 120 (90) *Ficc.* 162

'For he shall grow before him as a tender plant...' ('Brotará como raíz de la tierra sedienta') see *Isaiah

Forkel, Johannes

A fictional character in Borges's 'Deutsches Requiem', said to have lived from 1799 to 1846. The name recalls Johann Nicolaus Forkel, the first biographer of J.S. Bach, who lived from 1749 to 1818.

Fort William

A town in Inverness in north-west Scotland, at the foot of Ben Nevis.
Lab. 195 (162) *Aleph* 111

Fort, Paul (1872-1960)

A French symbolist poet of prolific output who published seventeen volumes of *Ballades françaises* (1922-58). He often set out his verses as folk songs in prose form to emphasise the greater importance of sound and rhythm than of rhyme. Aleph 12 (17): in 1912 Paul Fort was elected 'Prince des poètes' according to a referendum carried out by the daily political and literary journal *Gil Blas*.
Aleph 12 (17) *Aleph* 153

Fourth Eclogue see *Virgil

Francis of Sales (Francisco de Sales) (1567-1622)

A French Jesuit theologian who campaigned against the *Calvinists and became bishop of Geneva. Canonised in 1665, Francis of Sales was author of the immensely popular *Introduction à la vie dévote* (Introduction to a Devout Life) (1609), a religious work attempting to reconcile Christian and secular values, which was translated into all the main European languages. *Quevedo's Spanish translation appeared in 1634 (see *Obras Completas*, ed L. Astrana Marín, 1963, vol.1, 1370 ff).
Lab. 65 (38) *Ficc.* 48

Fray Bentos

A small town on the banks of the river Uruguay, famous for its meat-canning industry. In his youth Borges was a regular visitor to his cousins' ranch near Fray Bentos. See *Haedo.
Lab. 87 (59) *Ficc.* 118

Fredegarius de Tours (Fredegario de Tours)

The name assigned to the author, or authors, of a chronicle of the Frankish Kingdom. This contained *inter alia* an abridged version of the *History of the Franks* in nine volumes by St Gregory, bishop of Tours (*c.*540-594) which reflected the orthodox Christian views of the bishop and his aversion to the *Arian heresy. Fredegarius' chronicle appears in *Migne's *Patrology*. Aleph 70 (109): no record has been found of

Fredegarius denying (together with *Aristotle) God's power to change the past.

Aleph 70 (109) *Aleph* 77

Freud, Sigmund (1856-1939)

An Austrian physician and neurologist, the founder of psychoanalysis. Freud's greatest innovation was to explore the unconscious mind as manifested in dreams and the effects of infantile sexuality and its repression. His psychoanalytical method was based on 'free association', the relation of thoughts as they occur. Borges appears to be deliberately silent about Freud's influence on literary expression and literary criticism. In an interview with Richard Burgin he dismissed Freud as 'a kind of madman...labouring over a sexual obsession', arguing that his system of causality is too simple for the complexity of the world.

Fict. 70 (77) *Ficc.* 82

Gaetulia (or Getulia)

A country of North Africa extending from the Atlas Mountains to the Atlantic coast. In the second century BC the people of Gaetulia joined Jugurtha (d.104 BC), king of Numidia, in his resistance to Rome. After the Mauretanians became Roman subjects in AD 40, the Romans made frequent sorties in Gaetulia. Lab. 136 (107): though there was no proconsul in Gaetulia (the region was not entirely subordinated), the Gaetulians served in the auxiliary forces of the Roman Empire.

Lab. 136 (107) Aleph 9

Galatea, La

*Cervantes's first book, an eclogue, written in 1583 and published in 1585. It is said to relate indirectly to the story of the author's courtship of Catalina de Palacio, whom he married in 1584, and to include among its characters many contemporary writers disguised under pastoral names.

Lab. 67 (41) *Ficc.* 52

Galilee (Galilea)

A region in northern Israel, the northernmost district of ancient Palestine, extending from the Mediterranean to the river Jordan. Christ spent most of his early life in Galilee, where the greater part of his public ministry and most of his miracles took place. See *Tetrarch.

Lab. 106 (76) *Ficc.* 144

Ganges

The sacred river of the *Hindus, who believe that bathing in its waters washes away all sins. The Ganges rises in the Himalayas, runs through the northern plain of India (now Bangladesh) and flows into the gulf of Bengal.

Lab. 136 (106) *Aleph* 8

Garay Street

The name of a street intersecting with Plaza *Constitución in the unfashionable southern part of Buenos Aires.

Aleph 11 (15) *Aleph* 151

Garcin de Tassy, Joseph Héliodore (1794-1878)

A French orientalist, a specialist in Arabic, Persian and Hindustani, who translated the *Parliament of Birds* in two volumes in 1857 and 1863.

Aleph 36 (52) *Ficc.* 43

Gaucho

The name for horsemen of Spanish, Negro and/or Indian blood who lived in the River Plate provinces and were known for their poverty, bravery and love of freedom. Traditionally nomadic, the *gauchos* worked in open cattle-ranching, but with the advent of wire fencing in the nineteenth century their free-roaming life came to an end. Today the term has connotations both of extreme bravery and laziness; the *gaucho* has become a literary, almost a mythical, figure. The etymology of the word is uncertain, and its interpretation can be taken as a barometer of the political climate. According to one theory, the word was originally *guacho*, from the Mapuche *huacho*, meaning orphaned, destitute. More recent research maintains that it originated in the border area between Argentina, Uruguay and Brazil, and means a deserter and cattle thief; it is still pronounced *'gaúcho'* there, and may stem from the Guarani *caúcho*, meaning a drunkard.

Lab. 30 (6) *Ficc.* 18

Gauss

Perhaps an allusion to the mathematician Carl Friedrich Gauss (1777-1855), whose theory of numbers influenced Kantor. See *Mengenlehre.

Lab. 168 (135) *Aleph* 64

Geneva (Ginebra)

A Swiss city. Throughout World War I Borges lived with his family in Geneva where he attended the Collège Calvin. He often visited the city, and he died there on 14 June 1986. Lab. 131 (101): Geneva was a focal point in the Reformation as the home of *Calvinism, a branch of the Protestant Church associated with strict moral codes.

Lab. 131 (101) *Ficc.* 181

Genghis Khan (Zingis Jan) (*c.*1162-1227)

The great *Mongol warrior and ruler of genius who, after subduing the nomadic tribes of Mongolia, turned his attention to neighbouring states. Genghis led a series of expansionist military campaigns of extraordinary atrocity and plunder which resulted in the establishment of the Great Mongol Empire.

Aleph 36 (52) *Ficc.* 42

Genoa

Genoa, a city and fortified port in north-west Italy which came under Roman rule in the third century BC and prospered as a port. After the fall of the Roman Empire, it was invaded first by the *Lombards and then by the Moors. By the twelfth century it was one of the most important maritime republics of the Mediterranean, promoter of the Crusades, coloniser of the Levant and a bitter rival of Venice. See *Venetian Republic.

Lab. 155 (124) *Aleph* 42

George, St (San Jorge) (d. *c.*303)

A Christian martyr who was adopted as patron saint of *England under Edward III in about 1348; crusaders returning from Antioch had made him popular. Lab. 194 (161) refers to the medieval legend of the triumph of St George over the Dragon, symbol of the Devil.

Lab. 194 (161) *Aleph* 109

Georgics (Georgicas) see *Virgil

German Reich (Imperio Alemán) (1871-1918)

Also called the Second Reich to indicate its descent from the First (the medieval Holy Roman Empire). The German Reich was initiated by Bismark in 1871. Kaiser Wilhelm II was Emperor during the latter period up to the end of World War I. Following the tradition, Hitler called

his regime the *Third Reich.
    Lab. 44 (20) *Ficc*. 98

Germany (Alemania)

A varying symbol in the context of different stories. Lab. 45-6 (20-1): the defiant and hostile attitude of the Chinese spy *Yu Tsun, who acted as a German agent, appears justified in the light of events of the previous half-century. The German empire, established in 1870, joined the nineteenth-century scramble for *China during the Sino-Japanese War (1894-5), and seized the port of Kioo-chow as a reward for supporting China. A German fleet was sent to patrol Chinese waters. In 1900 Germany joined the other European powers in suppressing the Boxer Rebellion, a formidable nationalist uprising against foreign penetration led by the Dowager Empress and her Manchu advisers. Kaiser Wilhelm II exhorted the German troops embarking for the east to emulate the *Huns of the fifth century in putting down the enemy. Though the German forces reached Peking after the rebellion had been defeated, the Kaiser demanded that the young Prince Chum, half-brother of the Emperor, be sent to Berlin on a penitential mission and even asked that he perform 'kow-tow' in front of him. Lab. 160 (128): in the context of *Droctulft's story, the marshes of Germany are the sign of a country still in the stage of barbarism, contrasted with the civilisation embodied in *Ravenna. Lab. 173 (141): in 'Deutsches Requiem' Germany is used in two sets of conflicting images. Uppermost lies the representation of the spirit of pure Germanism (Kerndeutsch) as expounded in the *Third Reich ideology of the master race. Briefly, this argued that the Nordic Aryans were the bearers of the highest form of civilisation and culture and that their purity had to be preserved for the salvation of mankind. Yet this image is offset by the wider, humanistic tradition exemplified by *Hegel, *Brahms and *Goethe and even by their appropriation of *Shakespeare.
    Lab. 45 (20) Ficc. 99, Lab. 160 (128) *Aleph* 49, Lab. 173 (141) *Aleph* 83

Geseminus

A misprint for *Gesenius.
    Aleph 81

Gesenius, Heinrich Friedrich Wilhelm (1786-1842)

A German orientalist and biblical scholar famous for his rationalist methods of exegesis. In 1830 he was subjected to violent attack in the Evangelical press under the editorship of *Hengstenberg. Gesenius was a friend of *Thilo, with whom in 1820 he travelled to Paris, London and Oxford to examine oriental manuscripts.
    Lab. 173 (141) *Aleph* 81

Gestapo

An abbreviation for the German Geheime Staatspolizei (German secret police) responsible for 'security' within the *Third Reich. Founded by Goering, and later controlled by Himmler, it had the power of arbitrary arrest of anyone considered to be an enemy of the state, and its decisions were not subject to judicial examination. It was declared a criminal organisation by the Nuremberg Tribunal of 1946.

Lab. 118 (89) *Ficc*. 160

Ghazali (1058-1111)

A famous Persian theologian. After a nervous breakdown, Ghazali suffered a spiritual crisis and for a time became a Sufi mystic. He tried to reconcile the tensions between theology and philosophy. His anti-rationalist *Tahafut-al-falasifa* (Destruction of Philosophy) attacked the Neoplatonism of Avicenna (Ibn Sina), holding that the world was deliberately created by God and not simply an emanation of a First Being. His use of the word Tahafut (destruction) implies something like the collapse of a house of cards. The same concept was used by *Averroes in his refutation of Ghazali.

Lab. 180 (148) *Aleph* 91

Ghimel

The third letter of the Hebrew alphabet with a numerical value of three. See *Aleph.

Lab. 55 (30) *Ficc*. 67

Gibbon, Edward (1737-1794)

An English historian, author of *The History of the Decline and Fall of the Roman Empire* (1776-88). The first three volumes cover the history of Rome from the Antonines in the second century to the fall of the Western empire in the fifth; the last three take it to the sack of Constantinople ('New Rome') by Mahomet II in 1453. Though Gibbon shocked some contemporaries by the scepticism displayed in his account of the rise of Christianity, his work was much admired by others, such as David *Hume, and remains a classic of English historiography. See *'Terribilis visu facies...'

Lab. 159 (127) *Aleph* 47

Ginzberg – Ginsburg – Gryphius

Three aliases of the character Scharlach in 'Death and the Compass'. The first two are common Jewish surnames: Louis Ginzberg (1773-1848) was an American Talmudic and Rabbinic scholar who wrote extensively on

Jewish subjects and edited the *Jewish Encyclopaedia*; David Ginsburg (1831-1914), who converted to Christianity in 1846, was the author of *The Kabbalah: Its Doctrines, Development and Literature*, first published in 1863. The narrator of 'The Unworthy Friend' is said to own books on the *Cabbala by Ginsberg. Andreas Gryphius (1616-1664) was a leading German lyric poet and dramatist with a predilection for 'sanguinary themes and the terrors of the supernatural'. His delight in the absurd is exemplified by the title of one of his comedies, *Horribilicribifax*.

Lab. 109 (79) *Ficc.* 148, Brodie 23 (26) *Brodie* 26

Ginsburg see *Ginzberg

Giotto di Bondone (1266-1336)

An Italian painter who abandoned the stylised forms of Byzantine art, aiming at a more realistic representation of the human figure, and was thus an important forerunner of the Renaissance. Brodie 34 (38): Giotto's Circle is also a pun, alluding to an incident recounted in Vasari's *Lives of the Painters* (1550). When Pope Benedict IX was seeking proof of Giotto's artistic capability before employing him to decorate Saint Peter's, Giotto 'with the turn of the hand produced a circle so perfect...that it was a marvel to see'.

Brodie 34 (38) *Brodie* 93

Gloriana

Spenser's name for Queen Elizabeth in *The *Faerie Queene*
Aleph 36 (511) *Ficc.* 42

Gnitaheidr

The place to which *Fafnir is said to have removed the stolen treasure in the Norse *Fáfnismál.
Lab. 193 (160) *Aleph* 108

Gnosticism (Gnósticos)

From the Greek *gnôsis*, knowledge: the collective term designating a number of early Christian sectarian doctrines. Because of its emphasis on direct knowledge of God and the secret of salvation, and its adherents' claim to possess this knowledge, Gnosticism was declared heretical by the Church Fathers. For the Gnostics, knowledge meant not rational cognition but a revelationary experience 'transforming the knower himself by making him a partaker in the divine existence' (H. Jonas, *The Gnostic Religion*, Boston 1958). The essential feature of Gnosticism was its dualism. God is 'absolutely transmundane', alien to the universe, which he has not created and does not govern and to which he is as opposed as light is to darkness. The world is the creation of 'lower powers', Archons (rulers), who, though descended from God, do not 'know' God and obstruct knowledge of him. The earth is the domain of the Archons, whose leader is the Demiurge, or World Artificer. It is likened to a prison surrounded by cosmic spheres. Each Archon rules the earth and his particular sphere and bars the passage of souls wishing to escape and return to God. Mirroring the composition of the cosmos is the composition of man, whose origin is similarly twofold, his earthly body being bound by (seven) cosmic spheres, whereas 'pneuma', a spark of dormant divinity, is enclosed in his soul. The aim of Gnostic thinking is to liberate this imprisoned spark through 'knowledge'. Of particular relevance to Borges's work is the Gnostics' use of the labyrinth as a metaphor of a universe encompassing a plurality of worlds. Each section of the labyrinth corresponds to a different world through which the soul loses its way and wanders about, but whenever it seeks an escape 'it only passes from one world into another that is no less world'. Little was heard of the Gnostics after the second century, but their beliefs survived among other heretics, notably the Albigensians in the twelfth century. Lab. 125 (95): because their beliefs implied that Jesus was not the Redeemer of humanity, the Gnostics were looked upon as Antichrist.

Lab. 125 (95) *Ficc.* 169

Goethe, Johann Wolfgang von (1749-1832)

The most celebrated modern German writer, exceptional for the range and depth of his work and generally considered the last universal genius. In his great drama *Faust* Goethe presents a symbol of Western European man in his unceasing quest for all possible experience. Although man's activity is shown to have negative results, the spark that ignites him is regarded as divinely inspired and in harmony with Nature. Lab. 46 (21): by comparing the sinologist Albert with Goethe, the narrator attributes to Albert a transcendental understanding of the individual human condition. This idea is emphasised in Lab. 174 (141), where Goethe is referred to as 'the prototype of that ecumenic comprehension'. Lab. 179 (147): the allusion to hammer and anvil as metaphors for master and slave is derived from two of Goethe's poems, 'Koptisches Lied' and 'Epigramme 14'. See *Faust.

Lab. 46 (21) *Ficc.* 100, Lab. 174 (141) *Aleph* 83

Gog and Magog

Various legends in biblical and Muslim apocalyptic literature connect Gog and Magog with two powers under the dominion of Satan (e.g. Revelation 20). Lab. 184 (152): the incident referred to can be found in the

*Koran (Sura 18.92-8), where it is related that, when Dhul Qarnain (whom commentators have identified with *Alexander the Great) was journeying from the south to the north, he came upon people who asked for his protection, begging him to build them a rampart against Gog and Magog who were ravaging their land. They offered him tribute, which he refused, saying, 'The power which my Lord has given me is better than any tribute.' With their help he built a strong wall to protect them. According to a Syriac legend, Gog and Magog attempt every night to escape from their confinement by digging under the wall, but before morning God repairs the breach.

Lab. 184 (152) *Aleph* 96

Goldoni, Carlo (1707-1793)

An Italian playwright born in Venice, where he spent most of his life. Goldoni revolutionised Italian theatre, which until then had depended largely upon the conventions of the *commedia dell'arte* (improvised performances of stock comic situations by masked characters). He brought realism to the stage with his satirical social comedies whose distinguishing feature was their fast and witty dialogue, showing the influence of Molière. Those written in the Venetian dialect are considered his best. Goldoni was a prolific writer, the author of some 250 plays of which 150 are comedies. In 1765 he was engaged to teach Italian to the daughters of Louis XV, but his pension was withdrawn during the French Revolution and he died in poverty. His memoirs are considered an important document of eighteenth-century life.

Aleph 14 (19) *Aleph* 155

Golfo Plácido

The 'Placid Gulf' on which lay *Sulaco in Conrad's novel *Nostromo*. See *Avellanos, *Estado Occidental, *Higuerota, José *Korzeniovski.

Brodie 81 (99) *Brodie* 111

Golgotha (Gólgota)

Otherwise known as Calvary: the hill on which Jesus was crucified.

Brodie 19 (19) *Brodie* 133

Goyim (Goím)

The plural of the Hebrew *goy*, meaning nation: a *Yiddish name for Gentiles, or non-Jews.

Lab. 115 (85) *Ficc.* 155

Gradus ad Parnassum

'A step to Parnassus': a dictionary given to schoolboys to help them write Latin verses. Mount Parnassus was the home of the Muses.
Lab. 90 (62) *Ficc.* 120

Gram

In the Volsungsaga, a magic sword wrought for *Sigurd by his tutor Regin, rival brother of *Fafnir. The sword was reputed to be so powerful that it could cleave a tree in two with a single blow, and so sharp that it could cut a thread of wool in water.
Lab. 193 (160) *Aleph* 109

Grand National Lines

The tramway company in *Buenos Aires, set up in about 1870, controlled and managed by a British firm; the streetcars, which were originally drawn by horses, were later electrified. Until the middle of the nineteenth century, tramways were the main system of transportation in Buenos Aires.
Brodie 74 (91) *Brodie* 77

Green, Julian (or Julien) (1900-)

A novelist of American origin who wrote both in French and English and is the only foreigner to have been elected to the Académie Française. Fict. 70 (77): Green's religious preoccupations, morbid at times, are reflected in his paranoid characters and hallucinatory language. Referring to one of Green's novels, which he praises for the 'rigour of its inventiveness', Borges compares it to Henry *James's *Turn of the Screw* and Kafka's *Trial* (Preface to *Bioy Casares's *La invención de Morel*).
Fict. 70 (77) *Ficc.* 82

Gregorovius, Ferdinand (1821-1891)

A German historian of Italy, the author of *Roman Journals* and books about the Papacy and Lucretia Borgia. Lab. 131 (101): Gregorovius lived for a time in Ferrara, one of the most important centres of the Papacy. His alleged observation 'that mention of the Phoenix in oral speech was very rare' is probably apocryphal.
Lab. 131 (101) *Ficc.* 181

Grisebach, Eduard (1845-1906)

A German historian who edited *Schopenhauer in a six-volume edition

published in 1891.
   Brodie 85 (103) *Brodie* 117

Grosso, Alfredo Bartolomé (1867-?)

An author of standard Argentine primary-school history texts, such as *Nociones de historia argentina* (1893) and *Curso de historia nacional* (1898). Brodie 24 (26): the reference is omitted in the English translation.
   Brodie 26

Gryphius see *Ginzberg

Guadalquivir

A river in southern Spain, known as Baetis in Latin and Wadi el-Kebir in Arabic.
   Lab. 180 (148) *Aleph* 91

Guadalupe

A church in *Palermo. Brodie 74 (91): its original congregation tended to be of members of the patrician class, descendants of the old *criollo* families, who were hostile to immigrant and middle-class newcomers.
   Brodie 74 (91) *Brodie* 77

Gualeguay

A rural town and department in the province of *Entre Ríos. Aleph 66 (103): the English translation does not distinguish between Gualeguay and *Gualeguaychú.
   Aleph 71

Gualeguaychú

A town on the river of the same name in the province of *Entre Ríos, opposite *Fray Bentos. There is considerable interchange between the two cities.
   Aleph 66 (103) *Aleph* 71

Guaraní

An Indian dialect, originating in the Amazon delta area, spoken in Paraguay and in some areas of north-east Argentina. Present-day Guaraní contains a large percentage of words derived from Spanish or other foreign languages. Brodie 32 (36): while Guaraní is generally used

by the poorer Indians and *mestizo* population living in the countryside, Spanish is spoken by the more affluent *criollo* population of the cities, who reserve Guaraní for communication with servants.
  Brodie 32 (36) *Brodie* 91

Guayaquil

The largest city in Ecuador, a port on the Pacific south west of the capital Quito, founded in 1536. It was here that on 26 and 27 July 1822 the two great figures of Latin American history, *Bolívar and *San Martín, met to plan concerted action to expel the final vestiges of Spanish power from Peru. Brodie 81 (99): the story 'Guayaquil' is based on this momentous meeting, and upon the legends surrounding the behaviour of the two great leaders. There is no record of what was said, but San Martín stepped down and handed over the command of his troops to Bolívar. Historians have offered different interpretations of the event. Bolívar's supporters maintain that San Martín's true aim was to secure Guayaquil for Peru and that, if Bolívar refused to accept the offer to serve under him, it was through deference to San Martín. Brodie 87 (104): the official version offered in Argentine textbooks is that San Martín stepped down as an heroic act of self-abnegation, knowing that his own troops, who were already in Peru, would fight under another general, whereas Bolívar's troops, who were in Ecuador, would be unwilling to move south and fight under another commander, because of their personal attachment to Bolívar. San Martín realised that neither he nor Bolívar could defeat the Spanish alone. He therefore made the sacrifice, knowing that Bolívar would pursue the fight until independence was established. The two great leaders had different priorities and temperaments: Bolívar, who has been likened to Napoleon in his passion and intensity, was a political genius whose aim was to establish democratic republics in the former Spanish colonies; San Martín, compared to Washington for his strength of will and grasp of practicalities, believed that military leaders should keep out of politics and that each country should establish the form of government best suited to itself.
  Brodie 81(99) *Brodie* 11

Guedalla, Philip (1889-1944)

A witty and irreverent English biographer, author of lives of Wellington (1931) and Churchill (1941).
  Fict. 70 (77) *Ficc.* 82, Aleph 31 (45) *Ficc.* 35

Guerra Grande (1843-1856)

The 'great war' which took place between the two main opposing parties of Uruguay, the *Blancos, led by *Oribe and backed by *Rosas, and the *Colorado forces of *Rivera, lieutenant of *Artigas, supported by the

Argentine *Unitarians. Brodie 73 (90): the second phase of the war, from 1843 to 1851, was known as the Great Siege and consisted mainly of the Blancos' siege of *Montevideo, which thereby earned the epithet 'New Troy'.
  Brodie 73 (90) *Brodie* 76

Gujarat (Guzerat)

A region in western India bordering the Arabian Sea.
  Aleph 32 (47) *Ficc.* 37

Gulshan i Raz

The House of Roses, completed in 1317 by Mahmud Shabistari, one of the most important philosophical poems in the Persian language. More than thirty commentaries on it are extant; the best known, by Lahiji, is the basis of an English version by E.H. Whinfield, *Gulshan i Raiz: the Mystic Rose Garden* (London, 1880). Lab. 196 (163): there is no mention of the Zahir in Lahiji's commentary.
  Lab. 196 (163) *Aleph* 112

Gurí

A term used by natives of Rio de la Plata for 'child' or 'little one'.
  Aleph 73

Gutiérrez, Eduardo (1853-1890)

An Argentine journalist and novelist who espoused the cause of the *gaucho*. He is chiefly remembered for his novel on the semi-mythical *gaucho* hero Juan *Moreira, but he was also a chronicler of everyday life in *Buenos Aires. Brodie 64 (76): the reference has been omitted in the English translation.
  Brodie 59

Haedo, Bernardo

Haedo was a family surname of Borges: his mother's cousin was Francisco Haedo. As a child Borges and his family spent summer vacations at the Haedo ranch near *Fray Bentos. A few miles north, on the banks of the river *Uruguay, there is a small town by the same name.
  Lab. 88 (60) *Ficc.* 118

Hai Feng (Mandarin)

A Chinese town east of Hong Kong.

Harald Hardrada (1015-1066)

The son of a Norwegian chief who fought against the Danes under King Olaf II of Norway. At the King's death, Harald took refuge in Russia and served under the Prince of Kiev; from there he enlisted in the army of the Byzantine Emperor Michael IV. His military exploits form part of Byzantine and Norse medieval history. King of Norway from 1047, Harald expanded Norse rule over Orkney, Shetland and the Hebrides, and claimed the throne of England at the death of Edward the Confessor in 1066, allying himself with the rebel Tostig against the new English king, *Harold II. He was defeated and killed on 25 September 1066 at Stamford Bridge.

Lab. 146 (116) *Aleph* 22

Harnack, Adolf (1851-1930)

A German religious historian and patrologist, famous for his formulation of *Gnosticism as 'the acute Hellenisation of Christianity'. Harnack was opposed to any form of 'Hellenisation' (the interpretation of early Christianity in the light of Greek tradition), holding that Greek sources were an intrusion into Christian theology. As a result he was critical of traditional Christian dogma. See Wilhelm *Bousset.

Lab. 153 (122) *Aleph* 39

Harold II (1020-1066)

The last Anglo-Saxon king of England, who was defeated and killed by William the Conqueror at the battle of Hastings. Harold assumed the crown on the death of Edward the Confessor in 1066 in the face of two other claimants, *Harald Hardrada of Norway whom he defeated at Stamford Bridge and William of Normandy.

Lab. 146 (116) *Aleph* 22

Hasidim

The plural of 'Hasid': Hebrew for pious, a term used for the followers of a popular religious movement which arose among Polish Jews in the eighteenth century as a reaction to rabbinical and ritual formalism. Under the charismatic leadership of their founder, *Baal Shem Tov, the Hasidim, while continuing to adhere to strict observance of the Law, emphasised the joyousness of religion and the ecstasy of prayer, claiming that man's salvation lies in faith rather than religious knowledge. Their pantheistic concept of God was expressed in the belief that material objects are in reality the image of the deity. One of the distinguishing features of Hasidism was the unquestioned authority bestowed upon the Tzaddik, or spiritual leader, regarded as a mediator between man and God and endowed with supernatural powers. This personality cult, which led to much abuse and superstition, contributed to the animosity felt by orthodox Jews towards Hasidism and the persecution and even excommunication of their leaders by some rabbis, who considered them a godless sect. Lab. 116 (85): the idea that this animosity could lead to murder has no basis in reality; yet it is not too fanciful for *Scharlach to have built his masterplan on the premise that his enemy, the detective Lönnrot, might think it possible.

Lab. 107 (77) *Ficc*. 145

Haslam, Silas

A fictional name, perhaps a tribute to Fanny Haslam, Borges's paternal English grandmother, who is recalled in 'Story of the Warrior and the Captive'. See *Borges.

Lab. 29 (5) *Ficc*. 16

Hazlitt, William (1778-1830)

An English critic and essayist. Lab. 132 (102): 'Hazlitt's infinite Shakespeare' refers to Hazlitt's *Lectures on the English Poets* (1818), where he wrote: 'He was just like any other man, but that he was like all other men.... He was nothing in himself; but he was all that others were or that they could become.' Borges paraphrases these words in 'From Someone to Nobody' (Other Inq. 148) and develops Hazlitt's idea in 'Everything and Nothing' (Lab. 284 (248)).

Lab. 132 (102) *Ficc*. 182

'He that glorieth, let him glory in the Lord' ('El que se gloría, glóriese en el Señor) see *Corinthians

'He was in the world and the world was made by him' ('En el mundo estaba y el mundo fue hecho por él) see St *John

Hebrew tabernacle (Tabernáculo hebreo) see *Tabernacle

Hegel, Georg Wilhelm Friedrich (1770-1831)

A German philosopher, one of the foremost representatives of nineteenth-century idealism. According to Hegel's definition of reality, individual facts are not rational in themselves but only if viewed as aspects of the whole. The whole is called the 'absolute'; it is spiritual, and can only be reached by a process of logic. Lab. 173 (141): this process, known as 'dialectics', is composed of a triadic movement of *thesis*, the original statement, *antithesis*, its counterpart, to which the first gives rise, and *synthesis*, the unification of the two. This synthesis then becomes the new thesis in the next stage of the movement. Lab. 103 (73): Hegel's dialectical system of knowledge also operates in his vision of history. Deeply religious, Hegel viewed the universe as a manifestation of God, the absolute, who arrives at final self-knowledge through the history of finite beings. The human mind, rising from mere consciousness, passes through various stages, culminating in religion and perfect knowledge. Hegel further expands this principle by observing the various dialectic and cyclical stages of human progress in the realisation of God's purpose.

Lab. 103 (73) *Ficc*. 139, Lab. 173 (141) *Aleph* 81

Hegira (Hejira)

From the Arabic *hijrah*, emigration: the term for the starting point of the Muslim era, dated at 622 AD, when Mohammed fled from Mecca to Medina. The second caliph, Umari, introduced the Muslim calendar, which began with the first day of the lunar month, 16 July 622. Lab. 146 (116): the seventh century after the Hegira would therefore correspond to our fourteenth century.

Lab. 146 (116) *Aleph* 22

Heidegger, Martin (1889-1976)

A German philosopher who influenced Existentialism. Borges criticises Heidegger's philosophy as one which 'plays at desperation and anguish' but basically aims at enhancing the importance of the 'ego' and flattering its 'vanity' (Other Inq. 166). Elsewhere he belittles Heidegger's achievement: 'He invented one of the German dialects, but nothing else' (*Borges mem.* 78). Brodie 83 (101): the sentiments attributed to Heidegger's 'refutation' can be traced to his *Rektoratsrede*, where he demonstrates his warm reception of National Socialism, emphasising its ideas of strong, even violent, personal leadership. Heidegger speaks of a people knowing itself and discovering its own essence in the state. He places the statesman among his list of genuine creators, demanding of his leadership 'the strength to be able to walk alone'. The suggestion of Hitlerian demagoguery echoes Heidegger's words (*Freiburger Studentenzeitung*, Nov.3, 1933): 'The Führer himself and he alone *is* the German reality of today and for the future, and its law.' In later years Heidegger repudiated this position.

Brodie 83 (101) *Brodie* 114

Heliogabalus, Antoninus (Antonino Heliogábalo) (*c*.204-222) (also Elagabalus)

A dissolute Roman emperor, originally named Bassianus. He served in the Roman army in Syria, where he was popular with the Roman troops for his exceptional beauty, and was appointed high priest of the sun god of Emesa, Elagabal. Elected emperor in 218 at the age of 15, he took the name Marcus Aurelius Antoninus and added 'Heliogabalus' in honour of the god whose secret rites he introduced into the capital. His brief reign, marked by debauchery and cruelty, exemplifies a decadent and turbulent imperial court. Jealous of the popularity of his abstemious cousin, Alexander, he attempted to murder him; he was later killed by the Praetorian Guard in a latrine, together with his mother. Lab. 59 (34): the anecdote of the emperor writing 'on shells the lots...destined for his guests' is told by Lampridius in the *Historia Augusta* (2.22.1).

Lab. 59 (34) *Ficc.* 73

Heliopolis

A city in Egypt important for the worship of the sun god Ra. Among its few remains are the obelisks known as Cleopatra's needles.

Lab. 131 (101) *Ficc.* 181

Hell (Infierno)

The place of eternal punishment for impenitents. Lab. 130 (100): the allusion to the Redeemer in Hell is an oblique reference to a Christian tradition that of all sinners only *Judas and *Cain, who lost hope, are unequivocally condemned to eternal damnation. Fict. 68 (75): *Inferno*, the first of the three canticas of *Dante's *Divine Comedy*, describes Hell and the sinners whose souls inhabit it. Canto X 97-102 concerns heretics and atheists, among whom is Cavalcante de' Cavalcanti. He is the father of Dante's friend Guido, one of the poets of the 'Dolce Stil Nuovo', the lyric school which based the concept of love and the idealisation of woman on religious and philosophical premises. Cavalcante asks Dante about his son, hoping he is still alive. This surprises Dante, who remarks that the damned, while apparently able to prophesy the future, are blind to what is happening in the present. To this Cavalcante answers: 'We see even as men who are far-sighted, / those things...that are remote from us; / the Highest Lord allots us that much light.' See *Ugolino, *Ruggieri.

Fict. 68 (75) *Ficc.* 80, Lab. 130 *Ficc.* 175

Hengstenberg, Ernst Wilhelm (1802-1869)

A German Protestant theologian and leader of the orthodox Lutherans, a bitter opponent of 'rationalism' as a method of Old Testament criticism.

In 1830 he mounted a violent attack on the rationalist *Gesenius.
Lab. 173 (141) *Aleph* 81

Henríquez Ureña, Pedro (1884-1946)

A critic and teacher from the Dominican Republic, once considered the foremost Latin American literary historian. He spent most of his later life in *Buenos Aires where he was one of the original contributors to *Sur*, the literary magazine founded by Victoria *Ocampo. Henriquez Ureña was a long-standing friend of Borges and collaborated with him in the publication of *Antología clásica de la literatura argentina* (1937).
Aleph 22 (30) *Aleph* 168

Heraclides Ponticus (Póntico) (*c*.390-330 BC)

A Greek philosopher, born in Heraclea (Pontus), a pupil of Speusippus and *Plato. Many books in philosophy, rhetoric, music and mathematics are attributed to him, though nothing survives. Diogenes Laertius states that Heraclides, a trickster by nature, once persuaded the people of Heraclea that, by giving him a golden crown, they would avoid the famine which threatened their city. Before dying he arranged for his corpse to disappear, wishing people to believe that he had ascended bodily to Heaven, but the plan was discovered and his name ridiculed.
Lab. 55 (30) *Ficc.* 67

Heraclitus (Heráclito) (d. 480 BC)

A Presocratic philosopher, of whose work only oracular fragments remain. His philosophy, in opposition to that of *Parmenides, was based on the principle of permanent movement in nature due to the continuously changing character of its primordial element, fire; the process takes the form of a perpetual conflict of opposites, struggle and unity. This concept found echoes in the dialectics of *Hegel. Lab. 145 (114): isolated epigrammatic remarks by Heraclitus on his contemporaries and predecessors survive, mainly pungent and contemptuous.
Lab. 145 (114) *Aleph* 20

Hermes

In Greek mythology the herald or messenger of the gods, the protector of herdsmen and the god of science, commerce, invention, the arts and, above all, travellers. In this last role Hermes was also the guide of the souls of the dead to their final abode (psychopompos). In art he is usually represented as a vigorous youth with winged helmet and sandals. Lab. 113 (83): being a guide in both life and death, Hermes is referred to as two-faced.

Hermetic books (*Libros herméticos*)

A collection of occult writings, known as the *Corpus Hermeticum*, dating from the first to the third centuries. Their origin was ascribed to the Egyptian god Thoth, who received from the Greeks the name Hermes Trismegistos ('thrice-great Hermes'). They include a text called *Asclepius*, thought to have been used by St *Augustine in the writing of *Civitas Dei*.
   Lab. 154 (123) *Aleph* 40

Herodotus (Heródoto) (484-425 BC)

A Greek historian, born in Halicarnassus, known as the 'father of history'. After travelling in Asia Minor, Greece and Egypt, Herodotus settled in the Greek colony of Thurii in Italy. His *History*, full of charm and subtlety, relates the struggle between Greece and Persia, with numerous digressions. Lab. 131 (101): Herodotus (2.87) gives details of the *Phoenix, having seen it in a painting, and describes the bird's ritual returns to *Heliopolis.
   Lab. 131 (101) *Ficc.* 181

Hertha

A Teutonic fertility goddess, formerly known as Nerthus, said by *Tacitus to have been worshipped by early German tribes (*Germania* 40). Hertha corresponds to the Nordic Jord, earth goddesss and mother of Thor. In Germanic sagas Hertha (or Erda) is the oldest and wisest of the gods to whom Wotan appeals for knowledge.
   Lab. 160 (128) *Aleph* 48

Hesiod (Hesíodo) (fl. 700 BC)

A Greek epic poet, a near-contemporary of *Homer and author of the *Theogony* and *Works and Days*. The *Theogony* details the history of the gods from their emergence from chaos to the moment when Pandora, the first woman, is entrusted by Zeus with a jar containing all the evils which she will let loose on humanity. Lab. 103 (73), Aleph 14 (18): in the *Works and Days* Hesiod combines the moral teachings of the *Theogony* with rural precepts: continuing the story of Pandora, he traces the decline of mankind from the golden age through the silver and bronze ages down to the present iron age. The later part describes the various tasks which face the farmer and the appropriate times of year in which to perform them, harmonising the rhythm of nature with that of human life.
   Lab. 103 (73) *Ficc.* 139, Aleph 14 (18) *Aleph* 154

Hibernia

The Latin name for *Ireland.
Lab. 157 (126) *Aleph* 45

Higuerota

A peak whose 'white head rises majestically' in the Cordillera of fictional Costaguana described in Conrad's novel *Nostromo*. See *Avellanos, *Eastado Occidental, *Golfo Plácido, José *Korzeniovski.
Brodie 81 (99) *Brodie* 111

Hindu see *Hindustan

Hindustan (Indostán)

The land of the Hindus, comprising the valley of the *Punjab and Upper *Ganges. *Ficc.* 38, *Aleph* 143: sometimes, as here, Borges uses the term for *India in general. Aleph 32 (46): the history of strife between Hindus and *Muslims in the Punjab and other regions of India is long and violent. Hindu religious practices are polytheistic and, though they fall into different forms of mysticism, all 'teach that the world is illusory', as Borges states (Other Inq. 152). Lab. 144 (114): recurrent mythic themes are to be found in most Hindu religions, such as time seen as an endless repetiton of the year, the notion of repeated creations, the idea of eternal return and the doctrine of transmigration. See *Wheel.
Aleph 32 (46) *Ficc.* 38, Lab. 144 (114) *Aleph* 20, *Ficc.* 38, *Aleph* 143

Hindustan Review

There is no record of a *Hindustan Review* in *Allahabad, but the *Hindustani* was published there, in Urdu, from 1931 to 1933.
Aleph 32 (46) *Ficc.* 36

Hinton, James (1822-1875)

An English surgeon, theologian, philosopher and member of the Metaphysical Society. Accepting from idealistic philosophy the doctrine that existence is limited by consciousness, Hinton tried to save the essence of Christianity by claiming the presence of a 'Universal Spirit' in the 'actuality' of things. His system acquired the name of 'actualism'.
Lab. 39 (14) *Ficc.* 29, Lab. 120 (90) *Ficc.* 162

Historia Naturalis

A rambling scientific treatise by *Pliny the Elder (AD 23-79) which deals with geography, anthropology, physiology, botany, agriculture, medicine and the arts. Compiled from vast reading, and citing about 500 authors, of whom about 150 were Roman, it is a major source of our knowledge of ancient life. Lab. 89 (61): the 'odd volume' in the story of Funes probably refers to book 2 where in chapters 3-7 Pliny writes about memory, calling it 'the boon most necessary for life'. Lab. 90 (62): 'ut nihil non iisdem verbis redderetur auditum' (7.24) may be translated: 'so that nothing heard can be repeated exactly.' Lab. 149 (118): at 5.8 Pliny describes the inhabitants of the most remote parts of the North African desert beyond *Gaetulia. Among these he mentions the troglodytes who 'dig out caves and use them as habitations, feed on the flesh of snakes, lack the use of language and speak not in words but in shrieks'. Pliny adds that the Garamantes, not having the custom of marriage, spend their time with different women, and that the Augylae only worship the underworld. These lines are quoted almost verbatim in the first chapter of 'The Immortal' (Lab. 137). Lab. 152 (121): the passage from book 7 where Pliny observes that no two faces in the universe are alike is to be found in chapter 1: 'human features...are so fashioned that, among so many thousands of men, there are not two in existence which cannot be distinguished from one another.' Aleph 76: the dragons alluded to can be found in books 8 (32-3) and 12 (33-4), where Pliny describes how every species of animal is 'cunning for its own interest'. He gives several accounts of how dragons (by which he means any long-toothed snake) attack elephants in the summer in order to cool off by drinking their cold blood, 'both combatants dying together, the vanquished elephant as it falls crushing with its weight the snake coiled around'. The reference is probably to the account of the contest quoted by Borges in his *Imaginary Beings* under the heading of 'The Dragon'.

Lab. 89 (61) *Ficc.* 120, Lab. 149 (118) *Aleph* 26, Lab. 152 (121) *Aleph* 38

Historical Museum (Museo Histórico)

A museum in *Buenos Aires, situated in Defensa Street, in the southern part of the city (*Barrio Sur).

Brodie 78 (95) *Brodie* 83

History of Fifty Years of Misrule (Historia de cincuenta años de desgobierno) see José *Avellanos

History of Shorthorn Cattle in Argentina (Historia del Shorthorn en la Argentina)

An agricultural text published by Stanwick in 1910. An earlier edition, *Historia del ganado Shorthorn*, was published by James Sinclair in London in 1904.

Brodie 18 (18) *Brodie* 131

History of World War I see *Liddell Hart

Hitler, Adolf (1889-1945)

The leader of the National Socialist Party in Germany, who was elected Chancellor in 1933. In defiance of treaty obligations he rearmed and led Germany into a disastrous war which changed the face of Europe. Lab. 178: preaching the supremacy of the Aryan race, his policy was a 'final solution': the complete extermination of the Jews. Six million died in German concentration camps. In 'A Comment on August 23, 1944', Borges speculates on the hypothesis that Hitler actually wished to be destroyed and collaborated in his own annihilation (Other Inq. 134-6).

Lab. 178 (146) *Aleph* 88

Hladik, Jaromir

A fictional character, the protagonist of 'The Secret Miracle', whose writings are referred to in 'Three Versions of Judas'. See *Vindicación de la eternidad*.

Lab. 118 (88) *Ficc.* 159, Lab. 129 (98) *Ficc.* 174

Hochschule

The German word for a university or its equivalent.

Lab. 44 (19) *Ficc.* 97

Holland, Philemon (1552-1637)

An English translator of the classics known as the 'Translator-General'. His rendering of *Pliny's *Historia Naturalis*, the first in English, is noted for its exuberance and poetic resonance and is believed to have been used by *Shakespeare.

Aleph 20 (27) *Aleph* 165

Homer (Homero)

The first and greatest Greek poet, of Ionian origin, who seems to have lived between the ninth and eighth centuries BC: the author of the *Iliad* and the *Odyssey*, both of which were transmitted orally (how far our present texts were remodelled by others remains a matter of dispute). According to legend Homer was blind. Nothing is known about him, but the homogeneity of the language and inspiration of the two poems, together with the consistency of their characters, points to a single originator. Borges studied at length the many translations of Homer's poems and discussed their different merits, displaying a partiality for the versions of *Pope. He was particularly interested in the range of interpretations that emerge in the translations, and the impossibility of distinguishing, within the text, between what is intrinsically Homer's and what is part of the heritage of language; he concluded that the original meaning of a text could never be recaptured (*Disc.* 105). Borges also felt a certain affinity with Homer, no doubt heightened by his blindness; he suggested that Homer, on losing his sight, realised that poetry was his destiny: compelled to look for experience within himself, he gained in inspiration (*Hac.* 9-13). Lab. 138 (108): 'the rich Trojans from Zelea...': these 'words in Greek' which the narrator of 'The Immortal' repeats in his delirium, are a quotation from the passage in the *Catalogue of ships in the *Iliad* listing the Trojan allies (2.824-7). The men from Zelea were led by Pandarus to whom *Apollo had taught his skill with the bow. Lab. 140, 148 (110, 117): a 'reprobation which was almost remorse': these words too 'belong to Homer' in so far as they refer to the insinuation of Helen's guilt when, after the abortive duel between Paris and Menelaus, she reprimands Paris for not having fallen on the battlefield (*Iliad* 3.385ff.). Lab. 144 (114): the poem about a war of 'frogs and mice' refers to the mock epic *Batrachomyomachia* intended as a satire on the *Iliad* and traditionally attributed to Homer. See Giambattista *Vico, *Smyrna.

Lab. 144 (114) *Aleph* 18, Aleph 35 (51) *Ficc.* 41

Hora de todos y la fortuna con seso, La (The Hour of all Men or Fortune in her Wits)

A satirical and philosophical work by *Quevedo, whose attack on the government of Philip IV led to his banishment. The work is a 'moral fantasy' in which people from different nations and professions face a tribunal of Gods. Lab. 68 (42): the passage likened to Don *Quixote's well-known debate 'against letters and in favour of arms' is the passage describing the Greeks as 'rich in books and poor in triumphs'. Quevedo regrets the lack of bullets, complaining that all the lead has been used to make letter-moulds for printing more books. 'Yet,' he argues, 'it was our battles that gave us our empire and our victories.' The most pungent line, and the one which most concisely expresses the spirit of the debate, is 'Nunca se juntó el cuchillo a la pluma que éste no la cortase' ('Never did the sword join the pen without the one cutting the other'), which denies the compatibility of the world of letters with the world of arms (cf. ed. Zaragoza, 1651, 125-8).

Lab. 68 (42) *Ficc.* 53

Hotel du Nord

According to Borges's Commentaries (Aleph 173 (268)), the Hotel du Nord stands for the Plaza Hotel in *Buenos Aires, one of the city's most elegant hotels.

Lab. 106 (76) *Ficc.* 143

Hrabanus Maurus (Hrabano Mauro) (c.776-856)

Archbishop of Mainz, religious teacher and author of erudite theological texts expounding the views of St *Augustine. His religious zeal, reflected in his life and writings, verges on extremism.

Lab. 131 (101) *Ficc.* 181

Hradcany

A famous castle and landmark in *Prague, once the seat of the kings of *Bohemia and after 1918 the residence of the President of the Czech Republic.

Lab. 121 (91) *Ficc.* 162

Hudson, William Henry (1841-1922)

A British naturalist and writer born in *Buenos Aires who spent his childhood and youth in Argentina on a ranch in close contact with the *gauchos. *The Purple Land* (1885) is a novel set in the Uruguayan pampas, based on episodes of its history and dominated by its geographical setting. The same qualities characterise Hudson's collection of stories *El Ombú* (1902) and the romance *Green Mansions* (1904). Borges describes *The Purple Land* as 'one of the few happy books on earth' (Other Inq. 144). Brodie 17 (17) refers to a passage from Hudson's *The Naturalist in La Plata* in which he quotes from Darwin's *Journal of the Voyage of HMS Beagle*: 'At sea, a person's eye being six feet above the surface of the water, his horizon is two miles and four fifths distant. In like manner, the more level the plain, the more nearly does the horizon approach within these narrow limits; and this, in my opinion, entirely destroys the grandeur which one would have imagined that a vast plain would have possessed.' In Borges's story the memory of the character Espinosa mixes this quotation with another of Hudson's from *Far Away and Long Ago* (1918) in which, remembering his childhood experience riding in the pampas, he observes that, sitting on a horse, a man can dominate the widest horizon.

Hugo, Victor Marie (1802-1885)

A French poet, author of poetic dramas and novels and one of the leaders of the French Romantic movement. Hugo was also involved in politics. He was a member of the Assembly in 1848 and was exiled for almost twenty years, but finally became a senator of the Third Republic. As a poet Hugo contributed to the innovation of French verse by introducing new themes and diction and new harmonic effects in the use of the stanza. His theatrical work is often based on historical events to which legendary elements are added, as in *Hernani* (1830). His patriotic sentiments are shown in his famous novels *The Hunchback of Notre-Dame* (1831) and *Les Misérables* (1862), as is the pursuit of social and political justice and the theme of moral redemption. Lab. 102 (72): though Hugo's characters are often seen to strive for redemption, thus displaying an affinity with Borges's Fergus *Kilpatrick, no reference to the latter has been found in Hugo's poetry.

Lab. 102 (72) *Ficc.* 137

Hume, David (1711-1776)

A Scottish philosopher who, to quote Bertrand *Russell, marks, in the history of Western philosophy, the end of the age of reason and the triumph of scepticism. Lab. 32 (8): in his *Treatise of Human Nature* (1739-40) Hume began by accepting the premises of *Berkeley and proceeded to demolish them. Whereas Berkeley affirmed that God's perception maintains reality in existence, Hume speaks of the 'probability' of knowledge, referring to the unreliability of any notion empirically derived from inferences which, he asserts, are neither demonstrative nor demonstrable (Other Inq. 174). Hume claims that we cannot prove the existence of an objective reality, even though we naturally posit it; all we can affirm is the existence of 'bundles of sensations'. Hume denies the validity of causation, saying that though certain objects or events in our past experience have so far always been related, we cannot conclude from this that they will be related in the future or that they are related in unobserved parts. Hume's sceptical conclusion is that the supposition that the future resembles the past is simply derived from habit (*Treatise*, book I, part iii, section iv). Hume's scepticism, which finds a passionate echo in Borges (Other Inq. 104), extends throughout his system to the point where he discards any practical purpose in philosophy except as an 'agreeable way of passing the time': the narrator of 'Tlön, Uqbar, Orbis Tertius' at the end of the story also preserves such a sceptical outlook. Lab. 182 (150): Hume's 'remote arguments' can be found in his essay 'On Miracles' where he argues that a phenomenon constitutes a miracle – by definition a breach of a law of nature – only if its 'testimony be of such a kind that its falsehood would be more miraculous than the fact which it endeavours to establish'.

Lab. 32 (8) *Ficc.* 20, Lab. 182 (150) *Aleph* 94

Hunain, Ibn-Ishaq (808-873)

The most important Arab translator of ancient Greek. Bilingual in Syriac and Arabic, he translated Hippocrates and Galen into Arabic and *Aristotle into Syriac. He also wrote many original works on medical and philosophical subjects. Ibn-Ishaq belonged to a tribe which had embraced Christianity in the form of Nestorianism, a doctrine which held that there are two separate persons in the incarnate Christ, one divine and the other human.

Lab. 181 (149) *Aleph* 92

Hung Lu Meng

A Chinese text of the seventeenth century by Ts'ao Chan, reputed to be the greatest novel in China. Originally in eighty chapters, an edition published after the author's death included an extra forty chapters which may have been forged. The novel is the saga of the Chia, an upper-class Chinese family, and has thirty major and four hundred minor characters. Its plot is based on multiple episodes in which fate, psychological motivation, realistic elements and supernatural intervention merge. It was translated into English in 1929 under the title 'The Red Chamber'.

Lab. 48 (22) *Ficc.* 102

Huns (Hunos)

Nomads who came from east of the river Volga, invading Europe in the fourth century as far as the Danube and establishing an empire in Central Europe. They acquired a reputation for military skill and ferocity, and became rich by exacting tribute from people whose lands they agreed not to plunder. In the fifth century the Huns attacked the eastern Roman Empire, advancing deep into Greece. Lab. 150 (119): in 452, led by Attila, they invaded Italy but were finally driven away by famine and plague. On his death, Attila's empire was divided among his sons and its power rapidly disintegrated.

Lab. 150 (119) *Aleph* 35

Hyderabad (Haidarabad)

A state in south central India. Lab. 195: Nizam is the title of the reigning prince.

Lab. 195 (162) *Aleph* 110

Ibarra, Nestor (1908-?)

A friend and follower of Borges in his Ultraist period, when a preoccupation with language and its etymology led him to indulge in the playful invention of a private language. Ibarra was one of Borges's first translators and an early critic of his work, and published a perceptive interview with him ('Borges et Borges', *L'Herne*, 1969). Lab. 31 (7): the article in the **NRF* is, of course, apocryphal.

Lab. 31 (7) *Ficc.* 19

Ibbur

A form of metempsychosis in which the soul of a man is believed to enter the soul of another during his lifetime. According to *Luria, this temporary reincarnation gave rise to the possibility that a righteous man who had died leaving some obligation unfulfilled could unite with the soul of a living man and make good his neglect. Conversely, the soul of a man freed from sin might return to earth to lend support to a weak soul unequal to its task. Aleph 36 (529: the diaeresis in the spelling of Ibbur is idiosyncratic).

Aleph 36 (52) *Ficc.* 42

Iberra

A family in *Lomas de Zamora, whose legend stems from a text of uncertain origin which was sent to Borges and which he published in an anthology *El compadrito* (1968). The five brothers and two sisters kept an illegal gambling house, where, at election time, locals were persuaded with free wine and *empanadas* to favour the Conservative Party. Brodie 52 (63): there are certain points in common between the story 'The Intruder' and the legend of one of the Iberra brothers, Julio. He was known for his quick draw in gunfights, lived in a primitive hut near *Turdera and was often hounded for stealing other men's women. In time all the Iberras were killed in *criollo* duels. Their type disappeared in about 1936, when local political bosses began to rely more on police protection than on private bullies.

Brodie 53 (64) *Brodie* 16

Ibn Ezra (Abenesra), Abraham (1092-1167)

A Jewish scholar, philosopher and poet best known for his penetrating biblical commentaries based on grammatical principles. He is reputed to have been the first biblical scholar to distinguish reason from faith, and is also remembered for some liturgical poems.

Lab. 120 (90) *Ficc.* 162

Ibn Hakkan (Abenjacán)

The name of three well-known viziers of the *Abbasid dynasty. This may be of some significance in the context of the story in which the apparent king Ibn Hakkan (Abenjacán) turns out to be Zaid, his vizier.
Aleph 73 (115) *Aleph* 123

Ibn Qutaiba (b. 828)

One of the great Muslim writers of the ninth century, who lived and taught in Baghdad. Apart from his religious commentaries, Ibn Qutaiba wrote on Koranic rhetoric and compiled an anthology of poetic themes. One of his works was regarded as 'a veritable manual of neo-classicism', since it exhorted writers 'to create antique verses on new thoughts'.
Lab. 182-3 (150) *Aleph* 94

Ibn Khaldun (Abenjaldún)

A fourteenth-century Arab historian, the descendant of a politically influential Seville family who migrated to Tunis. Ibn Khaldun is regarded as the first Arab historiographer. His best-known works are *The History of Muslim North Africa* and *Mukaddima* (1375-9). The latter deals with 'all branches of Arab science and culture' and is said to be unexcelled in the Arab world for its insight and clarity.
Aleph 23 (30) *Aleph* 169

Iliad (Ilíada)

An epic poem about the Trojan war attributed to *Homer, consisting of 24 books whose action is confined to the last few weeks of the siege of Troy, ending with the funeral of Hector and the ransoming of his body by Priam. Agamemnon led the Greeks, having called them to arms to defend the honour of his brother Menelaus whose wife Helen had been stolen by the Trojan prince Paris, but the bravest fighter in the Greek camp and the central figure of the poem is *Achilles: his name is invoked at the beginning and he is the only one fit to kill the Trojan hero Hector. See *Pope.
Lab. 135 (105) *Aleph* 7

Ilion

The city of Troy, named after Ilus, its mythical founder. See *Iliad*.
Lab. 144 (114) *Aleph* 19

Illescas

A battle in central *Uruguay in 1904 between the rebel party of Aparicio *Saravia and the National Army.
   Aleph 67 (105) *Aleph* 72

Imitatio Christi (Imitación de Cristo)

The Imitation of Christ, a collection of mystical reflections in emulation of the life of Christ written in four books by the Augustinian monk Thomas à Kempis (1380-1471). It describes the various stages of the soul moving away from worldly affections towards union with God. A devotional work of great sincerity, it has been widely influential in the Church.
   Lab. 71 (44) *Ficc*. 57

Indapur

A town in the Poona district of *India.
   Aleph 33 (48) Ficc. 38

India

Borges often alludes to the vastness of India and the variety of its people, referring to them as 'vertiginous' and emphasising their association with the non-rational and chaotic. Aleph 83 (130): recalling the saying that 'India is larger than the world', Borges uses India as a metaphor of the universe. See *Hindustan.
   Aleph 33 (48) *Ficc*. 37, Aleph 83 (130) *Aleph* 144

India Muerta

More than one battle took place in this locality in *Uruguay. The one referred to in Aleph 69 (107) is the battle of 1845 when *Urquiza, leading the *Federalist forces of *Rosas, defeated the *Unitarians who supported the Uruguayan followers of Fructuoso Rivera.
   Aleph 69 (107) *Aleph* 75

Inferno see *Hell

Ingenieros, Cecilia

A friend of Borges who told him the true story on which the plot of 'Emma Zunz' was based.
   Lab. 149 (118) *Aleph* 26

Ingenious Gentleman (Ingenioso Hidalgo)

An epithet of Don *Quixote.
   Lab. 65 (39) *Ficc*. 49

Introduction à la vie dévote see *Francis of Sales

Ios

A Greek island in the Cyclades said to be the burial place of *Homer.
   Lab. 135 (105) *Aleph* 7

Ipuche, Pedro Leandro

A Uruguayan poet of the Ultraist period (*c*.1925), connected with Borges
and the short-lived but important literary magazine *Proa*. Ipuche, who
wrote in the tradition of *gaucho* poetry, was admired by Borges for his
concern to gain the reader's friendship rather than attain perfection of
form. Borges dedicated an essay to him, 'La criolledá en Ipuche', in *Inq*.
(1925).
   Lab. 87 (59) *Ficc*. 118

Ireland (Irlanda)

The relationship between Protestants, settled in Ireland by Cromwell in
the seventeenth century and regarded by the Irish as colonisers and
usurpers, and Catholics, who make up most of the population, has been
marked by bitter conflict. Catholics were deprived of civil rights and their
lands bestowed on English landlords, who cared little for their tenants. In
1823 the Irish patriot Daniel O'Connell helped found the Catholic
Association whose aim was to obtain for Irish Catholics the same political
and civil rights as those of Protestants. It was suppressed in 1825. Lab.
102 (72) refers, in general, to the rebellion against the landed gentry
which took place at the time, particularly in the rural areas. The potato
famine of the 1840s led to a formidable agrarian agitation, supported by a
constitutional movement which later became the Land League, headed by
Charles Stewart *Parnell, through whose influence Gladstone introduced
a Land Act in 1881. The movement for Home Rule, i.e. self-government by
the Irish, found expression in Ireland and some support in the English
Parliament throughout the nineteenth century. In 1922, after bitter
conflict, it led to the establishment of an independent Ireland, apart from
the six northern counties of Ulster, where the Protestants were in the
majority, which remained part of the United Kingdom. Lab. 97 (68): this
solution was unacceptable to many Irish northerners, who felt
threatened, and to the southerners, who felt that the ideal of the Republic

121

had been betrayed. War broke out between the supporters of the Irish Republic and the government of Ireland to whom the British were providing military equipment. The fighting was particularly brutal between June and August 1922.

Lab. 97 (67) *Ficc*. 130, Lab. 102 (72) *Ficc*. 137

Isaiah (Isaías)

An impassioned Hebrew prophet of the eighth century BC. Isaiah's Messianic predictions embody the ideal of the kingdom of God on earth, pointing to a time of world peace, when the nations 'shall beat their swords into ploughshares and their spears into pruning hooks' and 'the wolf also shall dwell with the lamb'. Many of Isaiah's prophecies were interpreted as foreseeing the advent of Jesus. Lab. 129 (99): 'For he shall grow before him as a tender plant...': this passage from the Servant's song (53:2-3) foretells the suffering of the Lord's faithful servant. Traditionally these verses have been read as linking the story of the faithful servant Israel to a vision of the incarnation and suffering of Jesus. At the time of the fictional Runeberg's alleged writings (the first decade of the twentieth century) a controversial attempt was made to identify the subject of the prophecy with an historical figure. This could have been the starting point from which Runeberg began to question the identity of the servant as Jesus, transferring the role of the Redeemer to *Judas. Lab. 130 (99) refers to Isaiah's prophetic vision of the apocalypse. Exhorting repentance among the people of Israel, Isaiah threatened: 'And they shall go into the hole of the rocks, and into the caves of the earth, for fear of the Lord and for the glory of his majesty, when he ariseth to shake the terrible earth' (2:19).

Lab. 129 (99) *Ficc*. 174

Iskandar Zul Qarnain see *Iskander Zul al-Karnayan

Iskander Zul al-Karnayan (Iskandar Zu al Karnayn) Alexander Bicornis of Macedonia (Alejandro Bicorne de Macedonia)

Iskander, as *Alexander the Great was known in Persia, was represented on his coins with two horns. One school of Islamic scholars attributes the allusion in the *Koran to Zu'l-Qarnain ('he of two horns') to Alexander, others to a contemporary of Abraham. Borges probably refers to the former. A footnote to Night 464 in the 1885 edition of *Burton's translation of the *Thousand and One Nights* deals with the highly idealised Persian version of Alexander. The two horns, probably symbolising the East and the West, have been variously explained as referring to two protuberances on his head or helmet, or two leeks, or the ram horns of Jupiter Ammon. Aleph 22 (30): the footnote in Burton also refs to the legend of Iskander as related in the *Sikandar Nama e Bara*, or *Book of Alexander the Great*, by Shaikh Nizami (*c*.1141-1217), the greatest romantic poet in Persian literature. In Canto XXIII, entitled 'Sikander's Mirror-making', the story is told that 'when Sikander became the key of the world, the mirror by his sword appeared'. Alexander was reputed to have been the first to fashion a mirror, and though at the beginning 'no reflection came truly' it became a 'mirror of philosophy' into which anyone could look and behold the truth. See *Gog and Magog.

Aleph 22 (30) *Aleph* 168, Lab. 184 (152) *Aleph* 96

Islam

The Arabic word for resignation or surrender (to the will of Allah). Islam was founded in the seventh century by the prophet *Mohammed; its principal doctrine is expressed in the *Koran. Aleph 32 (46): God the Indivisible: the basic belief of Islam is the absolute unity of God, of Allah (the only God) and the predestination of all things by him. Lab. 175 (143): 'initial epochs of Islam' evokes a time of religious fervour.

Lab. 31 (7) *Ficc.* 18, Lab. 175 (143) *Aleph* 83, Aleph 32 (46) *Ficc.* 36, Brodie 33 (37) *Brodie* 92, *Brodie* 139

Israel

A term for all the Jewish people, irrespective of their country of origin or residence. As a people, they are bound by their allegiance to the Torah, the holy scripture.

Lab. 132 (102) *Ficc.* 182

Ituzaingó

A battle fought in the province of *Corrientes on 20 February 1827 between the Brazilian army and the combined forces of the Argentine Republic and *Uruguay, led by Carlos María de *Alvear. The Brazilians were defeated, and the war ended soon after.

Lab. 89 (61) *Ficc.* 120, Brodie 73 (90) *Brodie* 76

Ixion

A character in Greek mythology who was pardoned by Zeus for killing his father-in-law and taken up into heaven. When he tried to violate Hera, however, he was condemned to remain tied to a revolving wheel.

Lab. 151 (120) *Aleph* 37

Jaguar

The jaguar was considered sacred among the Maya: in the *Popol Vuh*

(*Book of the Common), the Maya religious text describing the genesis of the world, the word for jaguar, 'balam', conveys the idea of magical power and is used as a title equivalent to 'mighty'. In the same text, among the first men in creation there are three legendary heroes named Jaguar.

Lab. 203 (169) *Aleph* 115

Jalil (also **Al Khalil**) (b. *c*. 720/1)

Reputedly the founder of Arab philology and author of the first Arabic dictionary. See **Quitab ul ain.*

Lab. 182 (150) *Aleph* 93

James, Henry (1843-1916)

An American novelist and short-story writer regarded as a master of modern fiction. After spending a year in Paris, where he met *Flaubert, Zola and Maupassant, James established himself in England. The antithesis between European and New World values is the theme of such novels as *Roderick Hudson* (1877) and *The Europeans* (1878), and also of the unfinished and posthumous *The Sense of the Past* (1917) whose concept of future events determining the existence of the past captured Borges's interest (Other Inq. 12). Fict. 66 (73): in fifty-one years of writing James strove progressively towards greater and greater accuracy of language and a more and more thoughtful and exploratory narrative which, transcending the plot, displays a virtuoso precision and elegance of style. Brodie 31 (35): though most of the characters in James's stories belong to a cosmopolitan and often artistic and socially sophisticated élite, the conflict of cultures is generally presented as a contrast between life in American cities such as *Boston, associated with conventional morality but artistic sterility, and the intellectual and stimulating experience of European cities, such as London or Rome, where moral decadence was an underlying threat.

Fict. 66 (73) *Ficc.* 78, Brodie 31 (35) *Brodie* 89

James, William (1842-1910)

An American philosopher, the elder brother of Henry *James. William James was an exponent of pragmatism, the theory that our conception of reality depends on the practical effects it has, ideas being true only in relation to other aspects of our experience. James applied the pragmatic doctrine to psychology, religion and history, his most influential book being *The Varieties of Religious Experience* (1902). The life of each man is a specific event, and every action affects the course of history. There are no fixed laws or static principles.

Lab. 69 (43) *Ficc.* 55

Janus (Jano)

In Roman mythology the two-faced God of doorways who was able to observe both the exterior and interior of private houses and the entrance and exit of public buildings. He thus became the god of departure and return and of the sun's rising and setting, and so was the special patron of all beginnings. He was honoured on the first day of every month, and on the first month of every year (January).
    Lab. 115 (84) *Ficc.* 155

Jerusalem

The capital of Israel and formerly of Palestine, regarded by the Jews as their sacred city and as a holy city by both Christians and Moslems. Lab. 152 (121): Jerusalem witnessed the scene of the beginning of Christianity, the first teachings of Jesus and his apostles, and the first martyrs, though it did not become a central focus of Christianity until the Crusades. St *Stephen was stoned to death in Jerusalem c.AD 35. Aleph 36 (51): in the sixteenth century, at the time of Isaac *Luria, Jerusalem was an important centre of *Cabbalism, a tradition which has continued to the present day.
    Lab. 152 (121) *Aleph* 37, Aleph 36 (51) *Ficc.* 42

Jewish Gauchos (Gauchos judíos)

A novel by the Russian-born Jewish Argentine writer Alberto Gerchunoff (1833-1949), published in 1910 as part of the centenary celebrations of independence. The novel is a paean to work, fraternity and man's ability to rise above life's obstacles, as experienced in Argentina. Set in a Jewish colony in the province of *Entre Ríos, it tells of the hardships suffered by the early colonists and their eventual triumph over natural and cultural difficulties. Its over-idealised portrayal has led some to say that it depicts neither Jews nor *gauchos.
    Brodie 24 (26) *Brodie* 26

Job

One of the late books of the Old Testament, whose exact meaning has been debated through the centuries. The story illustrates steadfastness of belief in the face of disaster and divine injustice, and raises the question of the individual's place in the scheme of the universe. *Maimonides, in his *Guide to the Perplexed* (ch. 3, lines 22/3) attributes Job's defiant questioning of God's justice to his defective knowledge of God, limited to 'report and hearsay' as in 'most adherents of revealed religions'. After the theophany of the whirlwind, however, when he attained true philosophical knowledge of God, Job realised that no misfortune, however grave, can trouble a man. A more radical interpretation, and one which accords better with much of Borges's writings, is that there is no principle of divine retribution because 'justice is not woven into the stuff of the universe nor is God occupied with its administration'. The main theme of Job appears to be the perennial problem of innocent suffering; like the character Zur Linde, Job has no doubt of his innocence. The quotation from Job which serves as epigraph to 'Deutsches Requiem' can be taken as an ironic reflection on the power of blind belief, irrespective of its cause.

Lab. 173 (141) *Aleph* 81

John, St (Juan)

One of the twelve apostles, traditionally regarded as the author of the fourth Gospel. This differs from the other three (synoptic) Gospels by not setting out to give an account of Jesus's life and teaching, but being rather a meditative exposition of Christian doctrine. Lab. 127 (97): the quotation from John 12:6 mentioned twice on this page as proof of Judas's greed and betrayal reads as follows: 'This he said...because he was a thief and had a bag and bare what was put therein.' Lab. 128 (98): John 1:10 refers to the mystery of the Incarnation of the Word whose divinity was unrecognised by men. The use of this quotation as a 'perfidious epigraph' to the final version of Runeberg's text on *Judas is a veiled insinuation that Judas's divinity was unrecognised throughout history. Lab. 155 (124): this verse (10:10) is an extract from the parable of the Good Shepherd in which Jesus claims that the only means of access to the fold is through him, all other ways being those of thieves and robbers. The narrator suggests that the allegorical meaning of 'having life more abundantly' was misunderstood and taken to mean that life should include all forms of evil as well as good.

Lab. 127 (97) *Ficc.* 172, Lab. 155 (124) *Aleph* 42

John of Damascus, St (Juan Damasceno) (c.675-c.749)

A Greek monk and theologian, declared a 'Doctor of the Church', who was the author of many books against heresy. John wrote extensively on the doctrine of Mariology, or the divine maternity of Mary, her exemption from original sin and her assumption into heaven. His anti-heretical writings deal mainly with the nature of God and human free will, which he relates to reason and describes as a manifestation of man's choice of good. Lab. 153 (122): the term 'forms' said to have been used by John in connection with the 'Histriones' is an allusion to his staunch defence of images in the Iconoclastic Controversy. This dispute, which agitated the Greek Church in the eighth and ninth centuries, was about the veneration of icons and its conflict with the ancient Mosaic prohibition against the use of images. John defended images on the basis of the theological significance of the incarnation of God, and the importance that this assumption of human nature in the body of Jesus had upon Christian dogma.

Lab. 153 (122) *Aleph* 44

John of Pannonia (Juan de Panonia)

There is no theologian by this name in the history of Christianity. Borges may have been thinking of the Hungarian poet Ivan Cesmicki (1434-1473), bishop of Croatia, who wrote in Latin and adopted the name Janus Pannonius. Ancient Pannonia corresponded to areas of present-day Hungary, Croatia and Austria and was finally subdued by Augustus in 9 BC.

Lab. 150 (119) *Aleph* 35

John of the Rood

A possible allusion to the Spanish mystic poet John of the Cross (1542-1591).

Lab. 133 (103) *Ficc.* 184

John of Viterbo (Juan de Viterbo) (1432-1502)

An Italian Dominican, commonly referred to as Annius of Viterbo, who edited seventeen treatises of *Antiquitatum Variarum*, a collection of fragments by various ancient writers, and used astrology to predict the fall of the Turkish Empire. Though honoured in his lifetime, he later fell into disrepute. Lab. 130 (99): no reference has been found for the story that John of Viterbo was a sorcerer and went mad at the sight of the Trinity.

Lab. 130 (99) *Ficc.* 175

Johnson, Samuel (1709-1784)

An English critic and lexicographer whose reputation rests mainly on his *Dictionary of the English Language* (1755), his studies of *Shakespeare and his *Lives of the English Poets* (1779). A brilliant talker at all times, much of Johnson's wit would have been lost but for his friend James Boswell (1740-1795) who, from 1763, collected material for his *Life of Samuel Johnson*, which was published in 1791. It is generally regarded as the best biography in the English language. Borges liked to believe that Johnson the man was greater than Johnson the writer and recorded many of his sayings in his Introd. Eng. Lit. Aleph 35 (51): Johnson's saying that 'nobody...likes owing anything to his contemporaries' is alluded to also in Lab. 174 (142) and repeated in Other Inq. 61, and in *Leop. Lug.* 87. No source for this saying has been found.

Jonson, Ben (1572-1637)

An English dramatist, contemporary with *Shakespeare, whose best-known plays were *Every Man in his Humour* (1601), *Volpone* (1606) and *The Alchemist* (1610). Lab. 149 (118): the assertion that Ben Jonson defined his contemporaries 'with bits of Seneca' is an allusion to *Timber; or Discoveries made upon Men and Matter* (1640), a posthumous collection of essays whose text is derived in part from *Seneca the Elder, *Pliny and Quintilian. Seneca's inspiration is to be observed particularly in essay 63 on poets, 69 on style, 70 on famous orators, and 72 on other writers, including *Bacon. In 63, for example, referring to the undeserved applause bestowed on the poetry of John Taylor (1578-1653), Jonson comments sarcastically: 'Not that the better have left to write or speak better but that they that heare them judge worse', an echo of Seneca's 'non illi peius dicunt sed hi corruptius judicant' (*Controversiae* 3, praef.). Writing of Shakespeare and the claim that 'he never blotted a line', Jonson commented: 'Would he had blotted a thousand.' Shakespeare, he explains, flowed with such facility that at times 'he should have been stopped': 'sufflaminandus erat', an allusion to the emperor Augustus' remark about the orator Atevius (Seneca, *Controversiae* 4.7)

Lab. 149 (118) *Aleph* 26

Joseph, Flavius (Flavio Josefo)

The name adopted by the first-century Jewish historian Joseph ben Matthias, one of the leaders of the Jewish revolt against the Romans in AD 66. Escaping death, he was taken prisoner by Vespasian, who later released him when his prophecy that Vespasian would become emperor was fulfilled. Josephus opted for Roman citizenship and assumed the name of Flavius, Vespasian's patronymic. His main historical works are *The Jewish War* (77/8 AD), a largely personal account of the war written from a Jewish point of view but with a regard for Roman susceptibilities, and *Antiquities of the Jews*, a history of the Jews from the creation of the world. The latter makes allusion to Christ, suggesting that it may be improper to refer to him simply as a man, but the passage is disputed (18.3.3). Lab. 131 (101): in the English translation 'the *Saturnales* of Flavius Josephus' *of* should read *or*.

Lab. 131 (101) *Ficc*. 181

Joyce, James (1882-1941)

An Irish novelist, author of *Ulysses* (1922) and *Finnegans Wake* (1939). These two works, which mark a complete break with the traditional concept and structure of the novel, inaugurated a school of admirers, and innumerable controversies. Lab. 71 (44): the style of Joyce's innovative prose, based on the frequent use of neologisms and the iconoclastic attitudes of his characters has made him one of the most challenging writers in modern literature.

Lab. 71 (44) F 57, Aleph 35 (51) *Ficc.* 41

Judas Iscariot (Judas Iscariote) (d. 30 AD)

One of the twelve apostles. The name Iscariot probably indicates that he came from Kerioth, in southern Palestine. Lab. 100 (71), 151 (121): according to the accepted tradition, Judas betrayed Jesus to the Roman authories for thirty pieces of silver, causing him to be arrested and executed. The episode is recounted in Matthew 26:14-16 and 47-49. Lab. 127 (97): the motive of the betrayal is uncertain. St *John's hint at Judas's avarice (John 12:6) is not supported by the other three evangelists. Though his actions were viewed with abhorrence in the Christian Church, an apocryphal gospel of the second century rehabilitated him and he was venerated by the Gnostic sect of the *Cainites. According to a Muslim belief, Judas defended Jesus and saved him from crucifixion. In the fourteenth century ad-Dimashqi mantained that Judas took on Jesus's appearance and was crucified in his stead. See *'Not one but all the things...'

Lab. 100 (71) *Ficc.* 135, Lab. 125 (95) *Ficc.* 169, Lab. 151 (121) *Aleph 37*, Lab. 191 (158) *Aleph* 106

Jujuy Street

A street in *Buenos Aires in the *Once district.

Brodie 18 (18) *Brodie* 132

Julius Caesar (Julio César) (100-44 BC)

A Roman general, politician and man of letters, who defeated *Pompey at the battle of Pharsalus in 48 BC, was appointed Dictator by the *Senate and was murdered four years later. The events of his campaigns in Gaul (58-52 BC) are related in the seven books of his *Commentaries* (*De Bello Gallico*). Lab. 89 (61): these reports, sent to the Roman Senate, aimed at justifying Caesar's policy and constitutional position. Despatched from his winter quarters, their lucidity and objectivity make them not only a reliable historical document but a literary masterpiece. The *Commentaries* on the civil war between Caesar and *Pompey (*De Bello Civili*), published unrevised after Caesar's death, are not held in the same esteem. Lab. 103/4 (73/74): during his dictatorship Caesar held total power in the city and the provinces. On 15 March 44 BC a group of republicans, including sixteen senators, knifed him to death in the Senate, before the statue of Pompey. Most but not all of the historical data given in Borges's story tally with the details of *Shakespeare's play, based mainly on *Plutarch. In *Julius Caesar*, on the morning of Caesar's death his wife *Calpurnia entreats him not to go into the Senate because of ominous rumours she has heard of graves opening to release the bodies of dead warriors. She has dreamed of his statue spouting blood like a fountain, and of the Romans washing their hands in it. Caesar is at first persuaded, but Decius Brutus mocks him and spurs him on to going, and Calpurnia's warnings go unheeded. Equally the petition presented by Artemidorus which denounces the members of the plot remains unread.

Lab. 89 (61) *Ficc*. 120, Lab. 103 (73) *Ficc*. 138

Junín

A modest rural town in the province of *Buenos Aires.
Brodie 15 (15) *Brodie* 127

Junín Street

A street in the centre of *Buenos Aires which in the early part of the twentieth century was full of brothels. It runs from the now lower-middle-class area surrounding *Once to the wealthy Barrio Norte.
Brodie 27 (29) *Brodie* 30

Jupiter

The greatest of the Roman gods, later identified with the Greek Zeus. See *Satyricon*.
Aleph 22 (30) *Aleph* 168

Justus Perthes

A German publishing house founded by Justus Johann Georg Perthes in Gotha in 1785. Its geographical section became internationally famous. In 1863 it first published the *Almanach de Gotha* (in French), a 'statistical, historical and genealogical annual of the various countries of the world'.
Lab. 28 (4) *Ficc*. 14

Juvenal, Decimus Junius (c.55-c.127)

A Roman satirist who attacked the corruption and depravity of Roman imperial society in particular and human weakness in general. Reputedly resentful and embittered through lack of promotion within the Roman civil service, Juvenal denounced favouritism at court and in the army and was probably banished by the Emperor Domitian to Egypt. His verses are distinguished for their epigrammatic wit and the ruthless portrayal of

brutal and disturbing scenes. See *'Ultra Auroram et Gangen'.
Aleph 82 (129) *Aleph* 143

Kabbala Denudata see *Knorr, Christian Rosenroth

Kaf

In Muslim mythology, the mountain range which surrounds the earth.
Aleph 36 (52) *Ficc.* 42

Kafka, Franz see *Qaphqa

Kai Kosru (Kai Josrú)

One of the early kings of ancient Persia. *Firdusi's epic, the *Shahnamah*,
contains much legendary material about Kai Kosru's life, including a
story of rival brotherhood, not dissimilar to that of the elder *Cyrus and
his brother *Smerdis. Aleph 22: with reference to the 'sevenfold cup' there
are allusions in various Persian writers, but not in Firdusi, to a cup with
seven lines belonging to Jamshid, an earlier legendary king of Persia.
Aleph 22 (30) *Aleph* 168

Kantian categories (Categorías kantianas)

The twelve concepts claimed by Kant to be necessary to a classification of
sensory experience, each corresponding to a function of human
understanding (see *Critique of Pure Reason*). They are divided into four
sets: quantity, quality, relation and modality. Each is symmetrically
subclassified into three aspects: unity, totality and plurality; reality,
negation and limitation; substance and accidence, cause and effect, and
reciprocity; possibility, existence and necessity. Fict. 69 (76): in his
'Criticism of the Kantian Philosophy', which forms an appendix to *The
World as Will and Representation*, *Schopenhauer attacks the rigidity of
these categories, saying that, in deference to his liking for symmetry,
Kant 'goes as far as to do open violence to truth' so that the system 'has
become the Procrustean bed on which Kant forces every possible
consideration'.
Fict. 69 (76) *Ficc.* 81

Katmandu

The capital of Nepal.
Aleph 33 (48) *Ficc.* 38.

Kemnitz

Perhaps an allusion to Martin Kemnitz (1522-1586), a German Lutheran theologian.

Lab. 129 (99) *Ficc.* 174

Khorasan (Jorasán)

Persian for 'land of the sun': a province in north-east Persia from which it has been frequently separated by political unrest. Lab. 196 (162): the veiled prophet of Jorasán is Al Moqanna, who ruled the region for fourteen years (c.765-79) in defiance of the armies of the *Mahdi. Because he had only one eye he veiled his face in green silk, claiming that he was God incarnate and that he wore the mask to spare his followers 'the dazzling and insupportable effulgence of his countenance'. When he was eventually besieged by the Mahdi's armies, he burned himself in order to destroy his remains, to confirm to his followers that he was God and would rise again. But his body was found and his deformity and deceit exposed. Borges gives a version of this story in 'The Masked Dyer Hakim of Merv' (Infamy 77).

Lab. 28 (5) *Ficc.* 15, Lab. 196 (162) *Aleph* 111

Kilgarvan

A small Irish town in County Kerry, *Munster. Lab. 103 (73): round towers are a feature of the Irish landscape; as an emblem of Ireland, they figured in the Irish national flag during the eighteenth and nineteenth centuries. No round tower is recorded in Kilgarvan.

Lab. 103 (73) *Ficc.* 138

Kilpatrick, Fergus

A fictional character in 'Theme of the Traitor and the Hero' whose name is quintessentially Irish. Fergus is the name of several Irish heroes who figure in early *Celtic literature, while Kilpatrick is a town in Scotland said to have been St Patrick's birthplace. Some similarity may be found between Fergus Kilpatrick in the dual role of traitor and hero and Fergus mac Roich in the saga of the *Táin bó Cuailinge* which deals with the war between Ulster and *Connaught. Fergus mac Roich was driven into exile by Conchobar, King of Ulster, and found himself fighting for Connaught against Conchobar and his brave son Cuchulain. See Robert *Browning, Victor *Hugo.

Lab. 102 (72) *Ficc.* 137

Kipling, Rudyard (1865-1936)

A British writer born in India. Kipling was educated in England but worked in India as a journalist from the age of 16 to 25, when he returned to England. His memory of India persisted, and he is most strongly identified with his images of life under the British Raj, as in *Barrack-Room Ballads* (1892), *Plain Tales from the Hills* (1888), *The Jungle Book* (1894/5) and *Kim* (1901). Aleph 82 (129): Borges, a great admirer of Kipling, was one of the first to recognise that beyond the occasionally jingoistic descriptions of Victorian India lay a deep appreciation of the country's essence distilled by Kipling's imagination. A feature of Kipling's writing that Borges claimed had influenced him was the minute accumulation of circumstantial detail to create atmosphere. Aleph 36 (51): Kipling's short story 'On the City Wall' from his collection *In Black and White* (1897) is similar to 'The Approach to Almotasim'; it concerns the bravery of the prostitute Lalun and the cowardice of her suitor, the Mohammedan Wali Dad, an unbeliever who has been educated as an Englishman. When a skirmish breaks out between Moslems and Hindus, Wali Dad pretends to plunge into the fight, but in fact hides away and wounds himself.
    Aleph 36 (51) *Ficc.* 42, Aleph 82 (129) *Aleph* 143

Knorr, Christian Rosenroth, Baron von (b. 1631)

Christian Hebraist and devoted student of the *Cabbala, whose teachings he believed afforded proof of the doctrines of Christianity, such as the identification of Jesus with Adam Kadmon (primordial man) and of the Trinity with the three highest sephirot (spheres, or divine manifestations in which God emerges from his hidden abode – also known as 'emanations'). Knorr wrote extensively on the subject, his major work being the *Kabbala Denudata* (1677-84) whose first two volumes comprise Cabbalistic nomenclature and other essays, and the remaining two writings by Isaac *Luria.
    Brodie 23 (26) *Brodie* 26

Kolzsvar

The Hungarian name for Cluj, originally a Roman colony and later the capital of Transylvania.
    Lab. 147 (116) *Aleph* 23

Koran (Alcorán)

From the Arabic *Qu'ran*, meaning recitation. The Koran is the sacred book of Mohammedanism, believed in *Islam to be the infallible word of God as revealed to *Mohammed by the angel Gabriel. Tradition dates it to the year 610. The Koran teaches the oneness of God, his righteousness and omnipotence, and his divine mercy and forgiveness. Lab. 182 (150): *Abulcasim's reflection 'that the Lord possesses the key to all hidden things and that there is not a green or withered thing on earth which is not registered in His Book' is probably a reference to the five Pillars of Islam (the Kalima, or belief that there is no God but Allah, prayer, almsgiving, fasting and pilgrimage) and a paraphrase of 'Not an atom's weight in earth or heaven escapes your Lord nor is there any object smaller or greater but is recorded in a glorious book' (Sura 10, Jonah, 61). Lab. 183 (151): the idea of the Koran as *the mother of the Book* deposited in Heaven and persisting in the centre of God in the words of *Ghazali, 'unaltered by its passage through human written pages and human understanding', stems from Sura 13, The Cave, 139: 'God abrogates, establishes and joins what he pleases; and with him is the Mother of the Book.' Borges discusses various interpretations of the Eternal Book in Other Inq. 118. Lab. 118 (88): 'And God had him die for a hundred years.' This quotation from the Koran (ch. 2, v. 259) is taken from the Sura named 'The Cow' and refers to an incident in which Allah gave proof of his power to an unbeliever by altering the passing of time. Aleph 73 (115): the epigraph to 'Ibn Hakkan al-Bokhari, Dead in his Labyrinth' stems from the chapter in the Koran entitled *The Spider*. The whole sentence reads: 'The false gods which the idolators serve besides Allah may be compared to the spider's cobweb. Surely the spider's is the frailest of all dwellings, if they but knew it.'

Lab. 118 (88) *Ficc.* 159, Lab. 181 (149) *Aleph* 92, Aleph 73 (115) *Aleph* 123

Korzeniovski, José

The original Polish name of the writer Joseph Conrad, author of *Lord Jim* (1900), *Nostromo* (1904), *Under Western Eyes* (1911) and many other novels. In 1886 Conrad qualified as a master mariner and acquired British citizenship. After sailing the seas for many years he settled in England and began to write in English, basing much of his fiction on his early sea experiences. Borges comments on Conrad's ability to perceive and project the 'poetic' quality of everyday life (Other Inq. 43), a quality he perceives also in Henry *James. Brodie 81 (99): the story 'Guayaquil' seems to include several references to *Nostromo*, which is set in the province of *Sulaco in a fictional South American country called Costaguana. The terms 'melancholy and pompous' with which Borges alludes to the first paragraph of his story probably reflect his view of Conrad's language, which he describes as introducing to English an epic and ceremonial ring 'proper to French prose'. See José *Avellanos, *Estado Occidental, *Golfo Plácido, *Higuerota, *Sulaco.

Brodie 81 (99) *Brodie* 111

Kühlmann, Ulrike von

A friend of Borges, mentioned in 'The Other Death' and the dedicatee of 'Story of the Warrior and the Captive'. In Borges's fiction the name Ulrica, used in 'An Examination of the Work of Herbert Quain' and given to the eponymous heroine of a story in *The Book of Sand*, seems to apply to the prototype of the northern European woman, proud, noble and unattainable.

Fict. 70 (77) *Ficc* 81, Lab. 163 (131) *Aleph* 52, Aleph 70 (108) *Aleph* 76

La Merced

An upper-class parish bordering *Palermo in northern *Buenos Aires.
Brodie 72 (89) *Brodie* 75

La Piedad

An old colonial street, now called Bartolomé Mitre, in central *Buenos Aires.
Brodie 75/6 (92) *Brodie* 80

Lacroze

The central Lacroze Tramway Line, which used to service the north-western suburb of *Buenos Aires. It has been replaced today by an underground system.
Lab. 167 (135) *Aleph* 63, *Brodie* 33

Laderecha

'The right hand': perhaps a deliberate play on words to denote a foreman; yet Borges claims that such a foreman actually lived, as recounted to him by *Reyles.
Brodie 38 (45) *Brodie* 102

Lafinur, Juan Crisóstomo (1797-1824)

Borges's great-uncle, a poet and teacher whose appointment in 1919 to the Chair of Philosophy at the newly formed Colegio de la Unión del Sud marked the movement from scholasticism to the doctrines of liberal thinkers such as Condillac and *Locke and laid the foundations of secular teaching in Argentina. Lafinur was criticised for upholding materialistic ideologies and was eventually forced into exile. Borges wrote a poem in his honour and dedicated to him his essay 'A New Refutation of Time', in which he praises his poetry and liberalism and comments ruefully: 'Like all men, he was given bad times in which to live' (Lab. 253 (218)). *Aleph*

154: the allusion to a Juan Crisóstomo Lafinur library – omitted in the translation – is based on fact.
Aleph 13 (18) *Aleph* 154, Brodie 32 (36) *Brodie* 91

Lafinur, Alvaro

A young cousin of Borges's father, considered by the family a ladies' man and a rogue. Borges records his indebtedness to Lafinur for initiating him into the mysteries of the brothels of *Palermo.
Aleph 16 (21) *Aleph* 158

Lafinur, Luis Melián

A Uruguayan uncle of Borges.
Lab. 93 (64) *Ficc.* 124

Laguna Colorada

A lake and district in the southern province of *Buenos Aires. See *Mesa.
Aleph 56 (84) *Aleph* 56

Laïs

A celebrated Greek courtesan. Lab. 191 (158): in her youth Laïs was paid with gold coins but in old age she had to content herself with less. Her plight is described by Athenaeus (12.81): 'Like the eagles she once snapped lambs in flight; now, old, she perches in hunger upon the temple, waiting to snatch meat from the altars. When she was young she was wild and proud of the golden coins she received. Now old and shapeless...she is so tame she will take money out of your hands.' The name became a general term for courtesans.
Lab. 191 (158) *Aleph* 106.

Lane, Edward (1801-1876)

An orientalist, the compiler of a *Thesaurus of the Arabic Language* and a translator of the *Thousand and One Nights* (1839) which followed Galland's eighteenth-century French translation. Lane's English version, heavily expurgated, was later superseded by Richard *Burton's. Borges describes Lane's work as erudite and accurate but laments its efforts to 'disinfect' the original by glossing over the coarser details and omitting what he considered immoral and reprehensible. Thus Lane created what might be termed an 'encyclopaedia of evasions' (*Etern.* 99). Brodie 91 (111): the reference to the 'annotations, interrogation marks and...emendations' in Brodie's manuscript humorously recalls the large number of explanatory notes added by Lane to his introduction and to each of the thirty chapters.

Lab. 188 (155) *Aleph* 101, Brodie 91 (111) *Brodie* 139

Lanús

A town and middle-class district in Greater *Buenos Aires, south west of the capital.

Lab. 166 (134) *Aleph* 60

Laprida Street (Calle Laprida)

A street in the fashionable district of *Palermo, in the Barrio Norte.

Lab. 40 (16) *Ficc.* 31

Laprida, Eusebio (1829-1898)

A sergeant-major who gained notoriety for his leadership during the wars between the Provinces and *Buenos Aires (see *Federalism). Placed at the head of 80 men, he defeated the regular army unit of 200 in a battle at the Cardoso Marshes on 25 January 1856. Aleph 55 (83): Laprida's defeat of the Indians took place not at Cardoso, as stated, but during a raid in 1879.

Aleph 55 (83) *Aleph* 55

Laquedem, Isaac

The name of the Wandering Jew in the Flemish version of the legend which appeared in Brussels c.1774. See Joseph *Cartaphilus.

Lab. 192 (159) *Aleph* 106

Larreta, Enrique Rodríguez (1875-1961)

An Argentine writer, president of the Asociación Amigos del Libro, who spent much of his life in France and Spain; his house in *Buenos Aires was filled with Spanish art. His novels include *La gloria de Don Ramiro* (1908), set in Ávila and in Toledo at the time of *Philip II, and *Orillas del Ebro* (1949) which was awarded a prize by 'la Dirección General de Propaganda Española'. Lab. 68 (42): a contrast may be established between *La gloria de Don Ramiro*, in which the author sets out to recreate the historic atmosphere of the sixteenth century by using archaic Spanish for the dialogues, and Pierre *Menard's version of *Quixote*.

Lab. 68 (42) *Ficc.* 53

Las Artes Street

A street now named *Bernardo de Yrigoyen. Its continuation, Carlos

Pellegrini, is a fashionable shopping centre flanking Avenida Nueve de Julio in the centre of *Buenos Aires.

Brodie 75 (92) *Brodie* 79

Lavalle, Juan Galo (1797-1841)

An Argentine hero, born into an aristocratic *porteño* family, who fought with *San Martín in the war of Independence, and with *Alvear in the war against Brazil. In 1828 Lavalle was elected by the *Unitarians as their military leader against the *Federalist movement. Aleph 54 (81): the *gaucho* militia (*Montoneros) mentioned here would have been followers of *Rosas who, when he was defeated by Lavalle in 1828, escaped in disguise with some of his troops to join Estanislao *López, the *caudillo* of the Santa Fe province. Lavalle was eventually defeated by the combined forces of Rosas and López on 26 April 1829. After ten years of exile in Montevideo he reluctantly returned to lead the Unitarian forces in another attempt to oust Rosas; he fought against Rosas and *Oribe when a revolt broke out in the province of *Buenos Aires and the port was blockaded by the French. On 2 September 1839 Lavalle allied his forces to those of the French, and his army of 550 men, embarked in French boats, landed near *Gualeguay and was involved in a series of military encounters. Brodie 73 (90): the 'sabrefest' is probably the battle of *Cagancha on 29 December 1839, in which Lavalle's party was victorious. The revolt was soon crushed and the blockade lifted. Lavalle did not attempt to enter the city. In 1840 he was defeated by Oribe at Quebracho Herrado and died soon after in Jujuy.

Aleph 54 (81) Aleph 53, Brodie 73 (90) *Brodie* 76

Lawrence, Thomas Edward (1888-1935)

An English scholar and military leader who played an important political role in the Arab world during World War I while serving in the British Army. Lawrence was sent by the British government to instigate and support an Arab rebellion against the Turks, then allies of Germany, in the belief that it would help conclude the war. The legendary events of this period of his life are told in his semi-autobiographical novel *The Seven Pillars of Wisdom* (1926). The book, packed with colourful characters and episodes in which fact and fiction mingle, describes the war against the Turks up to the conquest of Damascus in 1918, by which time the Germans were defeated. The accent of the first-person narrative suggests the moral degradation of the narrator. After the war Lawrence continued to campaign for the Arab cause. His eventful life ended tragically in a motorcycle accident. See *'There seemed a certainty in degradation'.

Lab. 125 (95) *Ficc.* 169

Leibniz, Gottfried Wilhelm (1646-1716)

A German philosopher and mathematician, born and educated at *Leipzig, who served as librarian and counsellor at the court of the dukes of Hanover. Leibniz's best-known works are *Theodicy* (1710) and *Monadology* (1714). Lab. 102 (72): in the second book he expands the principle that all substance is made up of an infinite number of spiritual beings, or 'centres of force', known as 'monads'. These are entirely self-contained, in so far as the activity of each excludes that of every other; yet each one mirrors the universe and they are all related by a 'pre-established harmony'. Although Leibniz's monads 'have no windows by which anything can come in or go out', this pre-established harmony makes it possible to infer from the state of any one substance a corresponding state of any other. Thus each monad, combining matter and form, is the microcosm of the whole. Lab. 32 (7): God, whose nature is discussed at length in *Theodicy*, is the supreme monad who pre-establishes the harmonious unity of the universe. Totally free of 'passive elements', he has a perfect knowlege of truth and goodness; the universe is the product of this perfect knowledge and, as such, this world must be 'the best possible'. Lab. 63 (337): at the stage in which perception is developed into thought Leibniz observes that all knowledge contains some basic 'root notions' which can rationally be referred to by universal symbols intellegible in all languages. These are described as *characteristica universalis*, though Leibniz never fully develops the doctrine. See *'Ne craignez point, Monsieur, la tortue'.

Lab. 32 (7) *Ficc.* 19, Lab. 63 (37) *Ficc.* 46, Lab. 102 (72) *Ficc.* 137

Leipzig

A German city and important cultural centre south west of Berlin. Lab. 147 (116): the presence of the narrator of the 'Immortal' in Leipzig after 1638 may be a pun on *Leibniz, who was born here in 1646.

Lab. 147 (116) *Aleph* 23

Lepanto

A Greek port, the site of an epoch-making battle between Spain and the Ottoman Empire on 7 October 1571. The Spaniards captured 117 enemy galleys. *Cervantes lost an arm at the battle, becoming known as 'el manco de Lepanto'.

Lab. 68 (42) *Ficc.* 53

Leusden, Johann (1624-1699)

A Calvinist theologian, professor of Hebrew at the university of Utrecht and one of the foremost biblical scholars of his time, who wrote several treatises on the bible and Hebrew philology. The 1739 edition of his *Philologus Hebraicus*, published in Basel, consists of three treatises: the *Philologus Hebraeus*, the *Hebraeo-Graecus* and the *Mixtus*. Lab. 111 (81): the 33rd dissertation mentioned by Borges is to be found in the *Mixtus*, and not in the *Hebraeo-Graecus* as alleged, and the passage is quoted almost verbatim, the original reading: '*Vel dies est sacer destinatus exercitiis sacris, qui incipit a solis occasu usque ad solis occasum diei sequentis*' ('This day, which commences when the sun goes down and continues until sunset the following day, is a holy day dedicated to spiritual pursuits'). The dissertation discusses the basic difference in the division of hours or prayer times between the Jewish day, reckoned from dusk to dusk, and the Christian day reckoned from dawn to dawn. This difference, it argues, would explain a discrepancy in the account of the hour of Jesus's crucifixion as related by Mark (15:25) and John (19:14). Because the Jewish calendar is calculated on a lunar basis, its months do not run parallel to the Christian (solar) months. Thus the murders in 'Death and the Compass' should not be understood as having taken place on the fourth day of either a Christian or a Jewish month, but according to a private code existing between criminal and detective in which the beginning of the day was reckoned at dusk according to Jewish custom and the date of the month according to Christian.

Lab. 111 (81) *Ficc.* 149

Leviathan

Hobbes's great work of political philosophy, published in 1651, in which he discusses the nature and function of the state and the duties of the individual. Aleph 11 (15): the quotation which serves as epigraph is taken from the famous concluding section on 'The kingdom of darkness' in which Hobbes, for whom ethics and politics cannot be separated from religion, rails against Papists and Presbyterians for their challenge to the authority of the sovereign. Suspicious of the Papists' allegiance to Rome, he attacks them for what he terms their superstitious attachment to *Aristotelian or speculative metaphysics. As the father of modern materialism, Hobbes held that the universe was corporeal, enjoying the dimensions of magnitude, namely length, breadth and depth. This belief led him to argue against the existence of an incorporeal soul, separated from the body yet feeling the torments of fire and hell. In chapter 46, 'On darkness from vain philosophy and fabulous traditions', Hobbes discusses the definition of certain basic philosophical terms such as body, time, place, matter and form. In the quotation he is mocking scholasticism for its refusal to see eternity as an endless succession of time, but rather as a standing-still of the present. This quotation is followed by a parallel discussion of place, in a paragraph whose title is more immediately related to 'The Aleph': 'One body in many places and many bodies in one place at once.' Here Hobbes argues for the separateness of places according to the division of parts, scoffing at the incongruities of the schoolmen who try to rationalise the incomprehensible by having us believe that 'by the Almighty power of God, one body may be at one and at the same time in many places; and many bodies in one and the same time in one place; as if it were an acknowledgment of the Divine Power to say that which is, is not; or that which has been has not been.'

Aleph 11 (15) *Aleph* 151

Lhomond, Charles François (1727-1794)

A French grammarian and historian, author of *De viris illustribus urbis Romae* (The Lives of Famous Romans), widely used in secondary schools in France, Belgium and Russia during the nineteenth century.

Lab. 89 (61) *Ficc.* 120

Liber Adversus Omnes Hereses (Book against all the Heresies)

An apocryphal text: perhaps an allusion to Irenaeus' second-century *Refutation of all the Heresies* in which the **Syntagma* by Justin Martyr is quoted. There is also an *Adversus Omnes Haereses* attributed by Jerome in his *De Viris Illustribus* to a certain Victorinus de Pettau (d. 304).

Lab. 125 (95) *Ficc.* 169

Liberator (Libertador)

A title of Simón *Bolívar.

Brodie 82 (100) *Brodie* 112

Libro de la invención liberal y arte del juego del ajedrez see *López de Segura

Liddell Hart, Sir Basil Henry (1895-1970)

A British military historian, author of a history of World War I, first published in 1930 as *The Real War, 1914-1918*. The second edition, published in 1934, was called *A History of the World War, 1914-1918*. Lab. 45/54 (20/29): Liddell Hart's account of the battle of the Somme, in whose department both the river Ancre and the 'city called Albert' are to be found, was written while he was convalescing from wounds received during the campaign. Reference is made to an attack by the British 13th Division which had been postponed from 29 June to 1 July 1916; there is no mention of rain having fallen before the battle. The long bombardment which preceded the attack destroyed all chances of surprise, and it failed with heavy British losses. Only in the area Fricourt /*Montauban did the British gain ground against the German defences (this is stated at p.252,

not p.22 as mentioned in Lab. 44 (19)).
  Lab. 44 (19) *Ficc*. 97

Life of Antoninus Heliogabalus (Vida de Antonino Heliogábalo) see Antoninus *Heliogabalus

'Like the philosopher...' ('Como el filósofo...') see *Pythagoras

'Like the spider which builds itself a feeble house' ('Son comparables a la araña') see *Koran

Lilliput

An imaginary island in *Swift's *Gulliver's Travels* (1726) whose inhabitants are only six inches tall. The diminutive scale of everything on the island sets off the pompous behaviour of its emperor and the intrigues of his courtiers. Lab. 94 (65): in Part One, ch. 2 Gulliver is asked to deliver up his belongings, which are then described in minute detail from the vantage point of the Lilliputians. Thus Gulliver's watch, 'a wonderful kind of engine', appeared to them as 'a globe, half silver, and half of some transparent metal ... which made an incessant noise, like that of a watermill'. The Lilliputians thought it must be an animal, or more probably a god. Gulliver records that the emperor 'was amazed at the continual noise it made, and the motion of the minute hand, which he could easily discern for their sight is much more acute than ours'.
  Lab. 84 (65) *Ficc*. 125

Lincoln, Abraham (1809-1865)

The sixteenth President of the United States (1860-5) who fought the Civil War to preserve the Union against the secessionist states of the South. In spite of the many factions opposing 'reconstruction' at the end of the war, he was re-elected in 1864. The Republican party was divided: Lincoln's attitude of 'malice toward none with charity for all' satisfied neither the Confederacy nor his own radical Republicans, and his policy on reconstruction was far from clear. In April 1865 he showed that he was willing to move towards the extremists of his party. Lab. 105 (75): after a cabinet meeting on 14 April 1865 Lincoln was shot dead in the theatre by one John Wilkes Booth. He was sitting with his wife and two other guests in a box to the right of the stage. The theatre was draped in red brocade and flags in honour of the President.
  Lab. 105 (75) *Ficc*. 141

Liniers

A street in *Buenos Aires in the district of *Almagro.
  Lab. 166 (134) *Aleph* 62

Liverpool

An industrial and commercial port in north-west England, once the leading cotton market of Europe, whose importance declined considerably after World War II.
  Fict. 70 (77) *Ficc.* 82

Locke, John (1632-1704)

An English philosopher whose influence upon modern thought rests chiefly on his *Essay Concerning Human Understanding* and *Two Treatises of Government*, both published in 1690. As an empiricist and anti-dogmatist, writing against the old philosophy of scholasticism, Locke examines the implications of new scientific ideas upon traditional concepts of religion and morality. The *Essay* is a critical assessment of the nature and purpose of understanding, claiming that, while man's understanding falls short of a total comprehension of reality, human knowledge is sufficient for the needs of mankind. Locke denies the existence of innate ideas and categories, arguing that the mind, at birth, is a *tabula rasa*, and that we get all our ideas from sense experience. Thus, as far as man's knowledge is concerned, general ideas are only abstractions from particular experiences. These preoccupations lead Locke to consider the nature of language and to observe its imperfections with regard to the subjective nature of its categories. Locke agreed that language is most useful when general names stand for general ideas and operations of the mind. Most of the intellectual argument of 'Funes the Memorious' stems from Locke's discussion of language in book 3, ch. 1 of the *Essay*, in which he considers the relationship of language and things, noting that whereas 'all Things are Particulars, the far greatest part of Words that make all Languages are General Terms'. The reason for this is necessity: since it is beyond human capacity to frame and retain distinct ideas of every particular thing, it is impossible for every particular thing to have a distinct and peculiar name; secondly, it would be useless if it did because this would prevent rather than facilitate communication; thirdly, it would not serve towards the improvement of knowledge which, though founded in particular things, enlarges itself by general views.
  Lab. 93 (65) *Ficc.* 125

Lomas (de Zamora)

A district in Greater *Buenos Aires, south of the capital. Once known as an English quarter, through its proximity to *Turdera and *Morón it has become a less desirable area for the middle classes.

Brodie 55 (66) Brodie 19, Brodie 75 (92) *Brodie* 78

Lombards

A Germanic nation who ruled in northern Italy between the sixth and the eighth centuries, when they were known as Longobardi. Coming from the west of Germany, under the leadership of Alboin, the Lombards crossed the Alps in 568 and occupied the whole of north, and some areas of central and south, Italy. Their rule was brutal and merciless; when they invaded Papal territories, Pope Adrian I called on the Frankish king Charlemagne, who defeated the last Lombard king Desiderius in 774 and destroyed his kingdom.

Lab. 159 (127) *Aleph* 47

London (Londres)

Borges's great attachment to London may be seen in his many references to the city, which he describes on several occasions as a labyrinth. Thus in Lab. 287 (251): 'the red and tranquil labyrinth of London'; Aleph 20 (27): 'a splintered labyrinth'; Aleph 78 (122): 'London...a better labyrinth'.

Lab. 94 (65) *Ficc.* 126, Aleph 20 (27) *Aleph* 164/5, Aleph 32 (46) *Ficc.* 36, Brodie 88 (106) *Brodie* 122

Longford

A county in central *Ireland to the east of *Roscommon.

Fict. 66 (73) *Ficc.* 77

Longobardi (Longobardos) see *Lombards

Lönnrot, Erik

A fictional name emphasising the theme of 'redness' in 'Death and the Compass'. Erik is associated with Erik the Red, the tenth-century Norse explorer whose exploits are recounted in the *Eriks saga*. Lönnrot is associated with Elias Lönnrot, one of the founders of modern Finnish literature who edited the Kaleva, a collection of Finnish folk songs, legends and riddles.

Lab. 106 (769 *Ficc.* 143

Lope de Vega see *Vega Carpio, Lope de

López de Segura, Ruy (fl. 1560)

A Spanish scholar and scientist, founder of the modern system of chess expounded in his *Libro de la invención liberal y arte del juego del ajedrez* (1561). A classic opening move of the game is named after him.

Lab. 63 *Ficc.* 47

López, Estanislao

A veteran of the Wars of Independence and *caudillo* of Santa Fe Province from 1818 to 1838. López was famous for the *montonero* tactics he learnt while fighting the Indians on the northern border, which allowed him to get the better of his less adaptable opponents in the regular armies. In 1829 he joined forces with *Rosas in a successful attempt to defeat the *Unitarian *Lavalle.

Aleph 54 (81) *Aleph* 53

Lord Jim

The protagonist of Joseph Conrad's eponymous novel published in 1900, an Englishman who controls a small community in the island of Patusan in the Far East. Previously a chief mate of the *Patna* sailing the eastern oceans, Lord Jim deserts his ship with its load of pilgrims when he believes it to be sinking. The *Patna* does not sink, and the rest of Lord Jim's life is marred by the memory of his cowardice. When the people of Patusan are threatened by a band of thieves, Jim tries in vain to protect them by pledging his life. Having failed to avert a massacre, he redeems his past by accepting the responsibility of so many deaths and facing execution. Aleph 68 (106): like *Razumov in Conrad's *Under Western Eyes*, Lord Jim is an exemplar of ambivalence between cowardice and bravery. See José *Korzeniovski.

Aleph 68 (106) *Aleph* 73

Los eruditos a la violeta

A satirical work (1772) by the Spanish poet and essayist José Cadalso y Vázquez. It attacks pseudo-erudition by offering would-be scholars lessons on how to appear to be learned without too much reading. The reference is omitted in the English translation.

Aleph 154

Lost Encyclopaedia (Enciclopedia Perdida)

An encyclopaedia compiled at the order of Yongle, the third emperor of the *Luminous Dynasty, which became known as *Yongle da dian* (The Great Work of Yongle), Yongle being the reign-title of the Emperor. The manuscript of 22,877 sections bound in 11,095 volumes was completed in 1408; two more copies were made in 1567. The original and one copy were destroyed in Nanjing; the other copy, kept in Hanlin Academy in Peking, was apparently already incomplete when the Academy was destroyed by fire during the Boxer uprising in 1900. A few lost volumes of the encyclopaedia are now scattered in libraries in China and elsewhere, including the British Library.

Lab. 49 (24) *Ficc.* 104

Louis XVI (1754-1793)

The king of France executed during the Revolution. Lab. 192 (159): when the royal family was escaping in disguise, Louis was recognised at Varennes by the resemblance to his effigy on a Louis coin.

Lab. 192 (159) *Aleph* 106

Lucerne (Lucerna)

A city in central Switzerland, during the Reformation a stronghold of Catholicism and from 1579 to 1874 the seat of the Papal Nuncio.

Lab. 39 (15) *Ficc.* 29

Lucian of Samosata (Luciano de Samosata) (*c*.120-200)

A Greek satirist, called the 'Blasphemer' for his attacks on religion. He wrote in a variety of genres, his most famous work being the *True History*, the first imaginary travelogue. In it Lucian claimed that, since nothing had happened to him that was worth writing about, he had turned to publishing untruths. He gave the following warning: 'This one thing I confidently pronounce for a truth, that I lie.' Aleph 22 (30): the mirror that Lucian saw in the kingdom of Endymion, which is 'that region that to us below seemed the moon', is described as follows: 'a mighty glass lying upon the top of a pit of no great depth, whereinto, if any man descends, he shall hear everything that is spoken upon the earth: if he but look into the glass, he shall see all the cities and all the nations as well as if he were among them. There had I the sight of all my friends and the whole country about: whether they saw me or not I cannot tell, but if they don't believe me they can go and look and they'll find my words true.'

Aleph 22 (30) *Aleph* 168

Lucinge, Princess of see *Faucigny Lucinge

Lugones, Leopoldo (1874-1938)

An Argentine poet, journalist and short-story writer. Most of Lugones's poetical work, though prodigiously varied, reflects the influence of the Spanish American modernist movement headed by Rubén Darío and of French symbolism (e.g. *Lunario sentimental*, 1909 and *Romancero*, 1924). Lugones was active in politics, first as a socialist but later as a nationalist and a supporter of fascism. Becoming involved in public education, he was nominated director of the Biblioteca de Maestros in *Buenos Aires. Borges's attitude towards Lugones changed through the years. Though in an early work he accused him of not having a single idea of his own (*Esperanza* 1926) and renamed his *Lunario* 'Nulario' ('a nothing'), nevertheless in his monograph on Lugones, perhaps as a result of his critical work on *Sarmiento and *Martín *Fierro*, he called him 'the greatest writer of Argentina'. In a prologue to more than one of his texts (*El hacedor, El otro, El mismo, Leopoldo Lugones*), perhaps to make up for the harshness of his previous criticism, he imagines himself presenting his work to an amiable Lugones, who in real life had never liked it.
  Brodie 32 (36) *Brodie* 91

Luke, St (Lucas)

A physician, probably a gentile, author of the third synoptic gospel. Luke's gospel addresses its message of universal salvation through the life, death and teachings of Christ to all men. Lab. 127 (97): Luke 22:3 reads: 'Then entered Satan into Judas surnamed Iscariot, being of the number of the twelve'; Luke 9:1 reads: 'Then he called his twelve disciples together, and gave them power and authority over all devils, and to cure diseases.' Lab. 155 (124): Luke 12:59 reads: 'I tell thee, thou shalt not depart hence, till thou hast paid the very last mite.' Stemming from a passage called 'This fateful hour', it is part of a speech in which Jesus announces that his words will bring about conflicts of interpretation and loyalties, but that men must find the right course for themselves, for in the end they will have to answer for all their actions.
  Lab. 127 (97) *Ficc.* 171, Lab. 155 (124) *Aleph* 41

Lully, Raymond (Ramon Lull) (1235-1315)

The first major poet and prose writer in Catalan. At the age of 31 Lully repented his profligate youth and dedicated the rest of his life to religious studies and the fanatical pursuit of missionary projects, until his zeal verged on madness. An expert in Arabic, he tried to teach Christianity in Tunis and Bougie and was arrested. Finally he was stoned to death outside the walls of Bougie while campaigning against *Islam. Though his writings abound in contradictions and eccentric speculations, Lully was called 'Doctor Illuminatus' in Spain and was for a while worshipped as a saint. Lab. 63 (37): Lully's *Ars Magna Generalis* (1275) is a treatise described in the frontispiece as a compendium of accessible answers to all questions on the arts and sciences. It begins by presenting three sectioned circles in which the principles governing the spiritual and physical worlds are arbitrarily set out under different letter headings. Rotating these circles on the same centre produces different letters, and Lully formulated his answers on the basis of their various combinations.

Lab. 63 (37) *Ficc.* 46

Luminous Dynasty (Dinastía Luminosa)

Probably a reference to the Ming Dynasty of China (ming: bright) which lasted from 1368 to the Manchu invasion in 1644, when the last Ming Emperor, Ts'ung-cheng, committed suicide. Lab. 49 (24): the third Emperor of the dynasty, Zhu Di, in the first year of his reign (1403) ordered the compilation of an encyclopaedic work containing 'all known literature'. See *Lost Encyclopaedia*.

Lab. 49 (24) *Ficc.* 104

Lund

A city of Sweden, ten miles from *Malmö, mentioned in tenth-century sagas. In the Middle Ages Lund was the capital of Denmark, and it remained the object of contention between Sweden and Denmark until it finally passed to Sweden in 1658, becoming a Lutheran bishopric.

Lab. 127 (97) *Ficc.* 171

Lunfardo

A term originating from the French 'Lombard'; the meaning 'thief' dates from the sixteenth and seventeenth centuries, when the Lombards were bankers and usurers in Paris. Brodie 66 (81): as appears from the English translation, the term is now given by extension to the slang used by the riff-raff of *Buenos Aires and surrounding areas. Much of its vocabulary has crept into colloquial *argentinismo* (Argentinian speech).

Brodie 65

Luria, Isaac (1534-1572)

A *Cabbalist, also known as 'The Lion', who was born in Jerusalem, spent his formative years in Egypt and became an important figure at the centre of Cabbalist teaching in Safed in northern *Galilee. Luria's only written work is a commentary on the 'Book of Concealment' (a section of the *Zohar), though he had numerous disciples in Safed who recorded his teachings. The primary concepts of the Lurianic Cabbala seek to explain the existence of evil by linking it to the mystical doctrine of metempsychosis. According to the school of Luria, each human soul is a spark from Adam, divorced from its original source from the time of the Fall but destined to return to it with the coming of the Messiah. Until then, however, it has to wander through all forms of existence, not only through the bodies of men, but through inorganic matter. Ideas of metempsychosis may have entered Judaism from Indian philosophy, or from *Orphic and Neoplatonic teachings. Luria elaborated on a particular aspect of this doctrine known as *Ibbur.

Aleph 36 (51) *Ficc.* 42

Lutf Ali Azur (1711-1781)

A Persian poet and biographer, best known for his *Atashkadah* ('Temple of Fire'), a collection of biographies of Persian poets with an anthology of their poems. Lab. 195 (161): though Borges is correct in referring to Luft as a 'dervish', for he became so in later life, the attribution of 'polygraph' seems less suitable, since his only other known work is a fairly slender *Divan*, or collection of poems. The story of 'the copper astrolabe' of Shiraz has not been traced in *Atashkadah*.

Lab. 195 (161) *Aleph* 110

Luther, Martin (Lutero) (1483-1546)

A German religious reformer of intense vitality who inaugurated the Reformation on 31 October 1517 by fixing on the church door at Wittenburg his ninety-five theses against the penitential system of the Church and the sale of indulgences by the Dominican Johann Tetzel. For this act he was excommunicated by Pope Leo X and his writings were burnt. Luther based his doctrine on the individual responsibility of all believers for adherence to the truth as expressed in the bible and on salvation by the grace of God alone. When in 1521 he was summoned by Charles V to the Diet of Worms he made the celebrated speech which ended with the words: 'Here I stand, I cannot do otherwise, God help me, amen.' In 1525 he married a nun who had renounced her vows. Lab. 176 (146): Luther's greatest influence on the German people was through his translation of the bible. He completed it in 1532, but revised it constantly until 1545. Through his translations and other writings he may also be regarded as the founder of the present literary language of Germany, that is, of New High German.

Lab. 178 (146) *Aleph* 88

Mabinogion

A collection of Welsh mythological tales dating from the fourteenth and fifteenth centuries. It comprises legends of Celtic and Norman origin, rich in supernatural and magical elements. The first English translation appeared in 1949. Brodie 89 (106): the episode of the two kings playing chess while their armies are engaged in battle is taken from 'The Dream of Rhonabwy' in which King Arthur and Owein play a game of 'gwyddbwyll' while Arthur's army is fighting the 'ravens' of Owein. The story may refer to a conflict between the old religion of the Celtic god Bran (or Vran), represented as a raven, hence the name of his followers, and Christianity, championed by Arthur. The game of gwyddbwyll was played on a board with two glass sets (one black and one white) of twelve pieces of similar size, each engraved with a different pattern; it was used at one time as a method of divination. Its translation into 'chess' probably indicates that Borges's source was a romantic Victorian edition of the *Mabinogion*. Borges also refers to this episode in his *Cuentos breves* where the source given is Edwin Morgan's *Week-End Companion to Wales and Cornwall*.

Brodie 89 (106) *Brodie* 122

Macao

A Portuguese colony on the South China Sea, the earliest European port in the Far East, dating from the sixteenth century. It was later identified with smuggling and gambling.

Lab. 135 (105) *Aleph* 7

Macbeth

Lab. 103 (73): in the context of the assassination of Fergus *Kilpatrick, the allusion to *Macbeth*, as well as to *Julius Caesar*, emphasises the literary quality of the 'scheme conceived' by the character Nolan and its predetermined nature. Warnings of death dominate the plots of both plays, unheeded by Caesar and misunderstood by Macbeth. See *Julius Caesar.

Lab. 103 (73) *Ficc.* 139

Macedonia

An ancient nation in the Balkan peninsula on the Aegean corresponding nowadays to parts of Bulgaria, Greece and Yugoslavia.

Lab. 153 (122) *Aleph* 39

Machado, Benito (1823-1909)

An Argentine military commander who in 1863 directed a campaign against the Indians in the southern pampas. Aleph 56 (84): the suggestion that Martín *Fierro was conscripted to his forces is not mentioned in the poem.

Aleph 56 (84) *Aleph* 56

Madras

A seaport in south-east India.
  Aleph 33 (48) *Ficc.* 33

Mahavira (*c.*599-527 BC)

The title given to Vardhamäna, the last of the twenty-four legendary patriarchs and founders of Jainism, a religion widespread in west India. Jainism conceives the universe as infinite and formed as a slender human figure with legs apart and arms akimbo surrounded by three layers of atmosphere. Mahavira preached severe asceticism, which involved renunciation of violence and all physical pleasures and respect for all living and non-living things.
  Aleph 85 (133) *Aleph* 148

Mahdi

Arabic *al-Mahdi*, meaning 'the guided one': the name given in Islam to the future restorer of the Islamic faith to the world. Lab. 189 (156) refers to the Mahdi Mohammed Ahmed (1844-1885) who put an end to Egyptian domination in the Sudan. Claiming divine inspiration, the Mahdi overcame the 8,000 strong army of General Hicks. In 1885, after a long siege, he captured Khartoum and murdered General Gordon.
  Lab. 189 (156) *Aleph* 103

Maimonides (also Moses ben Maimon) (1135-1204)

A Jewish philosopher, jurist and physician, born at Cordoba and forced to flee from Spain in the persecutions of 1149. He settled first in Fez and then in Cairo, where he became head of the Jewish community and also physician to the Sultan. Maimonides was the leading Jewish thinker of the Middle Ages. His *Commentary* on the *Talmud contains a codification of Jewish religious doctrine, its interpretation by existing authorities and his own comments on their moral and philosophical implications. His major philosophical work, written in Arabic, is the *Guide for the Perplexed*. Basing his interpretation of Judaism upon the systems of *Aristotle, Maimonides seeks to achieve a harmony between reason and faith. The *Guide* was translated into Latin as early as the thirteenth century and exerted a profound influence upon Christian as well as Jewish and Moslem thought. Lab. 122 (92): regarding dreams, in book 2 chs 36-8 of the *Guide* Maimonides discusses the relationship between prophecy, or divine emanations, and dreams. Breaking with traditional interpretations of the dream as a means of protection from anticipated danger, he develops his idea of the dream as a vision in which the action of the imaginative faculty becomes so perfect that you can see a thing as if it were outside you, and the thing which is produced in the dream appears as if by external sensation. Ch. 36 includes quotations of famous sayings, such as 'Dream is one sixtieth of prophecy', 'The windfall of prophecy is one dream' and 'If there be a prophet among you, I the Lord will make myself known to him in a dream' (Numbers 12:6). Although the discussion includes many ideas which seem closely relevant to Borges's story 'The Secret Miracle', the exact assertion attributed by the narrator to Maimonides has not been traced. The idea mentioned in the story that the final interpretation of dreams rests with God stems from Genesis 40:8.

Lab. 122 (92) *Ficc.* 164

Maipú

A battle fought on 5 April 1818, some ten miles south of Santiago, *Chile, in which General *San Martín finally defeated the royalist forces, thus securing the independence of Chile. This victory enabled San Martín to reorganise his army and embark on the last lap of his campaign for the emancipation of southern South America, notably the liberation of Peru.

Brodie 72 (89) *Brodie* 75

Maldonado

A small stream which marked the northern boundary of the city of *Buenos Aires. The surrounding area, *Palermo, was reputedly rough, as recalled by Borges in his 'Autobiographical Essay'. Today Maldonado forms part of the city's sewers and flows in pipes beneath the Avenida Juan B. Justo. Brodie 46 (55): the 'brook' referred to here is the Maldonado.

Brodie 45 (54) *Brodie* 40

Mallarmé, Stéphane (1842-1898)

A French poet who, together with Paul Verlaine, is regarded as the founder of the Symbolist movement, which had a marked influence in France throughout the twentieth century. Mallarmé also wrote a number of critical essays: his views on writing derive mainly from the principle that the world exists in order to be written about: 'Le monde est fait pour aboutir à un beau livre' ('The world was made to end in a beautiful book', misquoted by Borges as *'Tout aboutit à un livre' (Disc.* 121)). This idea is examined by Borges in 'On the Cult of Books' (Other Inq. 116-20). Lab. 67 (40): in his escape from reality, Mallarmé was influenced at first by Baudelaire, both poets having lost a parent in early childhood, but Mallarmé turned increasingly to the intellect, rather than the emotions, in his search for an ideal world. He saw the poet's task as feeling and describing the essences beyond reality. To convey this sense of distilled reality,

Mallarmé sought to pare down and condense his language: his later poems were often obscure, relying for their structure on the sound and association of the words employed.
Lab. 67 (40) *Ficc.* 51

Malmö

The third-largest city of Sweden, founded in the twelfth century, an important port on the Öresund Canal.
Lab. 130 (100) *Ficc.* 175, Lab. 165 (133) *Aleph* 61

Manantiales

A battle fought in the department of Colonia, *Uruguay, on 17 July 1871, when the revolutionary forces led by Timoteo *Aparicio were defeated by the army of the president, Lorenzo Batlle.
Brodie 38 (45) *Brodie* 101

Manchester

The leading commercial city in the north of *England during the nineteenth century. The choice of Manchester as the place of publication of Nahum *Cordovero's apocryphal work reflects its strong links with Jewish culture and its association with some of the oldest Sephardi families in England.
Lab. 149 (118) *Aleph* 25

Mantiq ut-Tair (Mantiq al-Tayr)

The Persian form of *Parliament of Birds*.
Aleph 36 (52) *Ficc.* 42

Marchenoir

A forest near Blois, the scene of numerous battles in the Franco-Prussian war of 1870.
Lab. 173 (141) *Aleph* 81

Marcus Flaminius Rufus (Marco Flaminio Rufo)

A fictional Latin name with the connotation 'flame' and 'red' (Rufus), contrasted with Joseph *Cartaphilus, an 'earthen man, with grey eyes and grey beard' (see Christ, *The Narrow Act*, NY 1969, 206).
Lab. 138 (108) *Aleph* 12

Mariano Rubio see **José de *Olavarría**

Marienburg (or **Marienberg**)

German for Polish Malbork, a town in the Polish province of Gdansk, formerly in East Prussia and closely associated since the thirteenth century with the Teutonic Order.
 Lab. 174 (142) *Aleph* 82

Mark, St (San Marco)

The author of the second synoptic gospel now considered the earliest of the three and the source of *Matthew and *Luke. With its sixteen chapters, it is the shortest of the gospels, its power lying in the simple narrative of events in the life of Jesus. Mark may have received his information direct from St Peter, which would account for his immediacy. The gospel was written in Hellenistic Greek, the popular dialect of the eastern Mediterranean. Its purpose is clearly evangelical. It emphasises the dramatic presentation of the passion and resurrection of Jesus as the means of achieving the Kingdom of God.
 Brodie 15 (15) *Brodie* 125

Marrakesh

A town in *Morocco, one of the residences of the Sultan. In the twelfth and thirteenth centuries it was the North African capital of the Almohad dynasty, under whose rule it enjoyed a temporary flowering of culture. Lab. 186 (154): *Averroes spent some years of exile in Marrakesh.
 Lab. 186 (154) *Aleph* 99

Mars (Marte)

The Roman god of war.
 Lab. 136 (106) *Aleph* 8

Martensen, Hans Lassen (1808-1884)

A Danish theologian, bishop and court preacher, author of several treatises on Christian ethics and dogma revealing a strong interest in theosophy. Martensen also wrote a sketch on the life of Jakob *Boehme.
 Lab. 129 (99) Ficc. 174

Martín Fierro see ***Fierro, Martín**

Martínez Estrada, Ezequiel (1895-1964)

A prolific Argentine writer whose work reflects a deep concern with his country's development. *Radiografía de la Pampa* (1933) describes the changes that took place in Argentina in the early 1930s under fascist rule. *La cabeza de Goliath* (1940) examines the relationship of *Buenos Aires to the rest of the country. *Muerte y transfiguración del Martín Fierro* (2 vols, 1948) is regarded as an outstanding work of literary criticism.

Lab. 39 (15) *Ficc.* 29

Masoller

A decisive battle on 1 September 1904 in northern *Uruguay between the rebel forces of Aparicio *Saravia and the National Army; Saravia was defeated and mortally wounded.

Aleph 68 (103) *Aleph* 72

Mastronardi, Carlos (1901-?)

A poet, essayist and journalist, a member of the group of writers identified with the avant-garde literary magazine *Martín Fierro*, which published some of Borges's early work.

Lab. 29 (5) *Ficc.* 16

Matthew, St (Mateo)

The author of the first gospel. Lab. 127 (97): Matthew 10:7-8 reads: 'And as ye go, preach, saying, The kingdom of heaven is at hand. Heal the sick, cleanse the lepers, raise the dead, cast out devils: freely ye have received, freely give.' Lab. 130 (99): Matthew 12:31 reads: 'Wherefore I say unto you, All manner of sin and blasphemy shall be forgiven unto men: but the blasphemy against the Holy Ghost shall not be forgiven unto men.' Lab. 152 (121): Matthew 6:7 reads: 'But when ye pray, use not vain repetitions, as the heathen do: for they think that they shall be heard for their much speaking.' Lab. 154 (123): Matthew 6:12 is part of the Lord's prayer. Matthew 11:12: the full verse reads: 'And from the days of John the Baptist until now the kingdom of heaven suffereth violence, and the violent take it by force.'

Lab. 127 (97) *Ficc.* 172, Lab. 152 (121) *Aleph* 38

Maude, Frederich Natush (1854-1933)

An English military historian, author of *The Evolution of Strategy*, technical essays, and studies of the great military campaigns of the past such as Leipzig, Jena and Ulm. Maude also translated *Clausewitz.

Mauretania (Mauritanos)

An ancient kingdom in north Africa corresponding now to north Morocco and central Algeria. The kings of Mauretania became Roman vassals as early as the second century BC. Two centuries later Mauretania was annexed to the Roman Empire by the Emperor Claudius and divided into two provinces. Lab. 135: (106): in the fourth century, during the tetrarchy of *Diocletian, Mauretania and other regions of north Africa were the scene of rebellions against the Roman army led by Maximian, the Emperor's colleague.
Lab. 135 (106) *Aleph* 8, Lab. 157 (126) *Aleph* 45

Mazorca

A political organisation formed in 1833 to advance *Rosas's *Federalist leadership. At first respectable, it soon became Rosas's secret police. Its name, 'ear of corn', was chosen to suggest the values of countrymen as opposed to townsmen. Rosas's enemies claimed that it was *más horcas* ('more gallows'), and it became a by-word for intimidation, vandalism and brutality. After Rosas's fall, it was abolished and its leaders executed. Brodie 79 (96): The English translation gives 'Rosas's henchmen'.
Brodie 85

Meinong, Alexius (1853-1921)

An Austrian philosopher who, in his theory of objects, or *Über Gegendstandstheorie* (1904), distinguished between objects that have 'existence' as physical objects and those that 'subsist' in our mind as concepts or theoretical entities, maintaining that the latter also have a form of existence. Accordingly he defined 'object' (*Gegenstand*) as that to which a mental act should be directed. Lab. 33 (9): Meinong's 'subsistent world' is illustrated by his example of the golden mountain which, though not present in the physical world, has a substantive existence as the product of our imagination.
Lab. 33 (9) *Ficc*. 21

Melo

A town in north-eastern *Uruguay.
Lab. 198 (165) *Aleph* 137

Melton Mowbray

A town north east of Leicester, popular among the English upper classes

as a centre of fox-hunting.
   Fict. 70 (77) *Ficc.* 81

Memphis

The largest city in Tennessee, on the Mississippi. In the 1820s it was undergoing rapid commercial and industrial growth.
   Lab. 39 (15) *Ficc.* 30

Menard, Pierre

A fictional character, perhaps drawn from Louis Menard (1822-1901). In an article by the symbolist writer Rémy de Gourmont (which Borges probably read), Louis Menard is described as a master of parody. He attempted to rewrite some of the lost Greek tragedies, including Aeschylus' *Prometheus bound*, and, as a hoax, wrote a piece which he attributed to Diderot. Like the fictional Pierre Menard, he indulged in anachronistic readings, thinking of Shakespeare when reading Homer, linking Helen with Hamlet and imagining Desdemona at Achilles' feet (see Emir Rodríguez Monegal, *Jorge Luis Borges: a Literary Biography* 123).
   Lab. 52 (36) *Ficc.* 45

Mengenlehre

German for 'set theory': a mathematical term designating the theory of G. Cantor (1829-1920) on the relationship between finite numbers and infinitude. Cantor examines the comparisons of infinite collections, starting from the observation of the equivalences in a series such as 1,2,3,4 which could equally express, or be expressed by, 2,4,6,8, so that 1 could be represented by 2, 2 by 4, 3 by 6 and so on. Thus any integer can represent all its multiples and all its multiples can be elevated to multiple power, so that 1 may be 6036 and also 6036 squared, and so on. Furthermore 1 can undergo equal fragmentation. The point ultimately arrived at is that any one cardinal number may be symbolic of any other, and of all others and, by extension, of infinitude; moreover there are a host of potentially infinite numbers. This theory led Cantor to the paradoxical conclusion that the universe is composed of an infinitude of points, as is a yard of the universe, or a fraction of that yard, making the most infinitesimal point on earth symbolic of the macrocosm. Borges discuses this theory in *Etern.* 77-9. In the *Mengenlehre*, the *aleph denotes a higher power than that of finite numbers. It also talks of a plurality of alephs.
   Aleph 22 (29) *Aleph* 168

Merlin

A legendary figure, originally a Welsh poet and prophet of the sixth century, but remembered chiefly as the enchanter in the twelfth-century Arthurian romance. In Geoffrey of Monmouth's narrative Merlin is identified with a boy from an earlier tale who has no father and whose magic helps Arthur's father to win his bride. Merlin is reputed to have instituted the Round Table, and to have helped Arthur defeat his foes by his counsel and magic. He was said to possess knowledge of the past and of the future. Aleph 22 (30): *The *Faerie Queene*, III, 2, refers to the mirror made by Merlin for King Ryence, which gave him the power to see all. It was in the form of a glass orb, shaped like the world, and enabled the viewer to look into the hearts of men and foresee the intentions of his enemies and the treachery of his friends.

Aleph 22 (30) *Aleph* 168

Merlo

A town on the outskirts of *Buenos Aires, to the west of the capital.

Brodie 49 (58) *Brodie* 46

Mesa, Manuel (1788-1829)

A military leader who fought in the Wars of Independence and later in the frontier wars against the Indians. Aleph 56 (84): in 1829, in *Laguna Colorada, Mesa was successful in recruiting a small contingent to fight on the side of Rosas. It was so popular that their numbers grew daily, joined by local *montoneros* and friendly Indians. On 29 January they were surprised by a force under *Lavalle and suffered heavy casualties. Mesa escaped with some of his men to join *Rosas, but he was attacked on the way, near *Pergamino, by Isidoro *Suárez, who sent him to *Buenos Aires where he was condemned to death and executed on 16 February 1829.

Aleph 56 (84) *Aleph* 56

Metrodorus (Metrodoro)

Metrodorus of Scepsis, in Mysia, was celebrated for his powers of memory and his hatred of Rome. *Pliny (7.24.1) wrote that Metrodorus perfected *Simonides' art of memory so that 'a man might learn to rehearse again the same words of any discourse whatsoever, after hearing them once'. He is also referred to by *Cicero, who says that 'he wrote down things he wanted to remember in certain "localities" in his possession by means of images, just as if he were inscribing letters on wax' (*De Oratore* 2.360).

Lab. 91 (63) *Ficc.* 122

Meyrink, Gustav (1868-1932)

The pseudonym of G. Meyer, an Austrian novelist who lived for many years in *Prague and converted from Protestantism to Buddhism. Meyrink's interest in occultism led him to study the *Cabbala, freemasonry, yoga and alchemy and to experiment with hashish. His best-known novel is *Der Golem* (1916), 'golem' being the Hebrew for embryo, or anything incomplete; it is based on the medieval Jewish belief that it was possible to infuse life into a clay or wooden figure by means of a combination of letters of any one of God's names. The most famous version of this legend became that of the sixteenth-century rabbi from Prague Judah Loew, who is said to have created a golem to serve in the synagogue. Every evening the rabbi removed a vital letter of the combination, but on one occasion he forgot and the golem took over in a frenzy. This masterpiece of fantasy (of which two films were made by Paul Wegener) combines this strange legend with experiences of Meyrink's own life in Prague. It contains metaphysical themes from which Borges drew inspiration for many of his stories. Borges also wrote a long poem 'El Golem', which he considered among his best (Sel. Poems 123). In Meyrink's novel the golem can be seen to symbolise the individual who has become the automaton of modern society, instilled with a soul that is alien to himself. Brodie 88 (106): there are certain autobiographical links between the narrator of 'Guayaquil' and Borges. In his 'Autobiographical Essay' Borges relates that when he first learnt German he read Meyrink's book in the original and later, in 1960, discussed the legend with the Jewish scholar Gershom Scholem in Jerusalem (Aleph 134 (216)). On the same theme he has written: 'Gustav Meyrink uses this legend...in a dream-like setting on the other side of the mirror and he has invested it with a horror so palpable that it has remained in my memory all these years!'

Brodie 88 (106) *Brodie* 121

Midrashim

The plural of the Hebrew word *midrash*, 'study'. The term refers to texts of scriptural exegesis which seek to discover the deeper meaning of the bible by enlarging upon the literal meaning of each detail of the scriptures. Lab. 130 (99): despite the implication of the syntax of the sentence, Midrashim are not a people or a sect.

Lab. 130 (99) *Ficc.* 175

Migne, Jacques Paul (1800-1875)

A French priest, theologian and publisher of theological literature. His most important publication is *Patrology* (1844-66), a collection of 'the teachings of the Fathers of the Church' consisting of 217 volumes of ecclesiastical writings in Latin up to the time of Pope Innocent III (1198-1216) and of 162 volumes of ecclesiastical writings in Greek up to 1439. The chief value of this work is that it contains texts that are not available in other editions. Lab. 153 (122): the introduction into *Patrology* of the writings of the character Aurelian is clearly apocryphal.

Lab. 153 (122) *Aleph* 39

Miklosich, Franz von (1813-1891)

An Austrian philosopher whose work focused on the nature of language and who in 1849 occupied the newly created chair of philology at the University of Vienna. Lab. 131 (101): though 'the page much too famous' is obviously apocryphal, Miklosich's linguistic studies included the origins of non-European languages such as Romany, the language of the gypsies.

Lab. 131 (101) *Ficc.* 181

Milonga

A popular tune, song or dance in Argentina. Borges wrote *milongas*, most of which are published in the collection 'Para las seis cuerdas' (*O.P.* 297) and some appear in English in Sel. Poems, 245-9.

Lab. 41 (16) *Ficc.* 32

Ministry of Finance (Ministerio de Hacienda) see *Saavedra

Minotaur (Minotauro)

In Greek mythology the monster with the head of a bull and the body of man born from the union of Pasiphaë, wife of King Minos, with a bull. Lab. 172 (140): the Minotaur was placed by Minos in a labyrinth built by Daedalus, where he devoured a yearly tribute of seven youths and seven maidens from Athens. Aleph 79 (123): *Dante presents the Minotaur as the guardian of the first circle of the 'violent', together with the centaurs (*Inferno*, 12.1-30). The assertion that Dante imagined the Minotaur as having the body of a bull and the head of a man is probably based upon a line from Ovid (*Ars Amatoria* 2.24) describing him as 'semibovemque virum, semivirumque bovem' ('a man half-bull, a bull half-man'). See *Ariadne, *Theseus.

Lab. 172 (140) *Aleph* 70 Aleph 79 (123) *Aleph* 131

Mir Bahadur Ali

A fictitious name composed of *Mir*, a title of respect used for the descendants of celebrated Mohammedan saints, *Bahadur*, a word common in all Altaic languages whose literal meaning is 'brave', often used as a surname or honorific title signifying hero, and *Ali*, one of the ninety-nine special names for God in *Islam, meaning 'The Exalted One'.

Aleph 31 (45) *Ficc.* 35

'Mirrors and copulation are abominable' ('Los espejos y la cópula son abominables')

The alleged original version of this aphorism, 'Mirrors and fatherhood are abominable', is itself a quotation from the story 'The Masked Dyer, Hakim of Merv' (Infamy 83).

Lab. 27 (3) *Ficc.* 14

Mishnah

Hebrew for 'repetition', 'instruction': the codification of the oral law in Judaism. As a collection of rabbinical discussions on the law of Moses intended to apply to the circumstances of everyday life, it forms the basis of the *Talmud and is thought to have been compiled towards the end of the second century by Rabbi Judah ha-Nasi. The assertion in Lab. 189 (156) stems from the Sabbath Tractate of the Babylonian Talmud, vol.1, pp. 41-3, which deals with the prohibition against carrying objects on the Sabbath. It reads as follows: 'A tailor must not go out with his needle near nightfall, lest he forget and go out (in the evening of the Sabbath), nor a scribe with his quill.'

Lab. 189 (156) *Aleph* 104

Mitchell's

A famous English bookshop in *Buenos Aires.

Aleph 69 (107) *Aleph* 75

Mithridates Eupator (132-63 BC)

Literally 'given by Mithras, the Sun god': 'Mithridates' was a name bestowed on a number of oriental kings, soldiers and statesmen. Mithridates Eupator was the last of the six kings of Pontus. He overran the Roman province of Asia and was Rome's most powerful enemy until deposed by Pompey. Lab. 91 (63): his memory has been turned into a legend of outstanding bravery and outsize strength and appetite. He spent much of his time practising magic and was thought to be invincible. According to *Pliny (7.24.1), 'Mithridates the king reigned over twenty-two nations of different languages and in as many tongues gave laws and ministered justice to them, without interpreters'.

Lab. 91 (63) *Ficc.* 122

Moab

An area east of the Dead Sea outside the Promised Land, part of present-day Jordan. Most of our knowledge of the Moabites is derived from the Old Testament. See *Moses.

Lab. 102 (73) *Ficc.* 138

Moctezuma (also Montezuma)

Aztec for 'The Lord annoyed': a metaphor describing the sight of the sun behind clouds, a title held by several personages in Mexican history. The most ancient of these was one of the leaders of the Tenoch tribes who invaded the lagoon where the city of Tenochtitlán was founded. The second was one of Tenochtitlán's rulers. Lab. 207 (173): the third Montezuma reigned over the Aztecs from 1502 to 1520 and is probably the one referred to in the story. Though a despotic king, he attended to the education of his people and made his country powerful. His superstition led him to welcome the Spanish invaders led by Cortés, whom he believed to be the personification of the god Quetzacoatl. Montezuma was fatally wounded by a stone thrown during a public meeting, an act that may have been arranged by Cortés himself. He died four days after the injury, having refused food and medicaments.

Lab. 207 (173) *Aleph* 121

Mohalaca

From *al-Mu'allaqat*, Arabic for 'the suspended ones': a term denoting a collection of seven poems by seven authors preserved by oral tradition from pre-Islamic times. Because of their outstanding quality, they were hung on the walls of *Islam's most sacred shrine, the Ka'ba in Mecca. See *Zuhair.

Lab. 185 (153) *Aleph* 98

Mohammed (Mahoma) (c.570-632)

Arabic for 'praised one': the name of the prophet and founder of *Islam to whom, according to the tradition, the angel Gabriel revealed the infallible word of God. Aleph 13 (17): the saying before bowing to the inevitable, 'If the mountain will not come to Mohammed, Mohammed must go to the mountain', refers to the story of Mohammed who, when asked for a miraculous proof of his teaching, ordered Mount Safa to come to him and, as it did not move, said, 'God is merciful. Had it obeyed my words it would have fallen on us to our destruction. I will therefore go to the mountain, and thank God that He has had mercy on a stiff-necked generation.'

Aleph 13 (17) *Aleph* 153

Mohkam

The most authoritative Arab dictionary of the Middle Ages, compiled by
*Abensida and comprising many volumes.
 Lab. 181 (149) *Aleph* 93

Moldau

The German name of the Vltava, a principal river in Czechoslovakia,
which runs through Prague.
 Lab. 118 (89) *Ficc.* 160

Molina Vedia, Amanda

A friend of Borges, who invented the name *Triste-le-Roy, which she
placed on the map of an imaginary island painted by her on the wall of
her bedroom. Borges used the name in 'Death and the Compass', which he
dedicated to her.
 Lab. 117 (87) *Ficc.* 143

Molinari

A fictional name, its obvious Italian association pointing to immigrant
origin, used to suggest a feeling of animosity. It may also have a veiled
reference to the poet Ricardo Molinari, a friend of Borges from his youth.
 Brodie 74 (91) *Brodie* 77

'Mon siège est fait'

'My siege is done': the reply given by René Aubert (1655-1735), abbé of
Vertot, when he rejected fresh documentation on the siege of Rhodes
brought to him after he had completed his account of the event
(d'Alembert, *Reflexions sur l'Histoire*).
 Brodie 86 (104) *Brodie* 119

Monaco

A small independent state on the French Riviera, a haunt of the rich
famous for its casino, yachting clubs, fashion industry and festivals.
 Lab. 62 (36) *Ficc.* 45

Mongols (Mogoles)

A general term for an important Asiatic ethnic group. It probably derives
from *mong*, meaning 'brave': bravery, accompanied by ruthlessnesss, was
one of the chief qualities of the Mongols. Lab. 161: riding from the deserts

of north and central Asia, the Mongols spread through Asia into eastern Europe. By 1227, on the death of their ruler *Genghis Khan, their dominion extended from the banks of the Dnieper to the China Sea. The empire was then ruled by the great Kubla Khan and his successors, men of culture and taste who ruled China and fostered the growth of the arts and literature. The emperor Buyantu, for example, is renowned for rescuing inscriptions of the Chow dynasty and placing them at the gate of the temple of Confucius in Peking. Unable to consolidate its command over its conquered peoples, the Mongol empire disintegrated. By the seventeenth century the Chinese emperor invaded Mongolia and the power of some tribes decayed; others became subject to Russia.

Lab. 161 (129) *Aleph* 49

Montaner y Simón

Barcelona publishers of the *Hispano-American Encyclopaedia* in 16 volumes, a reliable, accessible and informative work intended for family use. Borges often quotes from it, usually half-mockingly, refuting its over-simple assertions with more complex ideas (*Disc.* 61, 98, 113).

Brodie 74 (91) *Brodie* 78

Montauban

An area in France east of 'the city called *Albert'.

Lab. 44 (19) *Ficc.* 97

Montevideo

The capital of *Uruguay, a port on the River Plate. In colonial times Montevideo suffered from increasing reliance on *Buenos Aires, which in Uruguay's struggle for independence proved her chief local rival. In the middle of the nineteenth century it was twice seized by the Argentine dictator Juan Manuel *Rosas. Borges's nostalgic memory of Montevideo recalls the city as quieter and more rooted in tradition than his native Buenos Aires.

Montoneros

Gaucho guerrilla fighters who, in the civil wars which followed Argentina's independence, supported their local *caudillo* against the centralising policy of the *porteño* (*Buenos Aires) army. The *montoneros* fought mainly in the interior provinces; their allegiance to their leader was personal and direct, and they were largely indifferent to his political leanings. During the 1970s the term was adopted by young left-wing urban guerrillas.

Aleph 56, *Brodie* 76, 103

Moore, George (1852-1933)

An Anglo-Irish writer, author of novels, plays and short stories. Moore was educated in France and 'found his English style in French'. Borges remembers jokingly that Moore 'pledged to find fourteen errors in any of the sonnets of *Baudelaire' (*Borges mem.* 124). Lab. 149 (118): the reference to Moore's 'artifices' is to his contorted syntax and startling juxtapositions. To create an unbroken narrative, Moore introduced such stylistic devices as the substitution of the present participle for the verb in finite form, so as to achieve a more flowing sentence; the repetition of certain words within the same paragraph, to cement together the various sentences; and the change from narrative to conversation without indentation or inverted commas. He also introduced striking anachronisms, as in *The Brook Kerith* (1916), where Jesus is presented as the son of a carpenter who does not die on the cross and with whose living presence St Paul is confronted when preaching about the crucifixion; or as in *Heloïse and Abelard* (1921), where a twelfth-century French context provides the background for characters who behave as they would in modern times.

Lab. 149 (118) *Aleph* 26

More geometrico

Latin for 'according to the methods of geometry'. Lab. 112 (82): Spinoza's work in two parts on *Descartes's *Principia* is subtitled *More Geometrico Demonstrata*; his *Ethica* is subtitled *Ordine Geometrico Demonstrata*.

Lab. 112 (82) *Ficc.* 151

Moreira, Juan (1819-1874)

One of the last famous *gauchos*, who became a legendary figure during his lifetime. Moreira was born of a Spanish Galician father and *criollo* mother and brought up in the province of *Buenos Aires, where he lived peacefully until, victimised by the police, he was forced to become an outlaw. A high price was put on his head and he was eventually shot by the police. Soon after his death his story was fictionalised by Eduardo *Gutiérrez and published in serial form (1879-80). Mingling fact and fiction, Gutiérrez sought to expose the injustices suffered by the *gauchos* at the hands of the authorities. Moreira is shown to have lived a peaceful life until the age of thirty in Matanza, when he was hounded by a corrupt and abusive social system. The wit and manly courage with which he fought back turned him into a popular romantic hero and symbol of rebellion. The novel was dramatised by José de *Podestá.

Brodie 27 (29) *Brodie* 30, Brodie 48 (57) *Brodie* 44

Moreno

A street in *Buenos Aires that runs from the district of *Almagro almost down to the port.

Brodie 29 (31) *Brodie* 33

Morocco (Marruecos)

Arabic for 'farthest west', Morocco was a sultanate in north-west Africa inhabited by Arabs, Berbers, Europeans and Jews. It was conquered by the Arabs in the seventh century and by the Almohads in the twelfth and thirteenth.

Lab. 182 (150) *Aleph* 93

Morón

A district to the west of Greater *Buenos Aires, the scene of the battle of *Caseros (1852) in which *Rosas was finally defeated.

Brodie 49 (58) *Brodie* 46, Brodie 52 (63) *Brodie* 15

Moses (Moisés) (c.1500-1200 BC)

A major biblical figure, who led the Jewish people out of slavery in Egypt to the Promised Land. According to the biblical account, Moses received from God the Jewish law, also known as the Torah, *Pentateuch or Five Books of Moses. This moral and legal code is considered the Covenant binding the Jewish people as a nation. Lab. 129 (99): Moses 'did not see God's face' either at Mount Sinai, when he received the Commandments and a cloud covered the mountain (Exodus 24:15), or when he entered the Tabernacle and God descended as a pillar of smoke. On this occasion he beseeched God to show him his glory but received the answer: 'Thou canst not see my face: for shall no man see me and live.' He was told to stand in a cleft in the rock and God covered him with his hand as he passed, saying: 'And I will take away mine hand, and thou shalt see my back parts: but my face shall not be seen' (Exodus 33:18 and 23). Lab. 102 (72): after leading his people through the wilderness Moses was prevented from entering the Promised Land, which he could only glimpse from the land of Moab. This was as punishment for his disobedience at Meribah when, commanded by God to speak to the rock so that it should produce water, he struck it twice in a moment of anger, thus compromising what was intended to be seen as a miracle by an unbelieving people (Numbers 20:7-12).

Lab. 102 (72) *Ficc.* 137, Lab. 129 (99) *Ficc.* 175

Mother of the Book (Madre del Libro) see *Koran

Muharram

The first month of the Islamic calendar. The tenth of Muharram commemorates the Battle of Karbala fought in Persia in 680 between the Shi'ites and the Sunnites on the issue of legitimate leadership of the Islamic community. It ends the ten-day mourning period in memory of the martyrdom of the Holy Family of the Shi'ite leader Imam Hussein, grandson of the prophet Mohammed through his daughter Fatima, and is a day of holy celebration.
Aleph 32 (46) *Ficc.* 36

Munster

The largest province in Ireland, which includes Clare, Cork, Limerick, Waterford and Tipperary. It was once an ancient kingdom whose name appears in the sagas of *Celtic mythology. Munster was active during the Irish Civil War. In 1921 a Council of Action and twelve 'soviets' were established there by members of the Communist party of Ireland.
Lab. 97 (68) *Ficc.* 131

Muraña, Juan

An old-time *guapo*, described by Borges as an obedient fighting machine, whose only distinguishing features were his lethal accuracy as a shot and a total lack of fear (*Ev. Carr.* 69). According to Borges, Muraña had no initiative and was utterly servile to his current paymaster. While he killed many men, he himself was so insignificant that Fate could be said to be acting through him. (For another version of Juan Muraña, see *Ev. Carr.* 150)
Brodie 66 (81) *Brodie* 65

Mutiny (Rebelión)

The Indian Mutiny, also known as the Sepoy Rebellion ('sepoy' being a Persian and Urdu term meaning soldier, used in most vernacular languages of *India). It was one of the most traumatic events in British colonial history. Begun in 1857 by Indian troops serving in the army of the British East India Company, it ended in 1859 after the relief of *Delhi. The episode has been subsequently popularised for patriotic purposes by supporters of the Indian National Movement. During the rebellion the *Sikhs remained loyal to the British and helped overcome the rebels.
Aleph 84 (132) *Aleph* 146

167

Mysore

A state of southern *India with a capital city of the same name.
   Lab. 195 (162) *Aleph* 111

NRF (Nouvelle Revue Française)

An influential French literary magazine founded in 1909 by a group of distinguished writers and actors. Its aim was to re-examine artistic and intellectual values in the light of recent literary movements. It published the work of a number of as yet unknown authors, such as Kafka and Gide, and introduced leading foreign writers. It ceased publication during World War I and again between 1943 and 1953. Lab. 64 (38): the January 1928 number of the *NRF* contained passages by *Valéry, Proust and other famous authors.
   Lab. 31 (7) *Ficc.* 19, Lab. 64 (38) *Ficc.* 64

Nabucodonosor (more commonly Nebuchadnezzar)

The name of three kings of *Babylon, the most famous being Nebuchadnezzar II (*c*.630-562 BC) who drove the Egyptians out of Asia and annexed Syria to Babylon. Apart from being a brilliant commander, Nebuchadnezzar II patronised the arts throughout his empire and made Babylon one of the 'wonders of the world'. Lab. 154 (122): the 'Nabucodonosors of Nitria' who 'grazed like oxen and their hair grew like an eagle's' is an allusion to the story of Nebuchadnezzar's second dream: of a tree reduced to a stump, presaging the divine punishment of his arrogance by madness. The quotation stems from Daniel 4:33 and tells of the fulfilment of the prophecy of the king's downfall: 'he was driven from men, and did eat grass as oxen, and his body was wet with the dew of the heaven, till his hair grew like eagles' feathers, and his nails like birds' claws.'
   Lab. 154 (122) *Aleph* 40

Nadir Shah (1688-1747)

A robber chieftain who rose to become ruler of *Persia in 1736. Lab. 189 (156): no direct information on the astrolabe has been found, though there may be a tenuous association with the legend that during his invasion of India Nadir Shah captured the Koh-i-noor diamond.
   Lab. 189 (156) *Aleph* 103

Namur

A Belgian city and province taken by the Germans in World War I on 25 August 1914. It was also the scene of fighting in World War II. See

*Zorndorf.
  Lab. 173 (141) *Aleph* 81

Ñancay

A tributary of the Uruguay river flowing in the rich agricultural lands of southern *Entre Ríos province.
  Aleph 66 (104) *Aleph* 71

Napoleon (1769-1821)

France's most famous general, who became Emperor. His military exploits extended French dominion over a large part of Europe, and his ideas were a source of inspiration to the liberation movements of Latin America. In the Romantic imagination Napoleon typified a new spirit of individual freedom and power such as could 'challenge the world and subdue it with his genius'. See *Raskolnikov.
  Lab. 93 (64) *Ficc.* 124

National Academy of History (Academia Nacional de la Historia)

A learned society, with membership by invitation only, founded in 1893 for the writing of Argentine history.
  Brodie 82 (101) *Brodie* 113

National Gallery (Salón Nacional)

The leading art gallery in *Buenos Aires, now the Museo de Bellas Artes.
  Brodie 37 (41) *Brodie* 97

National Library (Biblioteca Nacional)

The National Library is now situated in the old part of *Buenos Aires, in *Barrio Sur. It was founded as the Public Library on 7 September 1810, immediately after the declaration of Independence. The first Director was Paul Groussac, a French scholar much admired by Borges. Borges's appointment to the directorship in 1955 came at a time when his eyesight was failing, an event poignantly remembered in 'Poem of the Gifts' (Sel. Poems 129). The library houses three copies of every book published in Argentina, and any related work published abroad. Of its 650,000 volumes, Borges remarked: 'It's almost infinity, isn't it?' The building is an imposing edifice, but in almost total decay.
  Brodie 73 (90) *Brodie* 77

Naturalis Historia see **Historia Naturalis*

'Ne craignez point, Monsieur, la tortue' ('Sir, don't fear the tortoise')

From a letter written by *Leibniz in January 1692 to Simon Foucher (1644-1696), a philosopher who applied the Cartesian method of doubt in the quest for truth. The letter stresses the need to illustrate the working of all accepted 'axioms' to further the progress of science. In particular Leibniz asserts the axiom that 'nature does not make jumps', from which it follows that all matter is infinitely divisible. With regard to motion, Leibniz agrees with Foucher that all space is infinitely divisible and adds that infinitely divisible space exists in a time which is also infinitely divisible. In the *contest with the tortoise, *Achilles need not 'fear the tortoise': the total time (and total distance) necessary for Achilles to catch up with the tortoise can be expressed as the sum of an infinite geometric progression in which each term is smaller than the previous one. While the number of terms is infinite, because the terms become infinitely small, their sum is a finite quantity. At that point Achilles reaches, and begins to overtake, the tortoise. This provides a mathematical resolution of Zeno's famous paradox. The ideas expanded in this letter reflect Leibniz's earlier work on the infinitesimal calculus.

Lab. 64 (38) *Ficc*. 47

Nebuchadnezzar see *Nabucodonosor

Newton, Sir Isaac (1642-1727)

An English mathematician and philosopher, author of the *Principia* (1687). Newton's most important discoveries include the principle of universal gravitation and planetary motion, his original calculations being based on the invariable time of the moon's orbit. Lab. 53 (28): with regard to space and time, Newton held that both exist in absolute as 'containers of infinite extension and duration' in which people, objects and events have their position.

Lab. 53 (28) *Ficc*. 109

Nibelungs (Nibelungos)

In the Norse sagas and German legend, a race of dwarfs named after Nibelung, their king. They become the possessors of the golden treasure that brings about the downfall of their people and their gods. Borges wrote on the Song of the Nibelungs in *Lit. germ.*, 89-97. See *Fafnir.

Lab. 193 (160) *Aleph* 109, Aleph 80 (125) *Aleph* 134

Nicholson, John (1821-1857) see *Delhi

Nietzsche, Friedrich (1844-1900)

A German philosopher whose belief that absolute truth is a philosophical invention had a marked influence on Borges. Nietzsche's writings must be understood against the background of the extreme physical suffering he endured which led eventually to his insanity. His philosophy is neither systematic nor expounded in a systematic form, but can be seen as a collection of different points of view reflecting the growing disintegration of his mind. In *The Birth of Tragedy* (1872) he changed traditional perceptions of classical culture as expounded by *Goethe. He highlighted the irrational or Dionysian streak which, he maintained, had co-existed with the more restrained Apollonian element. In *Beyond Good and Evil* (1886) he developed the idea of the *Übermensch* ('overman') as the person who has organised the chaos of his passions, achieved a distinctive individuality and become creative. The term has been popularly misconceived: it was not intended in a Darwinian sense ('superman' is a bad translation), but as implying a desire to reach out beyond one's condition. Life for Nietzsche was not a wretched stuggle for existence but a positive and dynamic striving for power. He revolted against Christianity, which he came to see as an enfeebled religion of comfort, and he preached a new master morality, inciting the *Übermensch* to trample underfoot the servile herd of the weak. He cited the sprouting plant and the babe in the womb as evidence of this natural will to grow, declaring that creation necessarily involves destruction, since life is always at the expense of other life. Thus he saw pity in negative terms, as based on sentimental morality, admiring instead *Schopenhauer's ideas of courage and destruction in pursuit of the realisation of one's own self. He regarded suffering, cruelty, dissimulation and revenge as virtues which developed strength and integrity. Speaking of the *Übermensch*, he wrote: 'We must be hard against ourselves and overcome ourselves; we must become creators instead of remaining mere creatures.' He considered *Goethe the model of the *Übermensch*. Some of Nietzsche's coinage and epigrammatic sayings glorifying courage were taken out of context by the Nazis and used to support the ideology of the master-race. Lab. 69 (42) refers to this misreading of Nietzsche's conception of power in militaristic terms. See *Zarathustra.
    Lab. 69 (42) *Ficc.* 54, Lab. 174 (142) *Aleph* 82

Night of Nights (Noche de las Noches)

In Arabic, *Laylat al-Qadr*, 'night of density', 'night of majesty': a night towards the end of Ramadan, the month of fasting, believed to be a holy night in which the *Koran descended from heaven via the angel Gabriel.

171

On this night the gates of the heavens open, angels descend to bring greetings to mankind and all prayers are answered – even salt water is believed to become sweet: 'Better is the Night of Qadr than a thousand months' (Sura 97:3). Lab. 51 (25): the one night 'at the middle of' the *Thousand and One Nights* refers to 'the story of the king and his son and the damsel and the seven wezeers'. This, the framework story of a cluster of tales reflecting the original framework story of the entire book, concerns the skilful telling of tales to delay an execution. According to *Lane, it starts at Night 567, ending with part of Night 606, and tells of a king who was enraged with jealousy when his favourite concubine alleged that his son had tried to seduce her. He gave orders to his Wezeers to put his son to death, but they, fearing that he would afterwards repent and blame them for not having dissuaded him, tried to divert him from his purpose by relating numerous tales. A similar story is told by *Burton concerning a demon, or Ifrit, in Night 602. Borges alludes to this night of self-revelation when the king hears his own story related in one of *Scheherazade's tales as 'magic among nights', and speculates on the unlimited possibilities of such interpolated repetitions (see Other Inq. 45).

Lab. 31 (7) *Ficc.* 18, Lab. 51 (25) *Ficc.* 106

Nilotic (Nilótica)

The Nilotic *Sudan, an area along the Nile south of *Egypt approximately equivalent to ancient *Nubia. Aleph 73 (116): its inhabitants are east central African tribes forming a distinct ethnic and linguistic group.

Aleph 73 (116) *Aleph* 123

Nîmes

A French provincial town in the Gard, famous for its Roman antiquities. *Ficc.* 57: 'Nîmes, 1939': this reference at the end of the story to the place and date of its writing is part of the fiction. The story was written in *Buenos Aires in 1938, when Borges was recovering from a serious illness. The English version omits this point.

Lab. 63 (37) *Ficc.* 46

Nishapur

The most important of the four great cities in *Khurasan, one of the great towns of Iran in the Middle Ages. Nishapur was subject to many changes of ruler and to repeated attacks; the sack referred to in Aleph 36 was that of 1221 at the hands of the *Mongols under *Genghis Khan. The tomb of Omar Khayyam is located in the outskirts of the town. Nishapur is also the native town of the Persian poet *Farid al-Din Attar, author of *Parliament of Birds*.

Nitria

An ancient valley in Libya near the Nile delta where flourished the cult of Serapis to whom sheep were sacrificed. Lab. 154 (122): in the fourth century a Christian monastery was founded in Nitria by Amun (c.320). Its monks lived in clusters of windowless cells and practised extreme asceticism. In 399 Amun and three other monks, who became known as the Tall Brothers, left the monastery for *Alexandria to support the movement started by *Origen and from there proceeded to *Constantinople to defend his ideas.

Lab. 154 (122) *Aleph* 40

Nizam see *Hyderabad

'No need to look for a three-legged cat' ('No hay que buscarle tres pies al gato')

A popular Spanish saying meaning that one should not go looking for trouble. The more usual version is 'No need to look for *five* legs', but there are precedents for Borges's version, notably in *Don *Quixote* (pt.1, ch. 13 and pt.2, ch. 10).

Lab. 107 (77) *Ficc*. 144

No One (Nadie)

Lab. 149 (118): the reference to 'No One' as *Ulysses (Odysseus) stems from an episode in the **Odyssey* (book 9). Trapped in the cave of the Cyclops, who is eating his companions one by one, Ulysses offers the giant some wine and tells him that his name is 'No One'. When the Cyclops is in a drunken sleep, he blinds him. The next morning, after the prisoners have escaped, the Cyclops cries out to his companions that 'no one' has tricked him and put out his eye. They therefore leave him alone. Once safely back on his ship, Ulysses shouts his real name across the waters.

Lab. 149 (118) Aleph 25

Nordstjärnan

Lab. 165 (133): there is no reference, in copies of La *Prensa* of January 1922, to either a mail or cargo boat of that name sailing out of *Buenos Aires. Maritime trade between Argentina and Scandinavia, however, was not uncommon.

Lab. 165 (133) *Aleph* 61

'Not one but all things attributed by tradition to Judas Iscariot are false' ('No una cosa, todas las cosas que la tradición atribuye a Judas Iscariote son falsas')

A quotation from *De Quincey on *Judas Iscariot in *Speculative and Theological Essays* (1857). Lab. 126 (96): the argument of the essay is, in De Quincey's words, based on speculations 'first broached by German theologians and by Archbishop Whateley'. The text reads: 'Not one thing but all things must rank as false which traditionally we accept about him' (*Writings*, ed. David Mason, vol.8, 177). Judas believed that 'Christ contemplated a temporal kingdom' and the liberation of his people from the Roman authorities. Therefore it was important that Christ should be forced into action by an outsider and should commit himself without hesitation. According to De Quincey, Judas believed he was fulfilling his master's innermost purpose by denouncing him, thinking that Christ's arrest would arouse all the people of Jerusalem. The essay concludes with a disquisition on the death of Judas, of which we have two different reports, one in *Matthew and the other in the Acts of the Apostles, adding that the Church is left to explain the contradictions of this 'memorable domestic tragedy'.

Lab. 126 (96) *Ficc.* 170

Novalis (1772-1801)

The pseudonym of Friedrich von Hardenberg, a mystical German Romantic poet and novelist. In *Heinrich von Ofterdinger* (1802, posthumously) Novalis presents in terms of a medieval allegory the message that the true meaning of the world, the poet's 'blue flower', is to be sought within oneself. Lab. 65 (39): the *Fragmente* is a collection of aphorisms expressing the new Romantic theory. In number 2005 of the Dresden edition Novalis writes: 'I demonstrate that I have really understood a writer only when I am able to act in the spirit of his thoughts, and when I can translate his works and alter them in various ways without detracting from his individuality.' Lab. 66 (40): this belief in the essential presence of an author in his text contrasts with Pierre *Menard's claim to be able 'to reach the *Quixote*' through his own experience, thus dispensing with the original authorial voice.

Lab. 65 (39) *Ficc.* 49

Nubia

An ancient region in north-east Africa, extending from the Nile Valley to the Red Sea.

Aleph 80 (124) *Aleph* 133

'Oh God! I could be bounded in a nutshell...'

Hamlet's reply to Rosencrantz's suggestion that, if he found Denmark to be like a prison, it was because his ambitions made it too narrow for his mind (Act 2, scene ii).
Aleph 11 (15) *Aleph* 151

Ob

A long river that crosses Siberia.
Aleph 15 (19) *Aleph* 156

Ocampo, Silvina (1905-)

An Argentine writer, the sister of Victoria *Ocampo and the wife of *Bioy Casares, who was a friend and collaborator of Borges.
Lab. 71 (44) *Ficc.* 45

Ocampo, Victoria (1893-1979)

An Argentine writer, an eminent figure on the Latin American literary scene. Between 1931 and 1970 she was the editor of *Sur*, a literary review which published Aldous Huxley, D.H. Lawrence, Jean-Paul Sartre and Albert Camus, as well as her compatriots and contemporaries, including Borges. She published most of her own writings in *Testimonios*, a series which began in 1935. They are brief essays on various subjects approached with insight and a perception of the fantastic. Elegant and aristocratic, Ocampo was one of the first Latin American feminists, and fought to uphold the rights of women authors; her 'Letter to Virginia' documents her beliefs.
Lab. 54 (29) *Ficc.* 97

Ocean (Océano)

The name by which the Greeks referred to the waters of the Atlantic, believed to be a river surrounding the earth. Lab. 137 (107): the mountain which gave Ocean its name is Mount Atlas, which stood at the extremes of the earth and was later identified with the mountain range in north-west Africa that still bears the name. Atlas was the giant described by *Homer (*Odyssey* 1.52) on whose shoulders stood the columns separating Earth from Heaven.
Lab. 137 (107) *Aleph* 9

Odes (Odas) see Abraham *Cowley

Odyssey (Odisea)

*Homer's epic describing the adventures of *Ulysses (Odysseus), king of Ithaca, and his return after the Trojan war: in Borges's opinion, an archetypal story (see *El oro de los tigres*, 129). Lab. 142 (113): when after twenty years, having sailed across the seas pursued by *Poseidon, he finally reaches Ithaca, Ulysses is recognised only by his nurse and his faithful dog *Argos, whom he finds abandoned and neglected. He enrols the help of his son Telemachus to rid the palace of his wife's suitors, whom he kills, and re-establishes himself on the throne.

Lab. 142 (113) *Aleph* 18, Aleph 14 (18) *Aleph* 155, Aleph 35 (51) *Ficc.* 41

'Oh time thy pyramids' ('Oh tiempo tus pirámides')

An allusion to a line from Borges's poem, 'Del infierno y del cielo', in *El otro, el mismo* (*Obra Poética*, 140) referring to the Day of Judgment when time will cease.

Lab. 80 (53) *Ficc.* 88

Olavarría, José Valentín de (1801-1845)

An Argentine military leader who joined the *Army of the Andes and took part in the battles of the War of Independence, *Chacabuco, *Cancha Rayada and *Maipú. *Brodie* 72 (89): Olavarría later fought under the command of Sucre in the Peruvian campaign, so he may well have fought at *Arequipa and *Ayacucho. Brodie 73 (90): back in *Buenos Aires, Olivarría enrolled in the action against the empire of Brazil and was wounded in the battle of *Ituzaingó in 1827. A supporter of *Lavalle in the conflict against the *Federalists, he was persecuted by *Oribe and forced to flee to *Montevideo, where he joined Rivera's forces and died soon after. Many details of his life coincide with details of the life of the fictional Mariano *Rubio, with whom he is said to have exchanged swords. This was a romantic custom among generals, and Borges recalls that his own grandfather had exchanged swords with General Mansilla on the eve of a battle in the Paraguayan War (see 25 Agosto, 86).

Brodie 72 (89) *Brodie* 75

Old Town (Ciudad Vieja)

The old city of *Montevideo, now the city's business centre.

Aleph 61 (94) *Aleph* 28

'On the City Wall' see Rudyard *Kipling

176

Once, Square of the (Plaza Once)

One of the oldest squares in *Buenos Aires. Though associated in Borges's memory with horse-drawn carts, it later became a cosmopolitan market of shopkeepers and street vendors. Borges remembers meeting his friend the writer Macedonio Fernández in the Café La Perla on the square (Aleph 142 (227)).

Brodie 18 (18) *Brodie* 80, Brodie 76 (93) *Brodie* 132

Once de Septiembre, Calle

A leafy street in the more traditional part of the *Belgrano district of Buenos Aires, omitted in the English translation.

Aleph 156

Orbis Tertius

In 'Tlön, Uqbar, Orbis Tertius' the name given to a proposed encyclopaedia to be written in one of the languages of *Tlön, relating to an imaginary planet, or to what our planet will become under the influence of Tlön. The Latin name stands in marked contrast with the Nordic 'Tlön' and the Arabic 'Uqbar'. Explanation of it in terms of what we call the 'third world' seems unacceptably out of context; a more satisfying theory would be that it refers to a view in later *Gnosticism that an *orbis tertius* existed as an intermediary between the spiritual *orbis primus* and the inferior, or casual, *orbis alter*. The attempt to resolve the duality of *orbis primus* and *orbis alter* is reflected towards the end of the story of 'Tlön', where it is said that the penetration of our world with 'objects' from Tlön would eventually result in an 'Orbis Tertius'. Another explanation may be found in the Copernican heliocentric system, according to which Mercury and Venus are the first and second planets orbiting round the sun and Earth the third.

Lab. 27 (3) *Ficc.* 13

Oribe, Manuel (1792-1856)

A Uruguayan military and political leader, head of the *Blanco party. Oribe fought against the Spanish in the Wars of Independence, joined *Alvear's forces in the war against Brazilian invasion and fought at *Ituzaingó. When *Uruguay regained its independence, Oribe became Minister of War and the Navy under the presidency of Rivera. Aspiring to the presidency himself, he then sought the support of *Rosas, whose forces had been driven out of Uruguayan soil by Rivera. Brodie 73 (90): Oribe and Rosas counter-attacked in what became known as the *Guerra Grande, during which Oribe's Blancos besieged *Montevideo for eight years.

Oriental

The old-fashioned name of the inhabitants of *Uruguay, formerly known as *Banda Oriental.
Brodie 33

Origen (185-254)

An early Christian theologian, one of the greatest of the Christian teachers, initiator of a scientific system of criticism of the Old and New Testaments and author of *De Principiis*. In 202 Demetrius, bishop of Alexandria, appointed Origen to supervise the exegesis of the sacred scriptures in order to fight heretical doctrines; he became jealous of Origen's reputation and later broke with him, asking that he be removed from his position and banished from Alexandria. Among the accusations Demetrius made against Origen was that, as a young man, he had mutilated himself in order to escape the temptations of the flesh (Lab. 153-4). Origen tried unsuccessfully to vindicate his position in a letter to the bishop of Rome; his former friend Heraclas joined his enemies, thus securing his own succession as bishop on the death of Demetrius (an episode which seems consistent with the motif of rivalry in 'The Theologians'). Origen's faith is based on a metaphysical system inspired by Neoplatonic and *Gnostic ideas. Like the Neoplatonists, Origen held that the soul, existing before the body, contains traces of the divine; by rediscovering and following these traces it arrives at full participation in the divine nature. Matter, though created by God as the sphere in which souls are tested and purified, stands in opposition to the divine in a situation which verges on Gnostic dualism; God is the regulating immutable idea, and Christ, his word (or 'logos') from eternity, is the mediator within the dualistic opposition.
Lab. 151 (121) *Aleph* 37

Orphic (Órfico)

Pertaining to the sect which takes its name from the mythical Orpheus, whose activities are recorded as early as the sixth century BC. Their creed rested on the principle of an original sin from which the soul eventually achieves liberation after the course of multiple lives, through asceticism and purifying rites. Lab. 155 (123): *Demosthenes in the *De Corona* (330 BC) refers to Salazian or Bacchic rituals, whose routine was very similar to Orphic rituals. Purification with mud and other duties once performed by his rival Aeschines are mockingly described by Demosthenes (259): 'to clothe the catechumens...to wash their bodies, to scour them with the loam and the bran, and, when their lustration was performed...give out the hymn, "Here I leave my sins behind / Here the better way I find" ' making sure that 'no one ever emitted an ululation so powerful' as himself.

Lab. 155 (123) *Aleph* 41

Ortega y Gasset, José (1883-1955)

A Spanish essayist, philosopher and journalist who lived in Argentina during the Spanish Civil War. Ortega y Gasset expounded the basic principles of his philosophy of life in his early *Meditaciones del Quijote* (1914) and *El tema de nuestro tiempo* (1923). Best known, however, are *España invertebrada* (1921: trans. *Invertebrate Spain*, 1937) in which he denounces Spain's lack of eminent intellectuals, and *La deshumanización del arte* (1925), in which he holds that art should not aim at imitating life. Brodie 32 (36): though Ortega y Gasset is considered one of Spain's most brilliant stylists, Borges often made derogatory remarks about his style, which he considered artificial, rhetorical and full of hollow metaphors. Borges only slightly modified his tone upon Ortega's death, when he wrote that perhaps, one day, he would find his fame 'less mysterious'.

Brodie 32 (36) *Brodie* 91

Othello (Otelo) see *Tamberlik

Oudh (Udh)

A town in north India annexed by the British in 1856. One of the seven holy places of the Hindus, Oudh is mentioned in the epic poem *Ramayana* and is also identified with episodes in the life of Buddha.

Aleph 82 (130) *Aleph* 143

Ouro Preto

The Portuguese for 'black gold', a city in *Brazil south east of Central Minas Gerais in the Serra do Espinaco. Founded in 1700 during a short-lived gold rush, it later decayed and was preserved as a living museum of the eighteenth century.

Lab. 39 (14) *Ficc.* 29

Pactolus (Pactolo)

A river in Lydia (now Turkey), famous for the gold contained in its sands.

Lab. 136 (107) *Aleph* 9

Palanpur

A city in north Bombay state.
   Aleph 33 (47) *Ficc.* 38

Palermo

A district in *Buenos Aires, originally the Italian quarter, to which Borges makes frequent reference. His family moved there soon after his birth from central Tucumán Street, when Palermo was 'on the shabby northern outskirts of the town', inhabited by 'shabby-genteel people', like the Borges family, and by others of a less respectable kind.
   Brodie 74 (91) *Brodie* 77

Pampan (Pampa)

The language of the primitive, nomadic Indians who lived on the pampas at the time of the Conquest. In the seventeenth century the Pampan were overrun by the *Araucanian Indians, with whom they merged. Today they are referred to by both names.
   Lab. 162 (130) *Aleph* 51

Paradiso

The third Cantica of *Dante's *Divine Comedy* in which the glory of Heaven and all the blessed is described. See Pier *Damiani.
   Aleph 70 (109) *Aleph* 77

Paraná

An important river in the River Plate system, rising in the province of Minas Gerais in *Brazil, flowing south and eventually ending in the River Plate and the Atlantic. It forms boundaries between Brazil and Paraguay, and between the provinces of Misiones and Corrientes and Paraguay. *Buenos Aires, due to its strategic position at the mouth of the river's delta, has potential control of all navigation along the Paraná, a controversial issue between *Federalists and *Unitarians in the aftermath of Independence, and one of the causes of Argentina's war with Paraguay. The Paraná has been the frequent scene of naval battles.
   Aleph 55 (82) *Aleph* 54

Pardo

A village in the district of Las *Flores in the province of *Buenos Aires.
   Brodie 57 (68) *Brodie* 21

Paredes, Nicolas

The most powerful local *caudillo*, or strong man, of *Palermo towards the turn of the century. In a passage fixing the stereotype of the *guapo*, Borges describes Paredes as the typically showy *criollo* – macho, swaggering, insolent, ostentatious, provocative and infinitely self-assured (*Ev. Carr.* 43).
   Brodie 44 (53) *Brodie* 39

Parerga und Paralipomena

'Byproducts and Leftovers': the title given by *Schopenhauer to his two volumes of collected essays, fragments, treatises, aphorisms and reflections published in 1851. It established Schopenhauer's reputation. Lab. 37 (12): the three prime reasons determining the victory of idealist pantheism which are reflected in the first volume can be summarised as follows. All knowledge, being representation of the Will, is rooted in the subject, in all knowing subjects. By shifting our standpoint once and for all and starting from what is represented instead of what represents, we can arrive at an understanding of the inner nature of reality (the Will itself) which cancels all dangers of solipsism. In grasping by immediate intuition our own inner nature (as Will), we are at the same time grasping the inner nature of *all* phenomena, since the inner, noumenal nature of all things consists in the one, single, indivisible and eternal Will. The same process by which we arrive at the understanding of our own psychology is applicable to our knowledge of the inner reality of what is represented by all the natural sciences. Theology is not an intellectual discipline but the expression of a human desire: it springs 'from the heart, i.e. from the Will'. 'Because a prayer is offered, a God is hypostatised' and within this framework gods 'can and do help when they are served and worshipped'. Lab. 175 (143): on the question of man determining his own destiny, Schopenhauer maintains that, starting again from the standpoint that all life manifestations are representations of the Will which is 'the kernel and essence of man', whatever 'occult power that guides even eternal influences can ultimately have its roots only in our mysterious inner beings' and concludes that 'in the last resort the alpha and the omega of all existence lies within us' (trans. E.F.J. Payne, Oxford 1974, 212).
   Lab. 37 (12) *Ficc.* 26, Lab. 175 (143) *Aleph* 84

Paris

The capital of France, and her intellectual and artistic centre. *Porteños* have traditionally accepted Parisian influence and sought to emulate the city's culture. Though 'Death and the Compass' is ostensibly set in Paris, the city is not named and, as Borges states, the places mentioned are meant to indicate certain parts of *Buenos Aires ('Commentaries', Aleph 173 (268)).

Lab. 190 (157) *Aleph* 104

Parliament of Birds (Coloquio de los pájaros)

A famous poem, *Mantiq ut-Tair*, by the Persian *Farid Edin Attar, an allegory representing the slow and arduous journey of the Sufi mystic's soul towards its source and final destination: unification with and annihilation in God. The seven valleys, or seas, to be traversed in search of the *Simurgh, or God, are those of love, knowledge, detachment, unification, bewilderment and, finally, annihilation. The poem, consisting of 40,000 couplets, contains a number of independent stories, each reflecting the main allegory. Aleph 36 (52): *Burton refers to this influential poem in his 'Terminal Essay' as an example of Persian poetic imagination which made the spheres of art and fancy as real as the world of nature and fact. He talks of Sufism as 'a creed the most poetical and impractical, the most spiritual and the most transcendental ever invented', a point he illustrates by his own poetical resumé of the poem.

Aleph 35 (51) *Ficc.* 41

Parmenides (b. c.515 BC)

A Presocratic philosopher born in Elea in southern Italy who greatly influenced the thought of later philosophers such as *Plato and *Aristotle. Most of Parmenides' ideas are expressed in a didactic poem *On Nature* of which only 160 lines have survived. Lab. 120 (90): the essence of his philosophy lies in the concept that 'being' is unchangeable and immobile, and cannot increase, diminish or be divided, or, as Borges quotes, 'has never been nor will be because it is now' (*Etern.* 9) The multiplicity of things is pure appearance, resulting from 'the polarity of two opposites', light and dark, whose existence, we are warned, is also 'specious and nominal'. Parmenides' 'being' stands in opposition to the 'becoming' of *Heraclitus, who saw movement as the essence of reality, and to all other philosophies for which the plurality perceived by our senses reveals a true aspect of reality. Through his denial of the reality of time, plurality and motion, Parmenides may be considered the first Western metaphysician. See *Eleatic paradoxes.

Lab. 120 (90) *Ficc.* 162

Parnell, Charles Stewart (1846-1891)

A militant leader of the Irish Home Rule movement. Born into an Anglo-Irish Protestant family, Parnell became a Member of Parliament in 1875 and leader of the Home Rule Association a few years later. He encouraged filibustering, and his organisation of rent boycotting against unpopular landlords, together with his association with popular uprisings, led to his arrest in 1881. The resulting spate of violence persuaded the Prime Minister, Gladstone, to release him the following year. Parnell supported Gladstone's unsuccessful Home Rule Bill in 1886. Lab. 97 (68): in 1889 Captain O'Shea, who had been Parnell's ally and a moderate supporter of the Home Rule campaign, filed a divorce petition against him for adultery with his wife Kitty. The subsequent scandal ruined Parnell's influence in politics. Irish opinion was split, and the Catholic clergy finally rejected him and declared him unfit to lead. Parnell continued his revolutionary campaign, but his appeal found a response only with the younger generation. See *Ireland, *Yeats.

Lab. 97 (68) *Ficc.* 131

Parsis (or Parsees)

Descendants of the *Zoroastrians who fled Persia to India in the seventh century to escape Muslim persecution. They still retain their religion.

Aleph 32 (47) *Ficc.* 37

Paseo de Julio

The former name of the northern section of today's Avenida L.N. Alem, a street in *Buenos Aires running parallel with the river. It used to be crowded with *conventillos* (slum dwellings) and houses of ill repute.

Lab. 166 (134) *Aleph* 62

Paso del Molino

A lower-to-middle-class residential district outside *Montevideo. In his youth Borges used to visit some cousins who lived there.

Aleph 28

'Past, The' see Ralph Waldo *Emerson

Patna

The name of the ship in Conrad's novel *Lord Jim*. See José *Korzeniovski.

Lab. 147 (116) *Aleph* 23

Patrology (Patrología) see Jacques Paul *Migne

Paul et Virginie (Pablo y Virginia)

An popular novel by Bernardin de St Pierre, published in 1787, the romantic tale of the pure love of Paul and Virginie, childhood sweethearts living in Mauritius, who become separated when Virginie is forced to travel to her native France. Eventually she returns to be reunited with her lover, but her ship is wrecked by a hurricane within a short distance of the shore. Had she consented to take off her clothes she might have swum to safety, but her modesty was such that she refused and perished. Paul, grief-stricken, follows her to his death.

Fict. 156 (172) *Ficc.* 193

Paul, St (Pablo) (*c*.5-10 – *c*.67)

The most important figure in the early history of the Church, whose theological principles were set out in his Epistles. Lab. 152 (121): while in Jerusalem to complete his education, Saul (as he was originally named) came across the followers of Jesus, whom he attacked and persecuted. He witnessed the martyrdom of *Stephen, though he did not participate in it, merely guarding the cloaks of those who were stoning him. Lab. 130 (99): while Saul was on the road to *Damascus on a mission to arrest some Christians, he was blinded, and converted, by a light 'from heaven' that shone 'round about him' (Acts 9:1-19, 22:5-16, 26:12-18). Paul died, a martyr, in Rome. See *Corinthians.

Lab. 128 (97) *Ficc.* 172, Lab. 152 (121) *Aleph* 37

Paul the Deacon (Pablo el Diácono) (725-799)

A Latin historian born of an aristocratic *Lombard family, the teacher and friend of one of the daughters of King Desiderius. At the close of the Lombard reign in Italy, Paul led the cultural revival initiated by Charlemagne. His most important work is his *History of the Lombards*, based on both oral and written sources, a valuable document of the life and culture of his people containing a number of curious anecdotes which create a vivid picture of the time. See *'Terribili visu facies...'

Lab. 159 (127) *Aleph* 47

Pavilion of the Limpid Solitude (Pabellón de la Límpida Soledad)

No specific record has been found of a Chinese pavilion of this name. In Chinese domestic architecture pavilions were traditional accessories to the main house, whither learned and wealthy Chinese commonly retired to write poetry. In choosing the name, Borges keeps within traditional terminology; the imperial palace in Peking, for example, includes the halls of 'Supreme Harmony', 'Heavenly Purity', 'Earthly Tranquillity', etc.

Pavón

A battle fought in the plain of Santa Fe, Argentina, on 17 September 1861 between the Confederate Nationalist forces under *Urquiza and the successful *porteño* army of *Buenos Aires led by Mitre. The issue was the reluctance of Buenos Aires to join the Confederation of Provinces as the nation's capital. Though not defeated, Urquiza withdrew, and Mitre's moral victory enabled him to negotiate between the people of Buenos Aires and the Confederation and organise a new national government.
Brodie 73 (90) *Brodie* 77

Paysandú

A department in north-west *Uruguay formed in 1837, bordering *Río Negro and containing the former territories of Salto and *Tacuarembó. The city of Paysandú is the second largest in Uruguay.
Lab. 132 (102) *Ficc.* 182, Aleph 66 (103) *Aleph* 71

Pennsylvania see *Pittsburg

Pentateuch (Pentateuco)

The first five books of the bible, considered by fundamentalist Jews to have been written in their entirety by *Moses under divine inspiration. Lab. 107 (77): with regard to the 'divine nomenclature', there are many biblical names which refer to different actions and attributes of God. In the Pentateuch the best-known passages are Exodus 3:13-15 and 6:2-3. In speculative *Cabbalistic literature, however, there is a common belief concerning different levels of esotericism which holds that every permutation of letters can be a name of God, so that ultimately the whole of the Pentateuch can be reduced to names of God. This idea is formulated in Lab. 85 (57): 'No one can articulate a syllable which is not...the powerful name of a god.'
Lab. 107 (77) *Ficc.* 145

Pergamino

A small river in the province of *Buenos Aires; also a city and a borough of the same name.
Aleph 55 (83) *Aleph* 53, Brodie 64 (77) *Brodie* 59

Pergamum (Pérgamo)

A city of Asia Minor fifty miles north of *Smyrna and fifteen miles inland. One of the most beautiful of Greek cities in the Hellenistic period, its library was second only to that of *Alexandria. In 130 BC Pergamum passed to Rome; its people were early converts to Christianity. Lab. 152 (121): no record is known of a Council held in Pergamum.

    Lab. 152 (121) *Aleph* 38

Persia

Present-day Iran, a country in south-west Asia. Borges's attraction for Persian literature can be judged from his frequent allusions to classical Persian poets such as *Farid Attar and Omar Khayyam, as well as to the *Thousand and One Nights*. Aleph 189 (156): Persia flourished under the reign of *Nadir Shah.

    Lab. 189 (156) *Aleph* 103

Persian Mystic: Attar see **Margaret *Smith**

Persiles and Sigismunda (Persiles y Sigismunda, Los trabajos de)

The title of *Cervantes's last novel published in 1617 and announced in the preface to part 2 of *Don *Quixote* as being 'either the worst or the best book written in our tongue'. Though full of amazing adventures, the work lacks the freshness and appeal of Cervantes's previous books; after the first eight editions public interest in it dwindled. Lab. 67 (41): the 'undoubtedly laborious tribulations' may refer to the vicissitudes suffered by this unpopular novel, or even to the effort of reading it, but is more probably an allusion to the full title in the original.

    Lab. 67 (41) *Ficc.* 52

Peruvian War

A campaign of *San Martín's across the Andes and his naval expedition to Peru in 1821.

    Aleph 55 (81) *Aleph* 53

Pharos

An island opposite Alexandria whose lighthouse was one of the seven wonders of the world. See *Proteus.

    Lab. 192 (159) *Aleph* 107

Philip the Second (Felipe Segundo) (1527-1598)

A king of Spain, son of the Emperor Charles V and Isabel of Portugal, who married in 1554 as his second wife Mary Tudor, Queen of England. Philip II dedicated his rule to unifying the Iberian peninsula and furthering the Spanish conquest of America. His religious fervour, which caused him to reactivate the Inquisition, affected the culture and art of Spain; a strong mystical note is evident both in the literature and the plastic arts of the time. Philip II conducted a successful campaign against the Turks, who were defeated by his younger brother Don John of Austria at *Lepanto in 1571. His policies in Europe, and in particular in the Low Countries in revolt against Spanish rule, brought him into conflict with Queen Elizabeth. In 1588 his Armada was defeated by the English navy.
    Lab. 68 (42) *Ficc.* 53

Philippics (Filípica) see *Theopompus

Philologus Hebraeo-Graecus see Johann *Leusden

Philosophie des Als Ob

From the German *als ob* meaning 'as if': a philosophy which, starting from the postulate that reality is not knowable, holds that pragmatically justifiable theories and systems are equally valid. The theory was formulated by the idealist positivist Ernst Vaihinger (1852-1933) in *Die Philosophie des Als Ob* (1911).
    Lab. 34 (10) *Ficc.* 23

Phoenix (Fénix)

A mythical bird of red and gold plumage worshipped in ancient Egypt, a symbol of immortality associated with the cult of the sun. The phoenix lived for 500 years and then burned its own nest; a new phoenix emerged from the flames and took the ashes of its dead father to *Heliopolis (Herodotus 2.73). The burning phoenix became a Christian allegory of the resurrection of the body and the eternal life of the soul. The phoenix also appears in the mythologies of *Islam and in the sacred books of China. In Imaginary Beings Borges devotes two entries to this fantastic bird (p.45, on the Chinese Phoenix, and p. 117). In the second he quotes from *Herodotus' account and from *Tacitus, who speculates on 'the intervals of the phoenix's visits' (*Annals* 6.28). He also refers to a myth recalled by *Pliny (10.2) according to which the phoenix lives a whole Platonic year, after which the history of the world repeats itself. From this, Borges adds, it was concluded in antiquity that the phoenix is 'a mirror or an image of

this process'.
   Lab. 131 (101) *Ficc*. 183

Phrygia (Frigia)

A country in western and central Asia Minor subject in turn to the Lydians, Persians, Seleucids and Attalids. In 116 BC most of Phrygia was absorbed into the Roman province of Asia, and in 25 BC the remaining eastern part was included in the province of Galatia.
   Lab. 153 *Aleph* 40

Pilar

The Basílica del Pilar, one of the finest churches in *Buenos Aires, in the vicinity of the Recoleta Cemetery. It was built by the Jesuits in 1732.
   Lab. 193 (160) *Aleph* 108, Brodie 35 (39) *Brodie* 94

Pious (Piadosos)

The Sect of the Pious, another name for the *Hasidim.
   Lab. 108 (78) *Ficc*. 146

Pittsburg

A prosperous industrial city in Pennsylvania. Pittsburgh is associated with some of the wealthiest and most powerful families in America, such as the Carnegies and Mellons (steel and power generation), the Fricks (stockholdings) and Heinzs (food-canning).
   Lab. 62 (36) *Ficc*. 45

Plato (Platón) (427-347 BC)

An Athenian philosopher, the disciple of Socrates whose teachings he expanded in his early dialogues, illustrating Socrates' inductive system which aims at knowledge through a process of dialectic. Lab. 59 (34), 183 (151): the *celestial archetype, or Platonic model, refers to the 'forms' of which, as Plato states in the *Republic*, the world is the manifold reflection. Thus we perceive the world in its multiplicity through our senses, while we conceive of the existence of the 'forms' by abstracting the essential from the many manifestations of the one archetype. The forms, however, are not just concepts of our minds but exist independently of their physical representation in a hierarchical system of which the idea of God is supreme. Awareness of their existence (absolute knowledge) is seen in contrast with the perception of each particular appearance, derived from our sensory experience. Lab. 178 (146): Borges comments on Coleridge's statement that all men are divided between Platonists and

Aristotelians in these terms: that the former see reality as manifestation of a cosmic order, while the latter, for whom reality consists of each individual experience, know that that order could be a 'fiction of our partial knowledge'. This distinction is fundamental for Borges, in so far as it indicates two totally opposed attitudes to life which are reflected in all antagonistic situations. Carrying Coleridge's distinction into the world of language, Borges concludes that, while for the Aristotelians language is only a system of arbitrary symbols, for the Platonists it remains the symbol of cosmic order, 'the map of the universe' (Other Inq. 156). Lab. 102: with reference to the 'Platonic year', the allusion to the cyclical return of events which appears in *Yeats's collection The *Tower is derived in particular from the 39th paragraph of Plato's dialogue Timaeus. There he refers to the eight circuits marked by the revolutions of the heavenly bodies and explains how it is by them that we measure time. He then adds that 'the complete year' (which Plato computed to correspond to 36,000 years) 'will be fulfilled' when all the planets will 'finish together', having returned 'to their starting point'. In his essay 'Circular Time' Borges explains how this passage led many to assume that Plato envisaged the principle of recurring history, mentioning among these Thomas *Browne, who in his Religio Medici used the term 'Plato's year' with this meaning (Etern. 92). See *Aristotle, *Politicus.

Lab. 59 (34) Ficc. 73, Lab. 102 (72) Ficc. 137, Lab. 150 (119) Aleph 35, Fict. 68 (75) Ficc. 79, Lab. 178 (146) Aleph 88, Lab. 183 (151) Aleph 95

Plaza del Parque and the Portones

The old colonial square of *Palermo, now known as Tribunales, the site of the law courts. The tramway station, called Portones because of its tall doorways, was originally situated there and gave its name to the square.

Brodie 76 (92) Brodie 80

Pliny the Elder (Plinio) (23-79 AD)

A Roman writer, author of the 37 volumes of *Historia Naturalis, a source of information on every branch of natural sciences known to the ancient world. Pliny was exceptionally industrious and wide-ranging in his interests and wrote also on grammar, military strategy and Roman history. His scientific zeal was the indirect cause of his death for, in order to observe closely the eruption of Vesuvius, he set sail towards it and lingered too long and too near the volcano. For Pliny's dragons, see *Historia Naturalis.

Lab. 89 (61) Ficc. 120, Lab. 149 Aleph 26, Lab. 152 Aleph 38

Plotinus (Plotinio) (c.205-270 AD)

A mystic philosopher, born in Egypt, who studied in *Alexandria and taught in Rome. Plotinus developed Plato's teachings and became the chief exponent of Neoplatonism. His writings were posthumously edited by his disciple Porphyry into six 'groups of nine', or *Enneads*. According to Plotinus all forms of existence derive from the One and all strive ultimately to return to their original source and remain there. The divinity is a graded triad, its three hypostases being the One, the eternal source of all being; the Nous, the divine intellectual principle, mind or thought; and the Psyche, or All-Soul, the first and only principle of life and the cause of the existence of the cosmos. Matter lies at the periphery of the cosmos, and is conceived by Plotinus as a set of increasingly fragmented reflections proceeding from the One, to Nous and to the All-Soul, fading out into blank matter. Aleph 36 (52): the passage mentioned derives from the section 'On Intelletual Beauty' in *Enneads*. According to Plotinus, the idea of beauty is one and perfect, all lesser beauties being a reflection of the splendour of the one supreme beauty. In this passage (5.8.4) Plotinus describes a vision of perfect unity in which everything is motionless and whole and part of everything else.

Aleph 36 (52) *Ficc*. 42

Plutarch (Plutarco) (*c*.46-*c*.120)

A prolific Greek biographer from Chaeronea, in Boeotia, whose *Parallel Lives* of Greeks and Romans (of which 23 pairs and 4 single lives survive) and *Moralia*, a varied collection of ethical, religious, physical, political and literary studies, made him the most influential Greek writer in the Renaissance. Lab. 157 (126) alludes to Plutarch's description of Caesar's reaction to the news that *Pompey had been murdered on the orders of the King of Egypt: 'From the man who brought him Pompey's head he turned away with loathing as from an assassin; and on receiving Pompey's seal ring, he burst into tears' (*Life of Pompey* 8). Lab. 151 (120): the dialogue *On the Obsolescence of Oracles* (*Moralia* 29) discusses the reasons why the advice and prophecies of the Greek gods were no longer to be heard in his day in the traditional places where oracles used to be consulted. Plutarch suggests that this is the result of Roman rule and the effect of the Romans' practical mentality on the Greeks' awareness of the metaphysical. The dialogue also discusses the possibility that more than one world exists. Plutarch, however, refutes the Stoic hypothesis that these worlds are supervised by several Zeuses, on the grounds that 'it is preposterous that there should be many supreme gods bearing one name' or 'an infinite number of suns, moons, Apollos, Artemises and Poseidons in the infinite cycle of worlds'. Gods, Plutarch continues, though born with the world and ending with it, are not tied to its physical nature like statues fixed to a pedestal; not participating in this nature, they are totally incorruptible and free from all limitations.

Lab. 151 (120) *Aleph* 36

Pluto (Plutón)

In classical mythology, the god who reigned in the underworld (Hades), a symbol of darkness and death.
Lab. 148 (118) *Aleph* 25

Podestá

A well-known family of circus actors who took part in the performances of *Juan Moreira*. Their leader was José (or Pepe) Podestá (b.1858), a clown and trapeze artist who first achieved renown with his creation of the clown 'Peppino el 88', a didactic comic figure who criticised many aspects of *porteño* social and political life in the 1880s. In 1884 Pepe Podestá played the part of Juan *Moreira in a pantomime version of the story, with other members of his family. Two years later he added extracts from the novel to his performance. Its success inaugurated a whole series of imitative plays, to which the Argentine theatre traces its origins. Other more immediate consequences were the audience's identification with, and angry reaction to, the unfortunate *gaucho*'s oppression. Brodie 64 (76): the reference is omitted in the English translation.
Brodie 59

Podolsk

A region of south-east Poland which passed to Russia in 1793. A heavy concentration of Jews lived in Podolsk, which became the centre of many important events in Jewish history. During the sixteenth century a spread of *Cabbalistic teachings prepared the ground for the rise of the false Messianic movement of Shabbethai Zvi. In the eighteenth century Podolsk became the cradle of *Hasidism, whose founder, *Baal Shem Tov, was born and lived there. Owing to centuries of poverty and persecution, it became a breeding ground for superstition and religious intolerance, which are said to have been more rife in Podolsk than in any other place within the Jewish Pale of Settlement.
Lab. 106 (76) *Ficc.* 143

Poe, Edgar Allan (1809-1849)

An American writer of poetry, literary criticism and fantastic tales, credited as the originator of the detective story; his character C. Auguste *Dupin inspired many writers of detective fiction, Borges among them. Lab. 67 (40): the phrase 'Poe, who engendered Baudelaire' refers to the French Symbolists' acknowledgment of Poe as their master for his insight into the hidden regions of the mind, his fusion of the senses and his rhythmical verse. Yet it was Baudelaire's masterly translation of Poe that transfigured the original and gave Poe an authority and directness to

191

which it never pretended in the original (see R.P. Blackmur's Afterword to *The Fall of the House of Usher*, NY 1960, 380). Aleph 74 (116): a well-known detective story by Poe, 'The Purloined Letter', the second of Dupin's stories, is a masterly tale of courtly intrigue, concealment and revenge. Dupin, by working out the mentality and reasoning of the culprit, deduces that the stolen letter has been left in full view, finds it and steals it back.

Lab. 67 (40) *Ficc.* 51, Aleph 74 (116) *Aleph* 124

Poem of the Cid (Poema del Cid)

An anonymous epic poem, regarded as the greatest literary masterpiece of Castile. Written *c*.1140, it is the earliest surviving poem of the Iberian peninsula. It narrates the exploits of Rodrigo Díaz de Vivar, the partly historical and partly legendary knight known as El Cid, meaning 'lord', and his love for his wife Ximena. El Cid fought for the Castilian king Alfonso VI, but on being wrongly accused and banished he became a soldier of fortune, fighting sometimes for the Christians and sometimes for the Moors. Though idealised, El Cid is basically an ordinary man, with greater spirit and courage but without the missionary zeal or crusader's ideology of his French counterpart in the *Chanson de Roland*. El Cid fights for *averes*, land and money, which were to be won, within an accepted code of honour, by fighting. The firm characterisation and the dramatic narrative, probably intended for oral performance, recaptures the life of a man who has inspired generations of Spaniards and remained Spain's favourite hero. Lab. 145 (114): the term 'rustic' probably refers to the subject matter of the poem: a frontier society, sober and dry like its habitat, the Castilian plateau, reflected in a terse style which conveys excitement without undue recourse to poetic ornament or dramatic intensity.

Lab. 145 (114) *Aleph* 20

Poesia, La see Benedetto *Croce

Poetics (Poética)

An influential book by *Aristotle on the art and functions of poetry. Lab. 181 (149): the words 'tragedy' and 'comedy', which baffled *Averroes, first appear in chapter 1 in a discussion of the media of poetic imitation. Aristotle states that tragedy and comedy use all the media – rhythm, music and formal metre. The difference between them is discussed in chapter 2, where comedy is said 'to aim at representing men as worse than they are nowadays, tragedy as better'. Aristotle's famous discussion of tragedy as a form of imitation is begun in chapter 6. See *Rhetoric*.

Lab. 181 (149) *Aleph* 92

Poitiers

A university city in west central France, important in French history from the Middle Ages to the sixteenth century. Joan of Arc was interrogated there in 1429.

Lab. 40 (16) *Ficc*. 31

Poland (Polonia)

An autonomous kingdom formed in 1815 from Polish territory previously absorbed by Russia. Owing to its geographical position, Poland has been frequently invaded and its political borders successively altered.

Lab. 102 (72) *Ficc*. 137

Politician see *Politicus

Politicus (Político)

One of *Plato's later dialogues, commonly called the *Statesman*, in which 'Young Socrates' discusses with a stranger from the *Eleatic school the nature and function of the statesman. The stranger compares the present age of Zeus with the mythical age of Kronos when God took charge of the universe and the creatures living in it. There was no labour, the land spontaneously yielded its products, men were born from the earth fully grown and gradually returned to infancy, when they disappeared again into the earth, to give rise to a new generation of mature beings. But in the age of Zeus, taking no heed of divine guidance we head towards disruption. Fict. 68 (75): the interlocutor referred to is the 'Eleatic Stranger' who alludes to the different legends of the backward revolution of the cosmos, such as that of the sun rising in the west and setting in the east, or those related to the age of Kronos. All these legends derive from a 'common origin' and illustrate the 'regressive' direction that statesmanship should take. For, if there was a time when God guided the world, the world, when left to itself, must 'by an inherent necessity' turn back to the source from which it received its original 'intelligence' (*Politicus* 268e-274e).

Fict. 68 (75) *Ficc*. 79

Polyolbion see Michael *Drayton

Pompey (Pompeyo) (106-48 BC)

A Roman general and statesman who in 60 BC joined *Julius Caesar and Crassus in the First Triumvirate. During Caesar's subsequent absence in Gaul, Pompey's senatorial influence grew. In 49 Caesar returned from

Gaul and the following year defeated Pompey at the battle of Pharsalus. Pompey was pursued by Caesar into *Egypt where the Emperor Ptolemy XIV, in whose hospitality he had trusted, had him murdered in the hope of winning Caesar's favour. See *Plutarch.

Lab. 157 (126) *Aleph* 44

Pope, Alexander (1688-1744)

An English poet and satirist. In 1711 Pope published his *Essay on Criticism*, an epigrammatic *tour de force* aimed at reproducing the style and paraphrasing the themes of Roman satire. *The Rape of the Lock*, a mock epic published in 1712, was also written on classical lines. The *Essay on Man* (1733-4), a work of vast scope, deals with the relation of man, nature and society. Lab. 135: Pope's most daring achievement was to translate the *Iliad* (1720) and the *Odyssey* (1725-6). These translations, though at times distant from the originals, aimed at reproducing their effects in the context of Pope's time. Pope was severely criticised. In his essay on the translators of *Homer, comparing different translations of the same passages, Borges praises Pope's version for the richness and spectacular quality of his language. As for 'accuracy', Borges considers that since the original meaning and intention of the author are irrecoverable, because there is no 'definitive text', to judge the quality of a translation by its 'faithfulness' is a futile task (*Disc.* 105 ff). Lab. 147 (116): before final publication, Pope's translation of the *Iliad* was delivered to subscribers in instalments.

Lab. 135 (105) *Aleph* 7

Porch (Pórtico)

An allusion to Stoicism, the school of philosophy founded by Zeno of Citium (*c.*300 BC), so called because Zeno taught in the porch (*stoa*) of Athens.

Lab. 192 (1159) *Aleph* 107

Poseidon

The Greek name (in Latin Neptune) for the god of the sea, originally the god of earthquakes and water. Poseidon was the son of Kronos, the brother of Zeus and after him, with *Pluto, the most important of the gods.

Lab. 151 (120) *Aleph* 36

'Pour encourager les autres'

A quotation from chapter 23 of Voltaire's *Candide* (1759), referring to the execution of Admiral Byng for failing to relieve Minorca. The complete sentence reads: 'In this country (England) it is good to kill an admiral from time to time to encourage the others.'

Lab. 119 (89) *Ficc*. 160

Prague (Praga)

The capital of Czechoslovakia, a city renowned for its architectural beauty which was virtually wiped out in World War II. Prague's Jewish community is one of the oldest in Europe. Jews played a prominent part in the cultural life of the city from the nineteenth century onwards, many, such as Franz Kafka, Max Brod and Franz Werfel, achieving international acclaim. Relations between Jews and non-Jews were relaxed, and Jewish topics and legends often appeared in the work of non-Jewish authors (see *Meyrink's novel *The Golem*). Lab. 118 (88): all this changed radically when *Hitler marched into Prague on 15 March 1939, setting into motion his plan for the elimination of the Jews: later that year the so-called Central Office for Jewish Emigration was established under the directorship of Adolf Eichmann. Brodie 88 (106): the few Jews who managed to escape went mainly to USA and Argentina.

Lab. 118 (88) *Ficc*. 159, Lab. 131 (101) *Ficc*. 182, Brodie 88 (106) *Brodie* 121

Prensa, La

One of Argentina's leading daily newspapers, founded in the late nineteenth century.

Lab. 165 (133) *Aleph* 61

Prince of Wits (Príncipe de los Ingenios)

An epithet of Cervantes. Aleph 15: in the prologue to *Don *Quixote* Cervantes ridicules the fashion for prefacing books with sonnets and epigrams by famous names and annotating them with Latin quotations and learned glosses.

Aleph 15 (21) *Aleph* 158

Pringles, Juan Pascual (1795-1831)

An Argentine military leader who fought for independence in the army of *San Martín, was present at the occupation of Lima and was decorated for bravery at the battle of *Ayacucho. In 1827 Pringles fought in the war against the imperial army of *Brazil, and later served the *Unitarian cause under General Paz, fighting against Facundo *Quiroga. On 17 March 1831, at Rio Quinto, Pringles's forces were defeated by Quiroga. Rather than surrender his sword to the enemy he broke it and threw himself into the river. Brodie 32 (36): of the many portraits of Pringles the best known is that by Antonio Contucci (1876), exhibited in his native city of San Luis.

Brodie 32 (36) *Brodie* 91

Procrustean (Procrusto)

'Appertaining to Procrustes.' In Greek mythology Procrustes had two iron beds of different sizes on which he forced strangers to lie. Those who were too short he hammered out and those who were too long he lopped. Lab. 151 (120): a procrustean argument is one unfairly cut to size to fit the point it aims to prove. Aleph 22 (29): the publishers 'Procrustes & Co.' is a black joke.

Lab. 151 (120) *Aleph* 36, Aleph 22 (29) *Aleph* 167

Prometheus (Prometeo)

'The forethinker': in Greek mythology a Titan who brought fire back to earth when Zeus had hidden it away. Lab. 151 (120): for this, or another offence, Zeus chained Prometheus to a rock and set an eagle to devour his liver. As he was immortal, his liver was renewed each night. Eventually he was rescued by Hercules.

Lab. 151 (120) *Aleph* 36

Proteans (Protéicos) see *Proteus

Protector

A title given to *San Martín.

Proteus

In Greek mythology a prophetic sea god, the son of Oceanus and Tethys, who had the power of assuming any shape he wished in order to avoid capture. Lab. 192 (159): *Homer describes Proteus as living in a cave near the island of Pharos: 'He will seek to foil you by taking the shape of every creature that moves on earth, and of water and of portentous fire; but you must hold him unflinchingly and you must press the harder' (*Odyssey* 4.417-20). Because he could assume whatever shape he pleased, Proteus was regarded as typical of the ever-changing aspect of the sea and, in the Orphic tradition, as the original matter from which the world was created. Lab. 155 (124): 'protean' means having the ability to assume all kinds of appearances. Lab. 148 (117): when *Ulysses and his men manage to capture Proteus, they are told by him that they must sail back to the waters of the Nile and make propitiatory sacrifices to the gods. At this point Proteus uses the name *Egypt for the river Nile (*Odyssey* 4.355-8).

Lab. 148 (117) *Alèph* 24, Lab. 155 (124) *Aleph* 41, Lab. 192 (159) *Aleph* 107

Provincial Museum (Museo Provincial)

Probably the museum of the city of San Luis.
  Brodie 32 (37) *Brodie* 91

Punjab

Sanskrit for 'five rivers': a region in north-west India, west of what is now Pakistan. It was annexed to India by the British in 1849, after the two Anglo-Sikh wars. Though the *Sikhs became dominant in the Punjab at the beginning of the nineteenth century, a long history of conflict among Sikhs, Muslims and Hindus has torn the nation apart. In 1947, when the independent states of India and Pakistan were formed, the Punjab was divided into West Punjab, a Pakistani province with a Muslim majority, and East Punjab, a province of *India with a non-Muslim population. Aleph 86 (135): the English 'men and women from all the corners of the Punjab...' does not perhaps convey the composite character of the people of this nation as given by the original: 'una turba de hombres y mujeres de todas las naciones del Punjab...'
  Aleph 86 (135) *Aleph* 149

Pyrrhus (Pirro)

The mythical son of *Achilles and Deidamia, also known as Neoptolemus. See *Pythagoras.
  Lab. 55 (30) *Ficc.* 67

Pythagoras (Pitágoras) (sixth century BC)

A Greek philosopher whose ideas influenced much of Western thought. Pythagoras believed that nature rested on mathematical principles and was explainable in terms of numbers and their relations. He spoke of the connection between numbers and music, anticipating the concept of 'harmonic progression' in mathematics, and he also envisaged numbers in terms of shapes. The number ten was for him the essence of the numerical system, and its representation as the sum of the first four integers became a sacred figure. There are strong links between the Pythagorean intuition of reality and later *Cabbalistic cosmological theories (see *Cabbala). Lab. 55 (30), 155 (123): Pythagoras believed that the soul was immortal and transmigrated at death to another form of living being in a process of self-improvement and purification. Lab. 171 (139): Pythagoras is probably 'the philosopher' alluded to by Asterion who thinks that 'nothing is communicable by the art of writing'. Though this

definition may also apply to Socrates, whose thought has come to us via
*Plato, Borges (Other Inq. 116) specifically referred to this characteristic
of Pythagoras, quoting the German scholar Gomperz. Elsewhere he
explained that Pythagoras 'wished his thought to go on living and
growing in the mind of his disciples after his death'. He was perhaps
implying that the written word has a deadening effect on thought, while
the spoken word brings thought alive (*Siete noches*, 127, night 6).

Lab. 55 (30) *Ficc*. 67, Lab. 129 (99) *Ficc*. 175, Lab. 155 (123) *Aleph* 41

Qaholom

A Quiché word from *qaholah*, 'to beget', meaning 'father' and referring to
a primary spirit, the Great Father, who preceded creation. According to
the Quiché concept of dual divinity, Qaholom was accompanied by Alom
(from *alan*, 'to give birth'), the Great Mother. Lab. 203 (169): though there
does not seem to have been a pyramid of this name at the time of the
conquest of Mexico, pyramids were a predominant form both in Mayan
and in Aztec religious architecture. See *Book of the Common.

Lab. 203 (169) *Aleph* 115

Qaphqa

Though the pseudo-Arabic transliteration of this word gives it a Middle
Eastern ring, commensurate with its setting in Babylon, it is clearly an
allusion to Franz Kafka (1883-1924). Borges admired Kafka and openly
acknowledged his influence on the story 'The Lottery of Babel'. In an
essay entitled 'Kafka and his Precursors' he pays tribute to the Czech
writer, saying that he influenced not only those who wrote after him but
also those who came before him, by awakening in his readers an
awareness of the obsessive quality of certain works of literature which
pre-dated his own (Other Inq. 106).

Lab. 58 (33) *Ficc*. 71

Quaritch, Bernard (1819-1899)

An English bookseller and collector first employed by the firm of Bohn.
Quaritch started his own firm in Leicester Square and issued multiple
catalogues of foreign books, early publications and rare manuscripts,
developing the largest trade in old books in the world. He was the first
publisher of *FitzGerald's *Omar Khayam*.

Lab. 27 (5) *Ficc*. 16

Quebracho

The Quebracho uprisings in *Uruguay lasted from 26 to 31 March 1886,
when young rebels from *Montevideo tried to prevent the re-election of a

military government. Though they were defeated, their cause became politically important.
  Lab. 92 (63) *Ficc.* 123

Querétaro

A town and state in Mexico.
  Aleph 20 (27) *Aleph* 165

Quevedo y Villegas, Francisco Gómez de (1580-1645)

A Spanish writer whose fame rests mainly on his picaresque novel *El Buscón*, his satirical poems and his burlesque 'letrillas'. Both in prose and poetry Quevedo's style is highly imaginative and baroque, characterised by puns, conceits and neologisms; his satire is pungent, dynamic and ruthless. He wrote five moral fantasies, the *Sueños*, which denounced the corruption and hypocrisy of the time and was censored by the Inquisition. Borges remarked on Quevedo's moral strength and uprightness, and on his refusal ever to strike a pathetic note. Though admiring the concision and intellectual density of his language, Borges seems to regret Quevedo's almost scientific approach to style which led him to mistrust the use of metaphors and made of him 'el literato de los literatos', a writers' writer (Other Inq. 36). See *Hora de todos...*, *Francis of Sales.
  Lab. 43 (18) *Ficc*. 34, Lab. 63 (37) *Ficc*. 47

Quicherat, Louis-Marie (1799-1884)

A distinguished Latin scholar who collaborated in a series of dictionaries and published numerous works of reference and annotated editions of classical authors. His *Thesaurus poeticus linguae Latinae* (1857) is an inventory of words used in Latin poetry.
  Lab. 89 (61) *Ficc*. 120

Quilmes

An industrial and residential area in southern *Buenos Aires on the banks of the River Plate. Though at one time favoured for weekend villas, particularly by the British, Quilmes has since become unfashionable, a heavily industrialised area, known mainly for Quilmes Beer, the largest brewing company in the world. Aleph 12 (16): Quilmes is not a seaside resort, though the river estuary does indeed look like a vast sea, sufficiently wide to have been the scene of naval battles.
  Aleph 12 (16) *Aleph* 152

Quitab ul ain

The first Arabic dictionary, compiled by *Jalil. It is not arranged alphabetically, but according to groups of sounds known as the 'order of Jalil'.

Lab. 182 (150) *Aleph* 93

Quixote, Don (Quijote)

The masterpiece of Miguel de *Cervantes Saavedra, regarded as the first modern novel for its blend of realism and fantasy. The story of the incredible adventures of a mad knight, it parodies the romances of chivalry and the values they upheld. *Don Quixote* came out in two successive volumes. The narrative in Part I (1605) is constantly interrupted by extraneous stories. The author responded to criticism and in Part II (1615) confined himself mainly to the relation of events. By chapter 44, however, the narrative begins to digress once more into episodes extraneous to the life of the hero and his companion Sancho Panza. Apart from its fantastic aspects and its technical innovations, the book has been considered a faithful record of life in Spain at the end of the sixteenth century, rich in social innuendo and implied criticism, while the variety of scenes described affords vast scope for humour and pathos. Lab. 68 (42): the list of themes absent from Pierre *Menard's version of 'Don Quijote', such as gypsies 'or conquistadors or mystics or Philip the Seconds or *autos da fé*' is a subtle reminder that these themes are absent also from the original, thereby challenging our understanding of 'realism' in literature. The tenuous relationship between fact and fiction is discussed by Borges from another angle in 'Partial Enchantments of Don Quixote' (Other Inq. 43). Recalling the episode in Part II, where characters pass comments, as readers, on Part I, Borges suggests that this self-reference has the disquieting effect of blurring the boundaries between fact and fiction, making the reader aware that if the character can also be a reader, the reader may also be a character in someone else's fiction. Lab. 69 (43): the phrase 'truth, whose mother is history...' stems from a passage in Part I, ch. 9 in which Cervantes, showing his concern for realism, is seeking to establish the credibility of his story. His device of casting doubt on a detail in order to add credence to the rest was learnt and used by Borges in his fiction. Thus Cervantes's narrator tells of the discovery of the original manuscript, a text in Arabic by Cide Hamete Benengeli, and warns his readers that they may expect some small deviations from the truth, because the Arab chronicler may at times fall short in his praise of a Christian knight. This he considers reprehensible, for a historian must not twist the path of 'truth, whose mother is history...'

Lab. 62 (36) *Ficc.* 45

Ramos Mejía

A part of *Buenos Aires in which the rich had weekend houses containing an English colony. It is now an industrial suburb.
  Lab. 27 (3) *Ficc.* 13, Brodie 15 (15) *Brodie* 127

Raskolnikov

The protagonist of Dostoievsky's novel *Crime and Punishment* (1866): a poor student in love with Sonia, a prostitute, who becomes the means of his spiritual regeneration. The crime of the title is the murder of an old woman, a repulsive money-lender; the punishment is the gradual racking of his conscience. Lab. 176 (144): in part 5, chapter 4 Raskolnikov confesses his crime to Sonia, saying that he committed it as a test of his daring because he wanted to become a *Napoleon.
  Lab. 176 (144) *Aleph* 85

Ravenna (Ravena)

A city in northern Italy 100 km south of Venice which in Roman times was a port and is now connected to the Adriatic by a four-mile canal. Ravenna was made the capital of the Western Empire by the Emperor Honorius in 402; it was conquered by Justinian's general Belisarius in 540 and became the seat of the governors of Byzantine Italy. The poet *Dante spent a large part of his exile in Ravenna and was buried there. Lab. 159 (127): in 728 the *Lombard king Luitprand took and destroyed Ravenna's suburb Classis. In 752 his successor Aistulf entered and sacked the city but, overcome by its beauty, spared its monuments.
  Lab. 159 (127) *Aleph* 47

Razumov

The protagonist of *Under Western Eyes* (1911), a novel by Joseph Conrad. As in *Lord Jim, the theme is cowardice and the story centres on the duplicity of the main character, who meets his just deserts. During his students days in St Petersburg Kirylo Sidorovitch Razumov has betrayed to the police the revolutionary Victor Haldin who took refuge in his lodgings. Sent to Geneva as a police agent to check on Haldin's contacts, he is welcomed as a fellow-revolutionary by Haldin's family and friends in exile. He succeeds in keeping up appearances until, weighed down by the guilt of his betrayal and shamed by the innocence of Haldin's sister, Natalia, and the undeserved trust and affection he is receiving, he confesses his treachery. To punish him, one of Haldin's comrades bursts his eardrums; the deaf Razumov is run over by a tram and remains permanently crippled.
  Aleph 106 (106) *Aleph* 73

Reboul, Jacques

Perhaps an oblique allusion to the writer Jean Reboul (1796-1864) who came from *Nîmes, where he was known as 'the baker of Nîmes'.
    Lab. 64 (38) *Ficc*. 48

Regules, Elías

A song-writer from the province of *Entre Ríos who combined the aggressive spirit of the *montoneros* with a vein of sweet sentimentality or, to use Borges's words, 'united the ornamental with the heartless – like the tiger' (*Ev. Carr*. 35).
    Brodie 59 (72) *Brodie* 52

Rembrandt, Harmenszoon van Rijn (1606-1669)

A Dutch painter, born at Leyden, renowned for his versatile portraiture. Brodie 33 (37): in his search for realism, Rembrandt made dramatic use of light and shade to emphasise the shape and movement of the human form and contrasts in the landscape.
    Brodie 33 (37) *Brodie* 92

Renan, Ernest (1823-1892)

A French orientalist, famous for his sceptical writings on the history of Christianity. His doctoral thesis, *Averroès et l'averroïsme*, was published in 1852. Lab. 180 (148): the epigraph is a quotation from this essay. Renan asserted that *Averroes, in his paraphrase of the *Poetics* of *Aristotle, shows an extensive knowledge of Arab literature but 'the most complete ignorance' of Greek literature, since no representative Greek poetry had been translated into Arabic. According to Renan, Averroes's knowledge was confined to the work of philosophical and scientific writers, and he was incapable of appreciating Greek poetry. Developing the theme of cultural gaps, Renan showed that the Latin version of Averroes's *Commentaries*, the one most widely used in medieval Europe for the propagation of Aristotelianism, was itself 'barbaric', being a translation of a Hebrew translation of a commentary on an Arab translation of a Syrian translation of a Greek text. Renan states that Averroes's fame was confined mainly to the Jewish and Christian world, where he was acclaimed for introducing and elucidating the work of Aristotle; in the Arab world, however, he was suspected of unorthodoxy and known chiefly for his refutation of *Ghazali. This view is disputed by Arab scholars. Lab. 180 (148): Renan discusses the number of changes undergone by Averroes's name from the Arabic 'Ibn Roschd' and lists sixteen different transcriptions: Ibin Rosdin, Filius Rosedis, Ibn Rusid, Ben Raxid, Ibn Ruschad, Ben Resched, Aban Rassad, Aben Rois, Aben

202

Rasd, Aben Rust, Averrosd, Averryz, Adveroys, Benroist, Averroyth, Avenroysta.

Lab. 180 (148) *Aleph* 91

'Reprobation which was almost remorse' ('Reprobación que era casi un remordimiento') see *Homer

Republic (República)

*Plato's most famous dialogue. Beginning as a discussion of the nature of justice, the *Republic* develops into a description of the perfect state. It is thus the earliest Utopia. Lab. 183: the Platonic model refers to Plato's famous theory of 'forms' discussed in books 5-8, according to which there are two levels of reality, the higher level of 'forms' (or ideas) and the lower level of 'images' (or likenesses). The 'form', made by God, has an absolute existence independent of our minds, whereas its particular appearance or manifestation of it in the world, being an imperfect copy and subject to change, has inferior status. Plato does not say that the appearance is *un*real: since it is a copy of a form it can partake of its reality, but it can never be fully identified with it. Differentiating between 'knowledge' and 'opinion', Plato asserts that the philosopher who is in love with truth may have knowledge of a form, since it is changeless and divine, but only 'opinion' of the changing world of appearance and sensation. Lab. 183 (151): this distinction gains particular relevance in its application to the *Koran.

Lab. 183 (151) *Aleph* 95

Retiro

A district in the centre of *Buenos Aires, made up partly of the fashionable Barrio Norte and partly, in the low-lying areas near the docks, of the rougher *Bajo.

Brodie 64 (76) *Brodie* 58

Revolution of 1890 (Revolución del noventa)

A rebellion against President Juárez Celman in July and August 1890. The rebels, mainly lawyers, students and recent immigrants, were protesting against the oligarchy of landowners who controlled the government and its inflationary policies. The rebellion was planned by the 'Unión Cívica' under Leandro *Alem and supported by Mitre and the clergy. After two days the rebels ran out of ammunition and asked for an armistice and a general amnesty, which were granted. After a few days Celman resigned; his successor, however, was from his own party and followed the same policies.

Revue des langues romanes

A literary review published from 1870 to 1945 in Montpellier, and, at intervals, in Paris, by the Société pour l'Etude des Langues Romanes. Lab. 63 (37): Borges refers to two separate issues, one of October and one of December 1909, but there seems to have been only one issue that year, covering May to December; it contained specialist articles such as *'Notes sur le vocabulaire de Maupassant et de Merimée'* by A. Schiuz, but no debate on the 'metric laws of French prose'.

Lab. 63 (37) *Ficc.* 47

Reyes, Alfonso (1889-1959)

A Mexican poet and essayist who was ambassador to *Buenos Aires 1927-30 and 1936-7. Reyes was a long-standing friend of Borges, who considered him his master in matters of style and often paid tribute to him. As a poet he participated in the 1920s modernist movement in Latin America.

Lab. 31 (7) *Ficc.* 19

Reyles Gutiérrez, Carlos Claudio (1868-1938)

A Uruguayan writer interested in rural life. Reyles was influenced by contemporary scientific and psychological theories and his books often dwelt on the effects of human and animal inbreeding in isolated environments. Brodie 38 (45): the assertion that Reyles's son told Borges the story upon which he based 'The Other Duel' is correct.

Brodie 38 (45) *Brodie* 101

Rhetoric (Retórica)

A treatise by *Aristotle dealing with the various aspects of oratory and setting out its functions and methods. Lab. 181 (149): in the *Rhetoric* Aristotle compares the activity of a good speaker to a theatrical performance, using terms such as 'acting' and 'stage' as well as 'tragedy' and 'comedy', whose meaning eludes *Averroes. Book 3, referred to by Borges, deals specifically with delivery. In chapter 1, 'The Parts of Rhetoric', Aristotle states that 'even writers of tragedy...have abandoned all those terms which are foreign to the style of conversation' (1404a, 30-5). In the same chapter, referring to the art of delivery, he writes that it 'was long before it found a place in tragic drama', adding that at first poets 'acted their own tragedies' (1403a, 20-5). Chapter 3, 'Frigidity of Style', points to the use of inappropriate metaphors by 'writers of comedy, because they are ridiculous' (1406b,5-10). Finally, chapter 14, 'Exordia', advises that the start of a speech should be 'equivalent to the opening scenes of plays' where 'the commencement is an intimation of the subject' (1415a, 5-10), and concludes by addressing the orator in theatrical terms: 'Bring yourself on the stage from the first in the right character...' (1417b,7).

Lab. 181 (149) *Aleph* 92

Riachuelo

A shallow stream marking the southern boundary between the city of *Buenos Aires and Greater Buenos Aires. It was the site of the first foundation of the city in 1536 before the early Spanish settlers moved up-river to Paraguay. For many years the mouth of the Riachuelo served as a second port, attracting nascent industries and a large immigrant population, which lived in crowded and unsanitary conditions.

Brodie 68 (83) *Brodie* 68

Rio Grande del Sur ('do Sul' in Portuguese)

The southernmost state of *Brazil bordering Argentina and *Uruguay. Lab. 96 (67): an area characterised by smuggling and contacts with neighbouring countries, its prosperity was largely due to the progressive agricultural methods introduced by European immigrants.

Lab. 30 (6) *Ficc*. 17, Lab. 96 (67) *Ficc*. 129

Río Negro

A river in *Uruguay which crosses the country from north east to south west; also the name of a department in western Uruguay on the river, on the opposite side of the Argentinian province of *Entre Ríos, the capital of which is *Fray Bentos. Lab. 92 (63) refers to the uprising of *Quebracho in 1886. Aleph 66 (103): before the fighting between the *Blancos and *Colorados in 1904 *Saravia was south of Río Negro, keeping watch over a government battalion which had been posted there.

Lab. 92 (63) *Ficc*. 123, Aleph 66 (103) *Aleph* 71

Ritter, Karl (1779-1859)

A German geographer and professor of history at the University of Frankfurt, author of *Die Erdkunde im Verhältnis zur Natur und Geschichte des Menschen* (Geography and the Study of Nature and History of Mankind). Ritter is regarded as the father of modern geography. There are two editions of his monumental work (1817-18, revised 1822), which has remained incomplete. The book presents the topography of a country as a leading element in its historic development.

Lab. 28 (4) *Ficc*. 14

Rivadavia

The longest street in *Buenos Aires, dividing the city into north and south. All the intersecting streets change their name as they cross it.
Fict. 154 (169) *Ficc.* 190

Roberts, Cecil E.M. (1892-1976)

An English writer, author of poems, plays and novels set largely in the 1920s. He was reputed for his 'special gift for easy-going, light-hearted romance'.
Aleph 31 (45) *Ficc.* 35

Robertson

Probably an allusion to the theologian Frederick William Robertson (1816-1853). After his ordination Robertson developed a form of asceticism so severe that it endangered his life. Haunted by innumerable doubts, he clung devoutly to the one principle of the 'unequalled nobleness of the humanity of the Son of God'.
Lab. 126 (96) *Ficc.* 170

Robinson Crusoe

The protagonist of Defoe's adventure story *Robinson Crusoe* (1719). Aleph 33 (48): the allusion to the footprint refers to the horror and fear felt by Crusoe as he realises that the island on which he has been shipwrecked is inhabited. Fear shatters his faith in God. At first he thinks the footsteps may be Satan's; then that they belong to someone even more dangerous, such as a savage; and ultimately that they may be his own. In the end his faith prevails and he prays to God and 'was no more sad – at least, not on that occasion'.
Aleph 33 (48) *Fict.* 39

Rodríguez Monegal, Emir (1921-1985)

A Uruguayan literary critic, a friend of Borges and the author of *Jorge Luis Borges: A Literary Biography of Borges* (1978), the best biography to date. Between 1966 and 1968 Monegal edited the journal *Mundo Nuevo* in Paris. He also edited the two-volume *Borzoi Anthology of Latin American Literature*.
Aleph 67 (104) *Aleph* 72

Rojas

A small town in the southern province of *Buenos Aires south of

*Pergamino. Aleph 56 (84): the incident alluded to figures obliquely in *Martín *Fierro* (pt 1, canto VIII, ll. 1265-1318).
Aleph 56 (84) *Aleph* 56

Rome (Roma)

The saying 'All roads lead to Rome', based on the transport system of the Roman Empire, can be taken to mean that all avenues of thought eventually lead back to their original source. In its literary sense the saying later became true of the Catholic world, whose centre is the Vatican.
Lab. 115 (85) *Ficc.* 155

Rosae Crucis (Rosa Cruz)

A secret society, named after the emblems of the rose and the cross, which were taken to be symbols of Jesus's resurrection and redemption. Its practices were based on ancient occult beliefs. In the seventeenth century two anonymous books in Germany told the story of a fictitious Christian, Rosencrutz, and of the society he founded. Now generally believed to be by Johannes Valentinus *Andreä, they aroused the curiosity of many eminent men, such as *Spinoza and *Descartes, who tried to meet members of the society. In time societies were actually founded and Rosicrucianism spread to London and later to Vienna, Russia and *Poland. Its history seems to provide a perfect example of a Tlönian *hrön* – an idea which, when believed, materialises.
Lab. 29 (5) *Ficc.* 16

Rosas, Juan Manuel de (1793-1877)

The governor of the province of *Buenos Aires from 1829 to 1831 and dictator of Argentina for almost two decades (1835-52). Although he fought as champion of the *Federalist cause, presenting himself as a self-styled *gaucho* and drawing much of his popularity from the *gauchos*, Rosas came from an old-established Spanish family whose fortune he multiplied to become the richest landowner in the country. As such, his interest was to pacify and eventually to unify Argentina in order to establish an export-oriented, land-based economy. To this end he began a reign of terror. He killed or exiled most prominent members of the *Unitarian party and ruled at home with the help of his private army, the *Mazorca. Having silenced opposition from the Unitarians, he systematically attacked other Federalist *caudillos*, until he was left to rule supreme. Eventually he was brought down by his staunchest supporter, the Federalist general *Urquiza, who, in alliance with Brazilian and Uruguayan forces, defeated him at the battle of Caseros (1852). At his downfall his arch-opponent *Sarmiento dubbed him the

'Unitarian' Rosas, meaning that through his ruthless campaign of dictatorial self-aggrandisement he had achieved the Unitarian aim of putting an end to civil war and uniting the country under one banner. Rosas was exiled to England and died in Southampton. Borges, who shared an ancestor with Rosas through his great-great-grandfather, wrote a poem on him recalling the ferocity of his rule and setting it against the annihilating effect of forgetfulness (Sel. Poems 15). Brodie 73 (90): in accordance with a decree of 1840, Rosas confiscated all property and goods belonging to the Unitarians and their families in order to finance his army and popular support.

Brodie 73 (90) *Brodie* 76

Roscommon

A county and town in central Ireland.
Fict. 66 (73) *Ficc.* 77

Rosenroth see Christian *Knorr, Baron von Rosenroth

Ross, Alexander (1590-1654)

A Scottish divine, author of poetical, philosophical and theological works in Latin and English. His most ambitious book, *A History of the World*, was intended as a continuation of the work begun by Sir Walter Raleigh. In his preface Ross claimed to be more conversant with the dead than with the living, a fact that Borges may well have had in mind when quoting him in the context of 'The Immortal'. Among Ross's Latin books are the eight volumes of *Virgilius Evangelizans* (1634), which presents the life of Jesus in the words of *Virgil. The first five books refer to biblical episodes and their allusion to the figure of Christ. Book 6 describes Christ's birth; book 7 the prophecies of his life and miracles; book 8 to 12 the life, death and resurrection; book 13 his ascension to Heaven and the coming of the Holy Spirit. Each passage is referred to the *Aeneid, Eclogues* or *Georgics* by book and line number. Lab. 149 (118): being composed of phrases from the writings of another author, *Virgilius Evangelizans* is an example of a 'patchwork' text alluded to in Nahum *Cordovero's *Coat of Many Colours*.

Lab. 149 (118) *Aleph* 26

Ruggieri

An archbishop of Pisa whose name appears among the traitors in *Dante's *Divine Comedy* (*Inferno* 33). In 1289 Ruggieri betrayed the trust of *Ugolino della Gherardesca, then Mayor of Pisa, accusing him of treason; as a result, Ugolino, his sons and grandchildren were starved to

death in a tower now known as *torre della fame*, 'the tower of hunger'.
Lab. 200 (168) *Aleph* 141

Runes, Runic crosses (Runas, Cruces rúnicas)

Runes were the characters of an early alphabet current in parts of northern Europe (Scandinavia in particular). The word is often used now to describe something secret and mysterious. Lab. 152 (122): the crosses which Borges defines as 'runic' are in fact wheeled crosses, the result of the fusion of Viking culture with Celtic Christianity. The *wheel was a prominent symbol in early Norse mythology, where it represented the sun.
Lab. 153 (122) *Aleph* 39, Brodie 98 (117) *Brodie* 148

Rurik

Also Ryurik, Rorik or Hrorikr: a semi-legendary ninth-century Varangian Viking prince, supposedly the founder of the Rurik dynasty which ruled Russia up to 1598. Rurik is thought to have come from Scandinavia at the invitation of the people of Novgorod to settle their internal wars.
Lab. 129 (99) *Ficc.* 175

Rusaddir

Present-day Melilla, a port in Spanish Morocco, founded by the Phoenicians and eventually occupied by Rome. In the fifteenth century it was taken by the Spaniards. A revolt of Spanish officers in Melilla in 1936 marked the start of the Spanish Civil War.
Lab. 157 (126) *Aleph* 45

Rusito

Slang term for *Ashkenazi Jews, from *ruso*, 'Russian' (as opposed to immigrants from the Middle East, who were known as *turcos*, 'Turks'). Most early Jewish immigration to Argentina was from Russia. *Brodie* 30: according to the historian R.B. Scobie (*Buenos Aires: From Plaza to Suburb*, 1974, 230), most Russian Jewish immigrants were victims of anti-Semitism. Children thereupon tended to adopt *criollo* speech and customs, and reject the language and ways of their parents. Brodie 27 (29): the English version uses 'Sheeny', a slang word for 'Jews', which does not specify their origin.
Brodie 30

Russel, Alley (Pasaje Russel)

A short passageway in what used to be a rough part of *Palermo, not far from Serrano, where Borges lived as a child.
Brodie 67 (83) *Brodie* 67

Russell, Bertrand (1872-1970)

An English mathematician and philosopher. Russell's *Principia Mathematica* (1910-13) develops the principle that pure mathematics is an extension of logic and that every authentic mathematical statement can be translated into a logical one. The most important stage of his philosophical thought is represented by *Our Knowledge of the External World* (1914) in which, having discarded both the idealist and realist positions, he replaces 'physical' entities (whose nature is problematical) with logical constructions which we feel to be intelligible. Thus we can avoid reference to the 'unobservable', except as something unknown which we can postulate. This theory is further illustrated in *Analysis of Mind* (1921). Later, Russell rejected this programme, though other philosophers continue to work in his tradition. Lab. 64 (38): in *Our Knowledge of the External World*, Russell dedicates a chapter, 'The Problem of Infinity...', to the historical analysis of philosophical questions associated with the concept of infinity. He presents the four arguments against motion produced by Zeno of the *Eleatic school, which are based on the principle that time and space are infinitely divisible. The second of Zeno's arguments is the *contest of Achilles and the tortoise, which Borges refers to in this story and elsewhere. Lab. 68 (42): Borges's reference to Russell in connection with 'the curious discourse of Don *Quixote on arms and letters' is a humorous allusion to the philosopher's political position. A pacifist and a conscientious objector during World War I, Russell was sent to prison for campaigning against conscription.
Lab. 34 (10) *Ficc*. 23, Lab. 64 (38) *Ficc*. 47

Ruzafa

Also Al-Rusayfah: a village in Jordan, near Amman.
Lab. 186 (154) *Aleph* 99

Saavedra

Probably a descendant of Cornelio de Saavedra, president of the historic Junta which deposed the Spanish Viceroy on 25 May 1810, declared the emancipation of the River Plate Province and established itself as the first *criollo* government in Argentina. Brodie 73 (91): employment in the Ministry of Finance is considered prestigious and consistent with the status of a member of an old and well-established family.

Sábato, Ernesto (1911-)

An Argentine scientist and writer, author of novels, such as *The Tunnel* (1948) and *On Heroes and Tombs* (1961), and of critical work such as *Uno y el universo* (1945) and *Heterodoxia* (1953). Sábato focuses on the condition of modern man, whose alienation often leads to despair. The psychological and philosophical concerns of his writings do not, however, detract from the depth of characterisation in his fiction. Sábato has always shown respect for Borges and interest in his work. When, at the annual literary competition of 1942, Borges failed to receive the first prize for his collection *The Garden of Forking Paths* Sábato was one of the twenty-one writers who protested and contributed to 'Reparation to Borges'. In 1968 he published *Tres aproximaciones a la literatura de nuestro tiempo* (Three Approximations to the Literature of Our Time) in which he wrote on three leading literary figures: Robbe-Grillet, Borges and Sartre.
Lab. 148 (118) *Aleph* 25

Saint-Simon, Louis de Rouvroy, Duc de (1675-1755)

A French soldier, diplomat and writer, the author of posthumously published memoirs of the reign of Louis XV and Louis XIV. Saint-Simon's flair for character-drawing, love of gossip, combination of prejudice and superstition and talent for catching the atmosphere of the historical moment make him unique among French diarists. Lab. 63 (37): these qualities, however, are not matched by style and grammar, which hardly make him a suitable candidate for an 'examination of the essential metric laws of French prose'.
Lab. 63 (37) *Ficc.* 47

Salado

A river in the province of *Buenos Aires subject to frequent flooding.
Brodie 17 (17) *Brodie* 129

Salammbô

A novel by Gustave *Flaubert (1821-1880), published in 1862, which reconstructs the life and culture of *Carthage at the time of the Punic wars. Rich in action and 'local colour', it probably originated during Flaubert's visit to Tunis in 1850. It is the story of the love of Hamilcar's daughter, the priestess Salammbô, for Mathô, a leader of the rebel mercenaries. After Mathô's defeat and execution, Salammbô dies of grief. Lab. 68 (42): the allusion to *Salammbô* should be considered in the light of Borges's comment that, no matter how rich Carthaginian literature may have been, it could never have included a novel like Flaubert's, for 'every writing belongs to its own time' (second prologue to *Luna de enfrente*, *O.P.*). Pierre *Menard's rewriting of *Quixote* as a 'document' of Nîmes in the twentieth century reflects that view by way of parody.

Lab. 68 (42) Ficc. 53

'Salomon saith, there is no new thing…' see Francis *Bacon

Salonika (Salónica)

A Greek port north west of Athens, once *Macedonia's natural outlet to the sea. Lab. 135 (105): the Spanish spoken in Salonika was probably Ladino (a mixture of old Spanish and some Hebrew). Salonika's Jewish colony was greatly augmented in the fifteenth and sixteenth centuries by an influx of Sephardic Jews from Spain.

Lab. 135 (105) *Aleph* 7

Salto

A town on the Uruguayan side of the River Uruguay which Borges used to visit in his youth. There is also a department of the same name. See *Amorim.

Lab. 88 (60) *Ficc.* 119

Samarkand (Samarcanda)

A city in the USSR, the oldest city of Central Asia, whose origin can be dated between 4,000 and 3,000 BC. Occupied by the Arabs and the Persians, Samarkand reached its height in the fifteenth century, as capital of the empire of the Islamic *Mongol ruler Tamerlane. Lab. 146 (116): playing chess in Samarkand is plausible. The game, known among both the Arabs and the Persians, was introduced into *Islam from *Persia and was given patronage at the court of Tamerlane.

Lab. 146 (116) *Aleph* 23

Samuel

The epigraph to 'The Intruder' is from 2 Samuel 1:26: 'I am distressed for thee, my brother Jonathan: very pleasant hast thou been unto me: thy love to me was wonderful, passing the love of women.' Some interpreters have seen undertones of homosexuality in Borges's story, a suggestion vehemently denied by Borges in private conversation with the authors.

Brodie 52 (63) *Brodie* 15

San Cristóbal

A department and city in the province of *Santa Fe, founded as a colony on land granted by the government to a London-based banking firm, Murrieta y Cía.
Brodie 25 (27) *Brodie* 27

San Francisco

A small town in *Uruguay where the *Haedo family owned a ranch. As a child Borges used to spend his summer vacations there with his family.
Lab. 88 (60) *Ficc.* 118

San Martín, José (1778-1850)

Argentina's greatest military leader, hero of the Wars of Independence and liberator of *Chile and Peru. Once the Spaniards had been defeated in Argentina, San Martín foresaw that his country's independence would not be won unless the royalist forces were expelled from the sub-continent. He set off from *Buenos Aires to enlist soldiers for his famous *Army of the Andes, which in 1817 he led into Chile. Here, after the battles of *Chacabuco and *Cancha Rayada, he finally defeated the Spaniards at *Maipú. He then led an expedition into Peru, where the Army of the Andes was joined by Chilean forces. On 9 July 1821, after securing several victories over royalist forces, he entered Lima – not, in his words, as a conqueror but as liberator of the Peruvian people – whereupon he was proclaimed Protector of Peru. Spanish troops remained in the Sierras, and San Martín realised that neither he nor Bolívar was sufficently powerful to defeat the Royalists on his own. Accordingly he sent troops to Bolívar in Quito and arranged a meeting, which finally took place in *Guayaquil on 26 July 1822. The conference clearly indicated the clash of personalities between the two men, as Bolívar distrusted both San Martín's military ability and his monarchical leanings. Fully aware of the predicament, San Martín conceded the leadership of his troops in Peru to Bolívar, returned briefly to Argentina and then, leaving the camp to his rival, departed for Europe, where he lived in self-imposed exile in Belgium. When he tried to return to Buenos Aires in 1829, he found Argentina torn by the strife between the *Federalists and the *Unitarians (respectively represented by *Rosas and *Lavalle). He refused to take sides and returned to Europe without even landing on Argentine soil. He died in Boulogne. Brodie 79 (95): San Martín remains to this day a sacred name in Argentine history, an example of bravery and abnegation. On this point Borges ironically recalls that when a Venezuelan writer once wrote that San Martín '*tenía un aire avieso*' ('had a sly look'), this was solemnly denied by an Argentine writer, who claimed that to say *avieso* and San Martín together was nonsensical: 'You may as well speak of a square triangle.' Brodie 88 (105): the masonic lodge referred to is the *Logia Lautaro*, of which San Martín was a member and where he exchanged revolutionary ideas.

Brodie 79 (95) *Brodie* 84, Brodie 82 (100) *Brodie* 112

San Salvador

A street in the district of *Palermo
Brodie 67 (83) *Brodie* 67

San Telmo

One of the oldest districts of colonial *Buenos Aires, founded by the Jesuits in the early eighteenth century. San Telmo has several fine buildings but is now considered a rough district. During the British invasions of 1806 and 1807 it was the centre of fierce resistance; its fighting spirit is illustrated in the popular song: *Soy del barrio de San Telmo / donde llueve y no gotea / a mí no me asustan bultos / ni grupos que se menean* ('I come from San Telmo, where it rains and does not drizzle. I am not frightened by bullies nor by gangs which move around'). Brodie 51: this song would give an ironic twist to the last sentence of the story, 'Rosendo's Tale'.

Brodie 51 (60) *Brodie* 48

Sant' Anna

A town in Livramento, Brazil, near the Argentinian-Uruguayan border, a rough area characterised by fighting and smuggling, mainly of cattle. Borges visited Sant' Anna with *Amorim and recalls his shock on seeing the violent shooting of a drunkard by a *capanga*. The incident was reflected in several of his stories: 'Tlön, ...', 'The Shape of the Sword', 'The Dead Man', ' The Other Death' and obliquely in 'The South'.

Lab. 41 (16) *Ficc.* 31

Santa Fe

A province north west of *Buenos Aires. Aleph 12: the 'alfajores', a typical Argentine sweetmeat made of sugared pastry, filled with chocolate, nuts or fudge, and manufactured in Santa Fe, differ from more traditional sweets by being larger, concave and more brittle. Regarded as a regional delicacy, they are difficult to obtain in Buenos Aires.

Lab. 161 (129) *Aleph* 50, Aleph 12 (16) *Aleph* 152

Santos

The busiest port in *Brazil, in the south-eastern state of Sao Paulo.
Aleph 22 (30) *Aleph* 168

Saravia, Aparicio (1856-1904)

A Uruguayan landowner and *caudillo*, uncultured and politically unsophisticated, whose magnetic personality secured him a following among the *gauchos* of the Interior. In 1897 he led the revolt of the *Blancos, a nationalist group demanding free elections and representation of all parties in the government, against the dictatorship of Idiarte Borda. Borda was assassinated in 1897 and the armed conflict ended in a peace pact, but the nationalist faction under Saravia was left isolated and on 1 January 1904 Saravia again led his troops against the Government of Batlle in an attempt to prevent elections in which his party was not represented. After a series of battles his side was finally defeated at *Masoller. Saravia was wounded and died in Brazil. After his death a legend sprang up that he would return. See *Illesca, *Tupambaé.
   Aleph 66 (103) *Aleph* 71

Sarmiento, Domingo Faustino (1811-1888)

An Argentine writer, historian and educationalist, and the country's President from 1868 to 1874. Sarmiento was born in the Andean province of San Juan and spent his early years in an atmosphere of growing caudillism – rule by local strong men on horseback – which, for him, epitomised barbarism. Sarmiento was largely self-taught. He admired European values, particularly English, and was influenced by the progressive ideas of liberal political and economic thinkers. He was a *Unitarian, fighting for the unification and Europeanisation of Argentina, and as such became an indefatigable opponent of *Federalism, which he considered retrograde and barbaric. His opposition to the *caudillo* Quiroga forced him into exile in *Chile. Here he wrote his most famous book, *Facundo*, in which he launched an outright attack on Federalism, using a 'barbaric hero', Facundo Quiroga. The ultimate target of his attack was *Rosas, to whose downfall the book contributed. Borges's admiration for Sarmiento and his ideas can be construed from his prologue to *Facundo*, where he says that the history of Argentina would have been different and better if, instead of 'canonising' Martín *Fierro, they had 'canonised' Facundo. Brodie 87 (105): during his exile Sarmiento was sent by the government of Chile to Europe to study school systems. While in Paris, he paid several visits to San Martín in his retreat on the outskirts of the capital. The General confided many details of the meeting at *Guayaquil. These conversations were the subject of Sarmiento's inaugural speech when he was elected a member of the *Institut Historique de France* on 1 July 1847 in the presence of San Martín. A copy of the speech, which shed new light on the Guayaquil controversy, was found in the archives of the Museo Histórico Sarmiento by the historian Antonio Castro, who disclosed his findings on 13 August 1947 in a lecture entitled 'Sarmiento y San Martín'. Sarmiento also wrote a series of articles under the title *Escritos sobre San Martín*, which includes a short biography of San Martín.

Brodie 87 (105) *Brodie* 120

Satornilus (Satornilo)

A second-century Syrian *Gnostic, known also as Saturninus of Antioch, who held that the angels, archangels, powers and dominions were created by the Supreme Unknown, the Father, but that the world and everything in it, including man, was created by seven of the lowest angels. Among these was the God of the Jews, whom the Divine Father sought to destroy by sending the Saviour. Satornilus held that Christ the saviour was a man only in appearance but did not possess a physical body. He also believed that man is not a complete human being until the Father gives him the 'spark of life', which at death returns to the divine fountain of life.

Lab. 125 (95) *Ficc.* 169

Saturn (Saturno)

A ferry which plied between *Buenos Aires and *Montevideo. It had an effigy of Saturn on its prow.

Lab. 90 (62) *Ficc.* 121

Saturnales

More correctly known as *Saturnalia*: a Latin work by the fifth-century author Macrobius. It consists of seven books. The first describes the origin and history of Roman festivals and tries to prove that all pagan theology, whether Roman, Greek, Egyptian or Assyrian, leads to the cult of the sun. *Heliopolis is mentioned in this context. Books 2 and 3 comment on various Roman writers, especially *Virgil. The remaining four books deal with assorted topics, from table conversation and the digestibility of foods to vertigo, whitening of the hair, blushing and the voice of eunuchs. Lab. 131 (101): the reference to 'the *Saturnales* of Flavius Josephus' is an error: *of* should read or.

Lab. 131 (101) *Ficc.* 181

Satyricon

An allegory in prose and poetry in nine books, the chief work of the fifth-century Carthaginian Martianus Capella, which was influential in the Middle Ages. Its full title (in English) is 'Satyricon, in which two books describe the marriage of Mercury with philology and the rest are each dedicated to one of the seven liberal arts'. Aleph 22 (30) refers to Jupiter's sphere in which 'the entire world is reflected as in a shining mirror' where one can see all the 'variety of the earth', its cities and its different living species, and all that 'each and all nations are doing'. In the mirror Jupiter marks 'those he wants to raise and those he wants to repress, those to be born and those to die'.

Aleph 22 (30) *Aleph* 168

Saul see St *Paul

Savoyard (Saboyano)

As is made clear in the English translation of Borges's story, the term refers to Xavier de Maistre (1763-1852), born in Savoy and author of *Voyage autour de ma chambre* (1795), which he wrote at the age of 27 while confined to his bed through injuries sustained in a duel. The *Voyage* is a light work in which each object perceived by the author in his bedroom prompts humorous reminiscences and small confidences.

Aleph 14 (18) *Aleph* 155

Sayers, Dorothy L. (1893-1957)

An English author, remembered chiefly for her detective novels featuring the character Lord Peter Wimsey. She regarded the detective story as a useful exercise of pure analysis which demanded no commitment to its subject matter. She is also known for her translation of *Dante's *Divine Comedy*.

Aleph 32 (46) *Ficc.* 36

Scharlach

The master-criminal in 'Death and the Compass'; in German the name means both 'scarlet' and 'scarlet fever'.

Lab. 106 (76) *Ficc.* 143

Scheherazade (Shahrazad)

The teller of the tales in the *Thousand and One Nights*, daughter of the vizier of King Shahriyar, who became her husband. It was the king's custom to kill his wives after the marriage had been consummated, but Scheherazade escaped by telling him stories and ending each night at the most gripping moment, so that he begged her to resume the narration the following night. By the time all the tales were told, she was able to present the king with his child, thus making her presence indispensable and dear to him. Brodie 91 (111): Borges expressed his fascination for Scheherazade's 'wondrous tales', describing her as 'more inventive than Allah' (*Borges mem.* 11).

Lab. 51 (25) *Ficc.* 106, Fict. 155 (170) *Ficc.* 191, Brodie 91 (111) *Brodie* 139

Scherzo

From the Italian, meaning 'joke': the third movement of a symphony, quartet or sonata in which one or more of the motifs reappears in a lighter tone and at a faster tempo.
Aleph 14 (19) *Aleph* 155

Schopenhauer, Arthur (1788-1860)

A German philosopher of the post-Kantian school, whose best-known books are *The World as Will and Idea* (1818; 2nd edn. 1844) and two volumes of essays entitled **Parerga und Paralipomena* (1851). Schopenhauer is the philosopher most quoted by Borges (about fifty times) in his stories and criticism. Solitary and retiring, Schopenhauer was relatively unnoticed until the publication of his essays, which brought him worldwide recognition. His philosophy is based on the principle that all that exists is a manifestation of the Will and is comprehensible only through the constructs of man's intellect engendered by the Will itself, such as time, space and causality. Lab. 53 (28): the reference to Schopenhauer's belief in a uniform absolute time follows: time, being like the rest of experience a representation of the Will, is not subject to variations connected with individual and particular states. Schopenhauer insists that through the constructs of our mind only the appearances of the world are revealed to us, and not its reality. Brodie 85 (103): with reference to Schopenauer's 'disbelief of history', it follows that history, resting on the category of time, belongs also to the world of phenomena. On this point Borges adds that, since for Schopenhauer 'the universe is a projection of our soul', 'universal history lies within each man' (Other Inq. 58). Outside the world of phenomena, only the reality of the self is knowable to man, as being part of the primary essence of all things, the Will. Lab. 99 (70): this, however, eliminates the concept of individuality, as suggested in 'I am all other men': all individuals are but a form or manifestation of the Will which moves and organises everything from the blind impulses of inorganic nature to the 'rationally' guided actions of man. Lab. 175 (143), Brodie 88 (106): yet, because man is the Will's prime manifestation, it can be said paradoxically that no human action is involuntary (since it is also a manifestation of the Will). Man can escape from the control of the Will, partially through the uplifting effect of the arts and, totally, by complete abnegation of the self through asceticism. For Lab. 37 (12) and 175 see **Parerga und Paralipomena*. For Fict. 69 (76) see *Kantian categories.
Lab. 37 (12) *Ficc.* 26, Lab. 99 (70) *Ficc.* 133, Lab. 53 (28) Ficc. 109, Lab. 174 (142) *Aleph* 82, Fict. 69 (76) *Ficc.* 81, Brodie 85(103) *Brodie* 116

Senate (Senado)

Lab. 103: in ancient Rome the Senate was the supreme council of state. Its prestige and authority, which grew during the Republican period, was threatened by the concentration of power in the hands of *Julius Caesar and gradually diminished after the establishment of the Empire.

Lab. 103 (73) *Ficc.* 138

Seneca, Lucius (*c*.55 BC – *c*.39 AD)

A Roman writer, born in Spain, often referred to as Seneca the Elder to distinguish him from his son, the Stoic philosopher appointed by Agrippina as tutor to her son Nero. Seneca the Elder was the author of a work on rhetoric, *Oratorum sententiae divisiones colores*, in which he rejected the artificial, often decadent language of some of his contemporaries in favour of the disciplined classical style of *Cicero and Livy. The argument is presented through examples taken from famous rhetorical teachers, which are divided into ten books of *Controversiae* (some only preserved in fragments) and at least one (surviving) book of *Suasoriae*. The sketches of the people described form an interesting comment on the literary life of the early Empire. Lab. 149 (118): Seneca's sharp observations and sarcastic judgments give his writings an epigrammatic quality which makes them eminently quotable. See Ben *Jonson.

Lab. 149 (118) *Aleph* 26

Sephardim

The plural of the Hebrew *Sepharad*, meaning Spain: the term applied to Jews who were resident in Spain and Portugal in the Middle Ages and their descendants, as distinguished from *Ashkenazim or German Jews.

Lab. 177 (144) *Aleph* 86

Sepher Yezirah

From the Hebrew *sepher*, 'book' and *yezirah* 'creation': a speculative text dating from between the third and the sixth centuries which seeks to explain the act of creation as a process involving the transition of the universe from its infinite state to its finite manifestation. It is concerned with the changes that took place in the deity as it existed before the Creation – that is, as an ineffable and unfathomable being – to a more personalised presence in the biblical story of creation. Creation is related as a process involving the combination of ten divine emanations, or primordial numbers with the twenty-two letters of the Hebrew alphabet. Together they form the 'thirty-two secret paths of wisdom' through which everything that is and will be exists. This belief illustrates the concept of the creative power of letters underlining the primordial function of language in the history of creation. It is said that 'the letters hover, as it were, on the boundary line between the spiritual and the physical world'. It should be pointed out that in Hebrew each letter is also a specific number, and in this sense a similarity may be detected between aspects of the *Sepher Yezirah* and *Pythagoras' theories of creation. See *Shem Hamephorash.

Lab. 107 (77) *Ficc.* 145, Lab. 119 (89) *Ficc.* 160

Serpent (Serpiente)

A symbol present in most mythologies and religions with varying meanings. In Christianity it is both an emblem of Christ and of saints and the disguise of Lucifer as the tempter in the Garden of Eden. Lab. 150 (119): the serpent is also a symbol of re-embodiment and multiplicity of lives. According to *Origen, it belongs to *Gnostic imagery, as the 'earth-encircling dragon' (*Contra Celsum* 6.25.351). The cult of the serpent occupies an important place in Gnostic mysticism, some of whose sects derive their name from it, such as the Ophites (from the Greek *ophis*, 'snake') and the Nassenes (from the Hebrew *nahas*, 'snake'). H. Jonas, *The Gnostic Religion* (1958), states that in the oppositional vein characteristic of Gnosticism, according to which symbols are interpreted against their traditional acceptance, the biblical God is seen as a symbol of cosmic oppression and the serpent, through its action in the Garden of Eden, as the symbol of redemption. The serpent's deed in inducing Adam and Eve to disobey their creator and taste the fruit of knowledge marks the beginning of all *gnôsis* (knowledge) on earth. One sect, the Peratae, regarded Jesus as a particular incarnation of the serpent since he brought lightness to a world of darkness. In Syrian-Egyptian *gnôsis* the serpent is seen more conventionally as a corrupter, taking the form of an earth-encircling dragon: an allegory of the evil spirit who rules the world.

Lab. 150 (119) *Aleph* 35

Serpent's bed (Lecho de las serpientes)

A *kenning* in the Norse Eddas, meaning gold. See *Sword-water.

Lab. 193 (160) *Aleph* 108

Serrano

A street in *Palermo where Borges spent his early childhood. He describes his house on Serrano Street as having 'two patios, a garden with a tall windmill pump and, on the other side of the garden, an empty lot'. This is in accordance with his definition of the Palermo of his day as 'the shabby northern outskirt of town' (Aleph 125 (203)).

Brodie 68 (83) *Brodie* 68

Serre

A river in the Ardennes and Aisne departments in the north of France.
    Lab. 44 (19) *Ficc*. 97

Seven Pillars of Wisdom see T.E. *Lawrence

Shakespeare, William (1564-1616)

England's greatest poet and playwright, author of more than 35 plays.
Lab. 99 (70): Borges tends to use Shakespeare's name as a symbol of all
humanity, the creator whose identity (not unlike that of God himself) is
dispersed in his multiple creation. He quotes Coleridge, for whom
Shakespeare is a 'literary variation of Spinoza's infinite God'; *Hazlitt,
who said that Shakespeare resembled all men but in himself was nobody;
and *Hugo, who compared the poet to the ocean, the seed bed of all forms
of life (Other Inq. 148). He later repeats this concept in an essay entitled
'Everything and nothing' (*Haced*. 43). Lab. 174 (142): Borges's reference
to 'the immense Germanic name' of Shakespeare stems from the fact that,
with the interpretative work of Lessing in the late eighteenth century
and the early nineteenth-century translations of August Wilhelm von
Schlegel, Shakespeare became one of the most influential forces in the
forging of the new German aesthetics of the anti-classicist and
anti-rationalist *Sturm und Drang* literary movement. He was admired
for the individuality and restlessness of his characters and the grandeur
of their ambitions and uncontrollable passions.
    Fict. 66 (73) *Ficc*. 78, Lab. 99 (70) *Ficc*. 133, Lab 103 (73) *Ficc*. 139, Lab.
174 (142) *Aleph* 82

Sharper's Cards (Los naipes del tahur)

An unpublished collection of literary and political essays by Borges
written in Spain in 1919 and showing the influence of Pío Baroja's biting
realism and ironic pessimism.
    Aleph 22 (20) *Aleph* 167

Shaw, George Bernard (1856-1950)

An Irish playwright, who began his career in London in 1876 as a music
critic and political journalist. Shaw's plays, often didactic, reflect his
social and political ideas and his rejection of Victorian moral values. They
include *Caesar and Cleopatra* (1901), *Man and Superman* and *Major
Barbara* (1905), *Saint Joan* and *Back to Methuselah* (1921). Borges was
particularly attracted to Shaw not only for his many paradoxes but for the
emphasis he placed on the values of the individual as against those of
society (Other Inq. 163). Lab. 149 (118): *Back to Methuselah* consists of five

linked plays whose time-span stretches from 4004 BC to AD 31,920. The theme of the last three is praise of longevity, which culminates in the last play of all, *As Far as Thought Can Reach*. People are born from an egg at the age of seventeen and, after four years of youthful pleasures, evolve into mature beings who, with the passing of time, are granted the experience of all that life can give. Lab. 144 (114): the saying that 'in an infinite period of time, all things happen to all men' is fashioned after the words of the She-Ancient to the Newly Born: 'Everything happens to everybody sooner or later.'

Lab. 149 (118) *Aleph* 26

Shem Hamephorash

From the Hebrew *shem*, 'name', and *mephorash*, 'pre-eminent': the pre-eminent name of God, which differs from all his other names by virtue of its significance. It is the Hebrew equivalent of the *Tetragrammaton, both words being periphrastic allusions, rather than direct references, to God.

Lab. 130 (99) *Ficc.* 175

Shylock

The Jewish usurer in *Shakespeare's *Merchant of Venice*, a character who has been interpreted in many different ways. Lab. 177 (144): the history of Shylock as set out in the fictional *Rosencratz Speaks with the Angel* is obviously apocryphal. There is, however, a long list of speculations about his origins. Among these figure an early ballad entitled *Ser Gernutus the Jew*, an English version of the Italian play *Il Pecorone*, the Persian story of the 'Seven Wise Masters of Rome' from the *Sinbad series, an English version of the *Gesta Romanorum* (c.1472) and the state trial of Rodrigo Lopez, Queen Elizabeth's Jewish physician.

Lab. 177 (144) *Aleph* 86

Siamese Twin Mystery

A detective novel by Ellery Queen (the pseudonym of Frederic Dannay and Manfred Bennington Lee), first published in 1933. The action takes place in the rich house of an eccentric doctor where murderer, victims, Inspector Queen and his son Ellery, together with other guests, are confined by a forest fire which has cut off all possible escape and finally destroys the house. The Inspector, diverted from the identity of the murderer which he had initially guessed, finally reverts to his original hypothesis.

Fict. 67 (74) *Ficc.* 78

Sigurd

In the Volsunga Saga the last of the Volsungs, who 'brings the *Fáfnismál* to an abrupt end' by slaying the dragon *Fafnir. He is known as Siegfried in the *Nibelungenlied*. See *Nibelungs.
   Lab. 193 (160) *Aleph* 109

Sikhs

Believers in a monotheistic religion which originated in the late fifteenth century in the *Punjab combining Hindu and Islamic elements. The Sikhs practise under the leadership of a Guru. They took up arms when persecuted by the *Mongols in the late seventeenth century, and by the early nineteenth century they were dominant in the *Punjab and remained so until its annexation to India in 1849. Though they were loyal to British rule and fought for the British in World War I, they joined Gandhi's movement during the unrest caused by the subsequent economic depression. Many Sikhs were killed in the massacre of *Amritsar (1919). Aleph 85 (133): at the time of the Mongol persecutions the Guru baptized five leading members of the sect, giving them a common surname, Singh (which means 'lion'), and thus turning the nation into a family. The surname is now spread throughout the Sikh population. See *Mutiny.
   Aleph 83 (130) *Aleph* 144

Sills, Milton (1882-?)

A stage actor and film star who made his debut in 1915. A precursor of John Barrymore, Sills played romantic roles and was popular with female audiences.
   Lab. 166 (134) *Aleph* 61

Simeon ben Azai

An early second-century Jewish scholar from Tiberias, a teacher of the oral law (or *Mishnah), renowned for his saintliness. Tradition held that only a sage was allowed to 'enter the Garden' (the euphemism used for theosophical speculations), but Ben Azai's piety was such that he could devote himself to theosophical speculation without injury to the soul. It was said that 'he who has seen Ben Azai in his dreams is himself on the way to piety'. Lab. 130 (99): according to a story in the *Talmud, Ben Azai 'beheld the mysteries of the Garden and died; God granted him the death of the saints' (Talmud, *Hagigah* 14b). It is difficult to decide whether Borges's use of the term 'rabbi' in connection with Ben Azai is a mark of respect or irony for, though Ben Azai's learning was great, he never achieved the status of rabbi.

Lab. 130 (99) *Ficc.* 175

Simonides (c.556-468 BC)

A leading Greek lyric and elegiac poet, few of whose poems survive. Lab. 90/1 (62/3): *Pliny (7.24.1) says that Simonides invented a memory technique (perfected by *Metrododorus) which enabled him to repeat anything he heard verbatim. Pliny probably derived this from *Cicero who attributed to Simonides the saying that, since vision is the sharpest of our senses, 'by an act of sight we keep hold of things that we can scarcely embrace by an act of thought' (*De Oratore* 2.357).

Lab. 91 (63) *Fict.* 122

Simurgh (Simurg)

From the Persian *si*, 'thirty', and *murg*, 'bird' (also *Sen-murgh*, 'the Great Bird'): the bird in the Hindu *Mahabharata*, where it is also called *Garida*. Borges quotes the legend of the Simurgh in a series of illustrations of the pantheistic belief that God is 'several contradictory or (even better) miscellaneous things' (Other Inq. 69). Aleph 36 (52): the Simurgh is the bird referred to as 'a bird that somehow is all birds'. See *Parliament of Birds*.

Aleph 36 (52) *Fict.* 42

Sin (also al Sin)

The Islamic name for *China.

Lab. 182 (150) *Aleph* 93

Sin Kalan (Sin-i Kalal)

Literally 'Great China': the Arabic and Persian name for the seaport of Canton during the *Mongol period. After contact with Hindu and Arab seamen and traders in the tenth century the city grew enormously. It was the first Chinese port to be visited regularly by European merchants.

Lab. 184 (151) *Aleph* 96

Sinbad (Simbad)

One of the characters of the *Thousand and One Nights* whose numerous sea journeys and adventures are spread over many nights. The tales of 'Sinbad the Sailor' are part of a group of independent stories later added to the original nucleus. Borges often draws a comparison between the seafaring Sinbad and *Ulysses (e.g. *Siete noches* 70).

Lab. 146 (116) *Aleph* 23

Sirkar

From Urdu and Persian: the Anglo-Indian word for the state or government.
Ficc. 37

Sisyphus (Sísifo)

In Greek mythology the son of Aeolus, punished for telling Asopus where Zeus had hidden his daughter Aegina. In Hades he was condemned to an endlessly repetitive task: rolling a stone uphill. 'Struggling with hands and feet alike, he would try to push it upward...but when it was on the point of going over the top...the pitiless stone rolled back down to the level' (*Odyssey* 11.593 ff).
Lab. 151 (120) *Aleph* 37

Sketch

A 'weekly journal of art and actuality' published in London from February 1803 to June 1959. Like the *Tatler*, though perhaps not aiming at quite such an exclusive readership, the *Sketch* contained glossy photographs of fashionable society.
Fict. 70 (77) *Ficc.* 82

Slatin, Rudolf Karl, Baron von (1857-1932)

An Austrian explorer and administrator in the Sudan. Lab. 189 (156): in 1892 he was Governor-General of Darfur, and he surrendered to the *Mahdi the following year. He escaped in 1895.
Lab. 189 (156) *Aleph* 103

Smerdis (Esmerdis) (6th century BC)

A Persian prince, the son of Cyrus and younger brother of Cambyses. He was murdered by his brother who was afraid he might usurp the throne during his absence in Egypt. Lab. 29 (5): Gaumata, an impostor claiming to be Smerdis, usurped the throne between 522 and 521 BC. He was deposed and killed by Darius I.
Lab. 29 (5) *Ficc.* 15

Smith, Margaret (1884-?)

An English orientalist. Her *Persian Mystic: Attar* (1932) consists of a short introduction and selected translations of the poetry of *Farid Edin Attar.
Aleph 36 (52) *Ficc.* 43

Smyrna (Esmirna)

A city on the west coast of Asia Minor. Lab. 135 (105): in 'The Immortal' the mention of Smyrna establishes an early link with *Homer, one of whose reputed (and disputed) birth-places it was.

Lab. 135 (105) *Aleph* 7

'So the Platonic year / Whirls out new right and wrong...' see *The *Tower*

Soergel, Albert (1880-?)

A German literary critic, author of *Dichtung und Dichter der Zeit: Eine Schildung der deutschen Literatur des letzen Jahreszente* (2 vols, Leipzig, 1911-28). In this panoramic study of German creative literature from about 1880, Sorgel traces the main influences, native and foreign, that have shaped German literature. Lab. 176 (144): Walt *Whitman is mentioned several times and has a separate entry with a photograph (vol.1, 533-6). The comparison with the character David Jerusalem is of course apocryphal.

Lab. 176 (144) *Aleph* 85

Soler

A street in the northern district of *Palermo running almost parallel to the house on Calle Serrano in which Borges lived as a child. Borges refers to this area as 'shabby' and 'genteel'.

Aleph 20 (27) *Aleph* 165

Soranus, Q. Valerius (fl. 100 BC)

A linguist and classical scholar, described by *Cicero as 'litteratissimus omnium togatorum' ('the most educated of all the Romans'). He was murdered at Pompey's instigation in 82 BC. Lab. 130 (99): the information that Soranus 'divulged the hidden name of Rome' is given by *Pliny (3.65) who recounts that it was held a sin to reveal the 'other name' of Rome 'religiously kept for the weal of the state'; Soranus 'soon paid the penalty', though it is not made clear what.

Lab. 130 (99) *Ficc.* 175

Southern district see *Barrio Sur

Southern railway (Ferrocarriles del sur)

A railway network serving the south of Argentina whose terminal is in Plaza *Constitución. It is now called Ferrocarril General Roca. *Ficc.* 151: there is no 'Ferrocaril Austral'.

Lab. 30 (6) *Ficc.* 17, Lab. 112 (82) *Ficc.* 151

Spectator

A weekly periodical first published in London in 1828. Described then as a review of 'educated radicalism', it is still traditionally associated with the literary views of the intelligentsia, though no longer of the left.

Fict. 66 (73) *Ficc.* 77

Spencer, Herbert (1820-1903)

An English philosopher, author of *First Principles* (1862) and *Principles of Ethics* (1879-93), who expounded the theory that the evolutionary forces which act in the development of animal life are also at work in man and in the moral structure of society, striving towards a goal which corresponds with the 'survival of the fittest'. Brodie 15 (15): the details relating to Spencer are autobiographical: in 'An Autobiographical Essay' Borges recalls that he first learnt about Spencer as a child, from his own father who was 'a disciple of Spencer' (Aleph 126 (204)). What particularly attracted him, as much as it did his father, was the importance Spencer gave to the individual and Spencer's defence of individual identity and freedom against the increasing intrusion of the state (Other Inq. 35).

Brodie 15 (15) *Brodie* 127

Spengler, Oswald (1880-1936)

A German philosopher of history, best known for his pessimistic work *The Decline of the West* (1918). Lab. 103 (73): Spengler argues against a linear interpretation of history, which he sees as consisting of aimless cycles of cultural configurations, of which western European civilisation is only one and already in decline. Lab. 174 (142): Spengler expresses the passing of cultures in terms of seasons, at times Apollonian, at times Faustian. By the latter term he means everything that is dynamic and speculative, a romantic longing for the unattainable. An ardent nationalist, he believed in the need for an aristocratic élite; today he is accused of laying the intellectual foundations of fascism. His concept of *Faust became the symbol of German dynamism at the time of the *Third Reich.

Lab. 103 (73) *Ficc.* 139, Lab. 174 (142) *Aleph* 82

Spenser

Richard *Church's biography of the poet Edmund Spenser (1552-1599) contained an extensive account of the composition of *The Faerie Queene*. Aleph 36 (51): the 'fault previously noted by Richard William Church (*Spenser*, 1879)', constituting a point of comparison with 'The Approach to Almotasim', may be found at page 130. Church writes: 'It is a heroic poem in which the heroine, who gives her name to it, never appears: a story of which the basis and starting point is whimsically withheld for disclosure in the last book which was never written!'

Aleph 36 (45) *Ficc.* 42

Spinoza, Baruj (1632-1677)

A Dutch Jewish philosopher, an admirer and follower of the rationalism of *Descartes and author of one of the most comprehensive systems of philosophy ever composed. His unorthodox views caused consternation among the Jews of Amsterdam who, in 1655, fearful of their position in a Christian environment, felt compelled to excommunicate him. Spinoza set out to deduce the nature of reality using a system conceived entirely through reason. His philosophy, expanded in *Ethics*, is essentially pantheistic and explains the universe as one substance or independent unity which must be its own cause. This belief led him to deduce that, since it comprises the whole of nature and its creation, this substance must be equivalent to God. Hence he concluded that God does not transcend the universe but is an impersonal force immanent in nature, an assertion that shocked his contemporaries. In *Ethics* Spinoza distinguished substance from its attributes and modes. Lab. 33 (9): substance, nature or God is infinite and manifests itself through an infinity of attributes, of which only two, thought and extension, are known to man. It is also divided into an infinity of finite modes (defined as 'parts' of the whole and ultimately indivisible from it), of which human beings are an example. For Spinoza there exists an exact correspondence between the 'modes' of one 'attribute' and the modes of any other, which makes the human mind a part of God's intellect, as the human body is a part of the physical system of nature. Though part of the absolute intellect, human thought can experience the absolute only through intuition, an insight Spinoza terms 'the intellectual love of God'; total knowledge is impossible since only two of God's attributes are known to man. Spinoza tries to achieve this intuition of God (or knowledge, or truth) through a logically deduced system of metaphysics in which arguments are advanced like geometrical theorems. Lab. 112 (81): this particular characteristic of Spinoza's method of exposition highlights the significance of the compass in 'Death and the Compass'. Borges was attracted to the idea of Spinoza 'creating' God in his elaboration of a rational system of metaphysics and wrote two poems to this effect. The juxtaposition of reason and intuition is a distinguishing feature of Borges's own writing as exemplified in his often used formulation *'álgebra y fuego'* ('algebra and fire'). See *More geometrico.

Lab. 33 (9) *Ficc.* 22, Lab. 112 (81) *Ficc.* 151, Brodie 23(25) *Brodie* 25

Staffordshire

One of Borges's many allusions to his family ancestry; his grandmother Fanny Haslam was born in Staffordshire. See Francisco *Borges.

Lab. 45 (20) *Ficc.* 99

Stamford Bridge

A village on the border of the East Riding of Yorkshire, seven miles from York, where *Harald Hardrada, king of Norway, was defeated in 1066 by *Harold, king of England.

Lab. 146 (116) *Aleph* 22

Stein, Gertrude (1874-1946)

An American writer and critic who lived and worked in Paris, presiding over an artistic salon and encouraging young writers; she was the friend and confidante of Matisse, Picasso, Braque and Douanier Rousseau, and a champion of the literary 'avant-garde' which included Hemingway, T.S. Eliot and Ezra Pound. The experimental nature of her fiction, as in *Three Lives* (1909), and of her poetry, as in *Tender Buttons* (1914), greatly influenced her generation.

Fict. 66 (73) *Ficc.* 77

Stephen (Estéban) (d. c.31)

The first Christian martyr and saint, stoned to death for proclaiming his belief in the divinity of Jesus. Lab. 152 (121): the episode of Stephen's martyrdom, believed to have made a deep impression upon *Paul, is related in Acts 7:58-60 in which it is said that Stephen's accusers laid their cloaks at the feet of a certain young man 'whose name was Saul'.

Lab. 152 (121) *Aleph* 37

Stockyards (Corrales)

A street in southern *Buenos Aires near the *Riachuelo, so-called because it led to the old *corrales* where cattle were sold and slaughtered.

Brodie 24 (26) *Brodie* 27

Suakin

A town in the *Sudan, on the Red Sea, formerly the port whence slaves were shipped to the Americas and Muslim pilgrims sailed to Mecca.
Aleph 77 (120) *Aleph* 128

Suárez

The name of several Argentine military men, including Borges's ancestor to whom the allusion in Aleph 54 (81) probably refers. Manuel Isidoro Suárez (1759-1843) was Borges's mother's maternal grandfather. Borges honoured his memory in two poems. Suárez fought in the Wars of Independence and is remembered as the victor of Junín. Aleph 54 (81): in the period leading to 1829, during the struggles between *Federalists and *Unitarians, Suárez fought on the side of the Unitarians.
Aleph 54 (81) *Aleph* 53

Sudan

The largest nation in north-east Africa, whose name derives from an ancient Arabic expression meaning 'land of the blacks'. Its population is largely Arabic in the north and African in the south; the many different tribes are divided by language and customs. Aleph 77 (120): tribalism is one of the main political problems of the Sudan.
Aleph 77 (120) *Aleph* 128

Suipacha Street

A fashionable street in the Barrio Norte district of *Buenos Aires.
Brodie 34 (38) *Brodie* 93

Sulaco

A town and province in the fictional country of Costaguana in *Conrad's novel *Nostromo*. See José *Avellanos, *Estado Occidental, *Golfo Plácido, *Higuerota, José *Korzeniovski.
Brodie 82 (100) *Brodie* 113

Summa Theologiae (Suma Teológica)

One of the most important texts of the Christian Church in which Aquinas (1225-1274) systematises and defines the theology of the Christian faith. Divided in three parts, each of about 1,500 pages, it discusses the nature of God, angels and man, the divine government of human acts and the state of grace (part 1); the theological and cardinal virtues (part 2); and the incarnation and resurrection of Christ and the sacraments (part 3). The material is arranged under different 'questions', each divided into 'articles' headed under a statement and presenting the objections to it, which are contested one by one. Aleph 71 (110) refers to the question 'whether God can make the past not to have been', which Aquinas answers in the negative, his principal reason being that changing the past would imply a contradiction and as such a diminution of God's power (part 1, q.25, art.4).

Aleph 71 (110) *Aleph* 78

Surakarta

The kingdom and capital of Java, whose population is largely Muslim. Lab. 189: the reference is probably to Surakarta's famous mosque, Mesjit Gede. The incident alluded to has not been traced.

Lab. 189 (156) *Aleph* 103

Swift, Jonathan (1667-1745)

An Anglo-Irish satirist and man of letters. In his best-known work, *Gulliver's Travels* (1726), the eponymous hero describes his journeys to various places, including *Lilliput where the inhabitants are a mere six inches tall and Brobdingnag which is inhabited by giants. Other creatures met by Gulliver are the Houyhnhnms (horses endowed with reason) and their enemies the *Yahoos (brutal beasts in the shape of men). Borges learnt from Swift the device of the 'foreign observer', an ironic means of presenting absurdity through the eyes of a naïve or uncomprehending onlooker. Other points of contact include the mixture of the serious and the absurd, economy of expression and attention to detail.

Lab. 94 (65) *Fict.* 124

Sword-water (Agua de la espada)

A metaphor for blood used in the Norse Eddas: an example of a *kenning*, a type of condensed metaphor found in Old Norse sagas. A kenning is always a compound consisting of two nouns, a head noun and a modifying noun, neither of which refers directly to the object designated, the comparison being usually by attributive association. Other kennings for blood are 'dew of wounds' or 'dew of sorrow'. Borges wrote extensively on kennings in *Etern.* (43-67) and *Lit. germ.* (141-151).

Lab. 193 (160) *Aleph* 108

Syntagma

Greek for 'collection': the earliest collection of heretical doctrines by Justin Martyr. Another text of the same title, also directed against heresy, was written at the beginning of the third century by Hippolytus of Rome, of which there remains only a fragment, *Contra Noetum*.

Lab. 125 (95) *Ficc*. 169

Tabaré

A romantic verse drama by the Uruguayan poet Juan Zorrilla de San Martín (1855-1931) first published in 1888. *Tabaré* tells the story of a *mestizo* in love with a Spanish girl who is kidnapped by an Indian chief. In the process of rescuing her, the young man is killed by the girl's brother who believes him to be the abductor.

Brodie 18 (18) *Brodie* 131

Tabernacle

The tent or portable shrine carried by the Jews during their wanderings in the wilderness. It consisted of an inner sanctum known as the 'Holy of Holies' and an outer chamber used as a temple. The extensive description in Exodus (25-31 and 35-40) deals with the construction of the tabernacle, its precise measurements, the material from which it was built, its ornamentation, and even the colour of its curtains, all of which are laid down in minute detail. The tabernacle was believed to constitute the dwelling-place of the Lord, its symmetry and harmony being a reflection of divine perfection. Lab. 153 (122): the reference to the quadrangular shape of the Hebrew tabernacle accords with the overall pattern of the dimensions given for its construction.

Lab. 153 (122) *Aleph* 39

Tachilhunpo (Tashilhunpo)

Tibetan for 'mount of blessing': one of the largest lamaseries in Tibet. It was founded in the fifteenth century and its Grand Lama is regarded as the reincarnation of the Buddha Amitabha, second in rank only to the Dalai Lama.

Aleph 35 (50) *Ficc*. 40

Tacitus, Cornelius (Tácito) (55-120)

Tacitus wrote the history the Roman Empire from 14 to 68 AD (*Annals*) and from 69 to 96 AD (*Histories*). At once passionate and epigrammatic, his work denounces the evil effects of power, the injustices suffered by the Romans at the hands of their emperors, and the servility with which senators and nobles bowed to their capricious rule. The surviving books of the *Annals* quoted in Lab. 46 (21) (books 1-4, part of 5, most of 6, and 11-16 incomplete) cover the reigns of Tiberius, Caligula, Claudius and Nero. The violent episodes depicted show Tacitus' acute perception of tragedy, to which Borges pays tribute in relation to Christ's crucifixion, saying that, though Tacitus did not refer to the crucifixion directly, its occurrence is suggested and implied in his portrayal of the time (Other Inq. 167).

Lab. 46 (21) *Ficc.* 100

Tacuarembó

Guarani for 'tall slender cane': a river in central *Uruguay which gives its name to a city and department. Lab. 41 (16): it rises not far from the Brazilian border near *Sant' Anna.

Lab. 41 (16) *Ficc.* 31, Lab. 96 (67) *Ficc.* 129

Tacuarí

A street in southern *Buenos Aires near Plaza *Constitución. See *Caseros.

Aleph 17 (23) *Aleph* 160

Tahafut-ul-falasifa

The Incoherence of the Philosophers, an attack by the anti-rationalist Islamic philosopher *Ghazali upon the Neoplatonism of Avicenna (Ibn Sina). Ghazali held that the world was deliberately created by God and not, as the Neoplatonists claimed, simply an emanation of a First Being. His use of the word *Tahafut* ('destruction') implies something like the tumbling down of a house of cards; the same concept was used by *Averroes in his refutation of Ghazali. See *Tahafut-ul-Tahafut*

Lab. 180 (148) *Aleph* 91

Tahafut-ul-Tahafut

Incoherence of Incoherence, a philosophical treatise published in about 1180, in which *Averroes seeks to refute *Ghazali's refutation of philosophy. Lab. 180 (148): the subject of chapter 11 is that divine nature cannot participate in the 'emotions' and passing 'inclinations' which occur in individual and material bodies. Averroes's argument in opposition to Ghazali is that there is no activity in God other than what there was from the start. Since God created only the universal and not the individual aspects of reality (*'ipse fecit universalia et non fecit particularia'*), it follows that God does not perceive the particular (*'ipsum non apprehendere particularia'*), whose existence is subsequent to creation. See *Aristotle.

Lab. 180 (148) *Aleph* 91

Talcahuano

A street in the centre of *Buenos Aires containing numerous antiquarian and second-hand bookshops near its intersection with *Corrientes.
Lab. 30 (6) *Ficc.* 16

Talmud

Jewish writings dating from the early centuries of the Christian era embodying the oral law, or *Mishnah, and discussions of its interpretation. Its emphasis is on ritual and legalistic aspects of Jewish tradition. See *Hasidim.
Lab. 106 (76) *Ficc.* 143

Tamberlik, Enrico (1820-1889)

A famous Italian tenor, possibly of Roumanian origin, who made his debut in Naples and sang in most of the world's opera houses. Among his most famous performances was Rossini's *Otello* with a libretto derived from *Shakespeare, first produced in Naples in 1816 (not to be confused with Verdi's opera of the same name whose première was held in 1887 after Tamberlik had retired).
Aleph 70 (108) *Aleph* 76

Tangier (Tánger)

A town in *Morocco, on the straits of Gibraltar. Lab. 182 (150): Tangier was an important Muslim centre at the time of the Almohad dynasty.
Lab. 146 (116) *Aleph* 22, Lab. 182 (150) *Aleph* 93

Tao te Ching (Tao te King)

A text dating from the third century BC illustrating the doctrines of *Taoism. Legend attributes it to an ancient sage, Tao te Ching.
Lab. 37 *Ficc.* 27

Taoism (Taoismo)

From the Chinese *tao*, 'the way': a philosophic and religious system which has been practised in China for more than 2,000 years. Over the centuries Taoist beliefs have mingled with Buddhism and with the preachings of *Confucius, leading to a similarity of ideas within the three systems. Tao views the universe as a hierarchy, the entirety of whose being is reflected in man: anyone who sets out to understand the structure of the world ends up by finding it within the workings of his own mind. All being is 'tao' and returns to it: from unity to multiplicity and back to unity. Within this unity the alternation of the complementary energy forces 'Yin' and 'Yang' is the origin of the apparent external variety of reality. While the ways of the world are many and lead to a scattering of the personality, the Taoist aims to retain a primordial conviction of unity, balancing the Yin and the Yang within himself. The elderly, closer to realising this condition, are also closer to sainthood. Hence the cult of longevity.

Lab. 49 (24) *Ficc.* 175

Tapalquén

An area in the south east of the province of *Buenos Aires near the hills of Tandil.

Brodie 64 (77) *Brodie* 59

Tapecito

The name given in *Uruguay to a half-caste Indian of *Guaraní descent.

Aleph 73

Taprobana

A gem-mining centre in Sri Lanka.

Lab. 60 (34) *Ficc.* 73

Tarik ibn Ziyad (Tarik Benzeyad)

An Arab leader who landed in Gibraltar in 711 and overran almost the whole of the Iberian peninsula, conquering it within the span of seven years. A legendary account of this event is told in the *Thousand and One Nights* (Nights 271-2), called 'The City of Labtayat' (perhaps Toledo). The story is told of a tower which was always kept shut. When a king died and another succeeded him, he would add a lock, until there were twenty-four. Eventually a king arrived from a different house and insisted on opening the tower. Having pulled off the locks, he entered and found figures of turbaned Arabs on horses and camels bearing lances, and an inscription warning that whoever opened the door would conquer the country. This was when Tarik ibn Ziyad sacked the city and killed its king. Tarik proceeded along the treasure-filled chambers of the tower, and when he came to the fifth chamber he found 'a marvellous mirror, great and round, of mixed metals, which had been made for Solomon, son of David...wherein whosover looked might see the counterfeit present-ment of the seven climates of the world'. Borges adapted and translated this story in Infamy (107).

Aleph 22 (30) *Aleph* 168

Tarnowitz (Tarnoitz)

A town in south-west *Poland, in the province of Katowice, formerly in Silesia, which belonged to Germany.
   Lab. 176 (144) *Aleph* 85

Tartarin see Alphonse *Daudet

Tartarus (Tártaro)

In classical mythology an abyss below Hades where the Titans were imprisoned by Zeus. Later it became a general term for the underworld.
   Lab. 137 (107) *Aleph* 9

Tatler

A glossy magazine with a strong upper-class appeal, founded in 1901.
   Fict. 70 (77) *Ficc.* 82

Taylor, Philip Meadow (1808-1876)

An Anglo-Indian administrator, journalist and novelist. Taylor was in the service of the Nizam of *Hyderabad until 1860, when he returned to England for health reasons. Lab. 195 (162): his novel *Confessions of a Thug* (1839) was instrumental in eradicating Thuggee under the British Raj. Thuggee originated in the worship of Kali, the Hindu goddess of destruction whose disciples were rewarded with the right to strangle and steal.
   Lab. 195 (162) *Aleph* 111

Temple

A street now known as Viamonte, in the fashionable Barrio Norte, named after the religious order of the Templars.
   Brodie 75 (92) *Brodie* 79

Temple of Fire see *Lutf Ali Azur

Tennyson, Alfred Lord (1809-1892)

An English poet who was appointed Poet Laureate in 1850 in succession to Wordsworth. Queen Victoria's favourite poet, Tennyson was the most representative versifier of the Victorian era. His *Idylls of the King*, a series of connected verses on the Arthurian legend, the first of which was written in 1842 and the last in 1885, was outstandingly popular. The distinguishing feature of Tennyson's poetry is his sensitivity to the sound of words. In an article on the translations of the *Thousand and One Nights*, Borges discusses the theme of the story-within-a-story, quoting a line from Tennyson as the perfect definition: 'Laborious orient ivory, sphere in sphere' (*Etern*. 133). Lab. 196 (163): the allusion is to 'Flower in the Crannied Wall' (1869) which reads: 'Flower in the crannied wall, / I pluck you out of the crannies, / I hold you here, root and all, in my hand, / Little flower – but *if* I could understand / What you are, root and all, and all in all, / I should know what God and man is.'

Lab. 196 (163) *Aleph* 113

'Terribilis visu facies, sed mente benignus, / Longaque robusto pectore barba fuit!'

'He was of frightening appearance but had a gentle nature / and his long beard fell on his strong chest': from the anonymous epitaph to *Droctulft which appears in full in *Paul the Deacon's *History of the Lombards* (3. 19). The lines are quoted by *Gibbon in chapter 45 of the *Decline and Fall* to describe 'the influence of climate and example' which the *Lombards underwent in contact with the culture of Italy. Gibbon remarks that the Lombards so succumbed to the influence of those they conquered that by the fourth generation 'they surveyed with curiosity and affright the portraits of their savage forefathers'. The lines are quoted also by *Croce in *La Poesia* as an example of poetry blossoming spontaneously in the most unexpected situations. See *'Contempsit caros ...'

Lab. 159 (127) *Aleph* 47

Teste, Edmond

A fictional character, the protagonist of *Valéry's early prose work *La Soirée avec Monsieur Teste* (1896). Lab. 67 (41): Edmond Teste is considered to be Valéry's *alter ego*: the opinions expressed by him during the course of his nocturnal conversations embody the literary ideas and intellectual pursuits of his author – concern with metre, syntax and punctuation, linguistic preciosity and a catholic interest in subjects as diverse as lithography, chess and philosophy. Pierre *Menard, who reflects many of Borges's interests and preoccupations, may be seen as a parody of Edmond Teste.

Lab. 67 (41) *Ficc*. 51, Fict. 66 *Ficc*. 77

Tetragrammaton

From the Greek *tettara*, 'four' and *gramma*, 'letter': the technical name in Judaism for the four Hebrew letters J H V H denoting the pre-eminent name of God: that which is separate from, and which exceeds, all other appellations. Of uncertain meaning, it is generally thought to be etymologically connected with an imperfect form of the Hebrew verb 'to be'. The tetragrammaton was uttered only by the high priest during worship in the temple, probably to safeguard it from desecration by heathens. It was held in such reverence that, after the destruction of the temple, its utterance was forbidden, and in the liturgical passages in which it appeared it was pronounced *Adonai* ('Lord'). In a non-religious context it was referred to simply as 'the Name'. Lab. 112 (82): there is historical precedent for Borges's irreverent and perhaps subversive use of the tetragrammaton in 'Death and the Compass'. As its utterance fell into disuse its original pronunciation became uncertain (though it is now thought to be represented in English by the sound 'Yahweh'). Moreover it often came to be written in an abbreviated or substitute form worked out by means of combinations based on the numerical value of the four sacred letters. This extreme reverence attracted a heretical belief in its magic and healing properties, and its letters were used in magic papyri and inscribed in amulets.

Lab. 107 (77) *Ficc*. 145

Tetrarch (Tetrarca)

From the Greek for 'ruler of one of four divisions': a term meaning 'vassal-ruler' given to minor despots in the provinces of Judaea and Syria in the Roman period. Lab. 106 (77): there was obviously no Tetrarch of Galilee at the time in which 'Death and the Compass' was set, but the name recalls Herod Antipas, son of Herod the Great, who was Tetrarch of Galilee during the lifetime of Jesus and who beheaded John the Baptist.

Lab. 106 (77) *Ficc*. 144

Tetuán

The capital of Spanish Morocco, a town and port on the Mediterranean dating from the expulsion of the Muslims from Spain in 1492. It served as a refuge also for some Spanish and Portuguese Jews, who formed their own community from 1511 onwards, preserving their language, customs and traditions. Lab. 189: from 1807 until 1912 Jews were consigned to their own quarter, called the *judería*.

Lab. 189 (156) *Aleph* 103

Thames

A street in *Buenos Aires running from Villa Crespo to *Palermo. Brodie 24 (27): Thames no longer intersects with *Triunvirato: by mentioning 'the corner' of these two streets, Borges is evoking the Palermo of his youth. Allusion to this corner of old Buenos Aires, which has long disappeared, conjures up the life of hoodlums and petty criminals nostalgically recalled in Borges's collection of poems *Para las seis cuerdas (For the Guitar)*. In

'The Puppet' a pimp meets his fate:

> Un balazo lo tumbó
> En Thames y Triunvirato;
> Se mudó a un barrio vecino,
> En la Quinta del Ñato.

> A pistol shot brought him down
> on the corner of Thames and Triunvirato;
> he moved to a new neighbourhood,
> the cemetery, called Quinta del Ñato. (Trans. Anthony Edkins)

Brodie 24 (27) *Brodie* 27

'The rich Trojans from Zelea that drink the black water of the Aisepos' (Los ricos Teucros de Zelea que beben el agua negra del Esepo') see *Homer

'The river nymphs and the dolorous and humid Echo' ('Las ninfas de los ríos, la dolorosa y húmida Eco')

A quotation from *Don *Quixote*, part 1, ch.26. The Knight of the Doleful Countenance, having decided to imitate the style of Amadis of Gaul (the hero of an early romance of chivalry), engraves lamentations on the bark of a tree and calls on the mythical creatures of the woods and 'the river nymphs and the dolorous and humid Echo' for consolation. Rodríguez Martín in his notes to the Clásicos Castellanos edition offers the following explanation for the epithets 'dolorous and humid'. The nymph Echo, daughter of Air and Earth, is condemned by Juno to silence except for repeating the last two syllables of anything said to her. She is called dolorous and humid because, having been rejected by Narcissus for her disabilities, she retires to the caverns and glens, where she is consumed by grief.
Lab. 67 (40) *Ficc.* 51

'The wizard who fashioned a labyrinth and was then doomed to wander in it' ('El hechicero que teje un laberinto y que se ve forzado a errar en él')

Perhaps an allusion to the myth of Daedalus. Daedalus, on the orders of King Minos, constructed a labyrinth for the *Minotaur to live in and trap his victims. Fearing that Daedalus would reveal the secret of his design, Minos imprisoned him in the labyrinth with his son Icarus. Daedalus thereupon made wings for himself and his son, and they both flew out of the labyrinth.

Lab. 179 (146) *Aleph* 88

Thebes Hekatompylos (Tebas Hekatompilos)

The ancient capital of Boeotia, home of the mythical king Oedipus and the scene of other Greek tragedies. Lab. 135 (106): the epithet 'Hekatompylos', 'with a hundred gates', is applied to Thebes by *Homer in his list of the Trojan allies to indicate its wealth and power (*Iliad* 2. 505). Lab. 151 (120): the king of Thebes who saw two suns refers to Euripides' *Bacchae* (918): Pentheus, king of Thebes, grandson of Cadmus, the city's founder, has been initiated in the Dionysian rites and sent mad; he appears on the stage in a daze and utters the words: 'Why now! I seem to see two suns; a double Thebes; / Our city's walls with seven gates appears double.'

Lab. 135 (106) *Aleph* 7, Lab. 151 (120) *Aleph* 37

Theopompus (Teopompo) (b. 380 BC)

A Greek historian, author of a history of Greece in twelve books of which only some fragments remain, and of *Philippics*. The latter is based on the reign of Philip of Macedon (360-336 BC) and contains long digressions on the nations with whom Macedon came into contact. The original text is lost, but fragments are quoted by *Plutarch and other later historians. Fict. 68 (75) refers to a passage from *Philippics* during a dialogue betweeen Silenus and Milenus. Silenus talks of a continent where, among other wonderful things, there grow by the River of Pleasure trees which produce fruit of a 'contrary nature': anyone who eats the fruit 'forgets what he loved and desired, grows younger and relives his life...becoming a youth, a child, an infant and then dying' (Aelian, *Varia Historia*, bk. 8).

Fict 68 (75) *Ficc.* 79

'There is no god but the God' ('No hay otro dios que el Dios')

The basic Muslim profession of faith: 'There is no God but Allah and Mohammed is his Prophet.' See *Allah.

Lab. 182 (150) *Aleph* 93

'There seemed a certainty in degradation'.

A quotation from chapter 103 of T.E.*Lawrence's *Seven Pillars of Wisdom*. The chapter is entitled 'Myself' and consists of a self-analysis on the author's thirtieth birthday. Near to fulfilling the ambitions of four years earlier, at the start of his Arab adventure Lawrence feels unworthy of the 'trust' and 'favourable opinion' he enjoys and wonders if all

240

established reputations like his are 'founded on fraud'. He confesses that, though he has always craved to be popular and famous and has been afraid of failure, he has also felt a deep attraction for base behaviour. 'There seemed a certainty in degradation,' he explains: a kind of safety, for no matter how high one could rise there was a limit below which one could not fall.

Lab. 125 (151) *Ficc.* 169

Thesaurus see Louis-Marie *Quicherat

Theseus (Teseo)

A mythical Greek hero, the son of Aegeus and the slayer of the *Minotaur. Among Theseus' other heroic adventures were the killing of *Procrustes and the defeat of the Amazons and Centaurs.

Lab. 172 (140) *Aleph* 70

Thessaly (Tesalia)

An area of north-central Greece inhabited at least since 1000 BC in which was situated the beautiful Vale of Tempe. Thessaly passed to Macedon in 344 BC and two centuries later became part of the Roman province of Macedonia. Lab. 143 (113): the river mentioned here could be the Peneus or one of its two tributaries, the Titaresios or the Enipeus.

Lab. 143 (113) *Aleph* 18

Thilo, Johann Karl

A colleague of *Gesenius, with whom he travelled in 1822 to Paris, London and Oxford to examine oriental manuscripts.

Lab. 173 (141) *Aleph* 81

Third Emperor (Tercer Emperador) see *Luminous Dynasty

Third Reich (Tercer Reich) (1933-1945)

From the German *Reich*, 'empire': a concept made popular by a treatise *Das Dritte Reich* ('The Third Reich') published in 1923 by A. Moller van den Bruck. It originated in the Christian tradition of the millennium described in the book of Revelation (20-22) and adopted in the twelfth century by the German theologian J. von Floris (1132-1202). Floris divided all time into three ages: the age of the Father (up to the birth of Christ); the age of the Son (up to 1260); and the age of the Holy Spirit, or *Drittes Reich*, a messianic age in which there would be a universal reordering of peoples and nations. Under National Socialism the idea of a Third Reich was reinterpreted in triadic *Hegelian terms, as the synthesis of the First Reich, the Holy Roman Empire, 962-1806, (the thesis), and the Second Reich, the empire of the Hohenzollerns created by Bismark in 1871, (the antithesis).

Lab. 118 (88) *Ficc.* 159, Lab. 178 (146) *Aleph* 87, Brodie 83 (101) *Brodie* 113

'This dog lying in the manure' (Este perro tirado en el estiércol') see Argos

Thousand and One Nights (Las Mil y una noches)

An anonymous collection of tales of Indian origin but of uncertain date translated into Persian and Arabic. Its nucleus was expanded with stories from Baghdad, anecdotes about rogues and tricksters from Cairo, and other independent tales, to make up a number intended originally as meaning simply 'a large quantity'. The stories can be divided into three kinds: 'histories', or long romances based on historical or allegedly historical events; anecdotes, short stories dealing with historical personages, mainly of the *Abbasid Caliphate; and romances and romantic fiction. The last category can be subdivided into: stories which are purely romantic, making free use of the supernatural; stories which appear to be purely fictitious but which reproduce the habits and manners of the Abbasid Caliphate and the Eyonbite Sultans of Egypt; and – the largest category, from which most European authors have drawn inspiration – stories which are purely fictitious, and stories of miracles and saints. There are also moral stories and some tales which serve as an excuse for dissertations upon various subjects. The most striking characteristic of the book is the extreme simplicity of its style, which belies most Western readers' expectation of tales 'showering barbaric pearl and gold'. The *Thousand and One Nights* first became known in Europe during the eighteenth century. Borges was an avid reader of the work, which he declared 'superior to the Koran' for its imaginative power. He often referred to it in his fiction and wrote an essay on its various translations (*Etern.* 99). As a boy he found *Burton's unexpurgated translation, published in London in 16 volumes in 1885-8, in his father's library. This edition was considered pornographic at the time because of its illustrations and sexual references, and Borges claims he had to read it secretly in the attic but was too carried away by the splendour of the narrative to notice its erotic content. A number of other editions are also mentioned by Borges. Many aspects of the book fascinated him, such as the circular form of the narrative which makes it the eternal book, the idea of multiple stories told within the framework of a single story, and the disquieting effect of the story which includes its own story-telling. Aleph 36 (52): vol. 10, 128-9, of Burton's *Arabian Nights* discusses the rise of Sufism (before 815 AD) and its influence upon Islamic thought and art. Burton defines 'Sufyism' as 'a revival of classic Platonism and Christian *Gnosticism with a mingling of modern Hylozoism; which, quickened by the glowing imagination of the East, speedily formed itself into a creed the most poetical and impractical, the most spiritual and the most transcendental ever invented.' See *Night of Nights, *Scheherazade.

Lab. 37 (13) *Ficc.* 27, Lab. 51 (25) *Ficc.* 106, *Ficc.* 43, Fict. 155 (167) *Ficc.* 188

'Thus fought the heroes, tranquil their admirable hearts...' 'Así combatieron los héroes...'

A pseudo-Chinese literary reference, untypical since military heroism is not a common theme in Chinese literature. In early Chinese poetry references to bravery were normally connected with hunting. In later periods military figures were presented as tragic victims who had died on distant borders and whose souls wandered unhappily, or as errant husbands who had abandoned their wives for long periods. Only in popular fiction do bandit-warriors attain heroic stature.

Lab. 52 (27) *Ficc.* 108

Tiber

The greatest river in Central Italy, by whose left bank *Rome was built.

Lab. 59 (34) *Ficc.* 73

Tientsin or T'ien Ching

A city in north-east China.

Lab. 49 (24) *Ficc.* 104

Tilsit

A city in the USSR formerly in East Prussia, famous for the meeting in 1807 of Napoleon and Czar Alexander which led to a peace treaty between France, Russia and Prussia.

Lab. 175 (143) *Aleph* 84

Times Literary Supplement (Suplemento literario del Times)

A weekly book supplement of *The Times*, first published in January 1902.

Fict. 67 (73) *Ficc.* 77

Tlön

One of two regions in an imaginary planet referred to in the literature of *Uqbar, the other being Mlejnas. Its description is said to be contained in *A First Encyclopaedia of Tlön*. Eventually material objects from this ideal region begin to invade reality. The nasal sound of 'Tlön' connotes a Nordic atmosphere always idealised in Borges's writings, contrasting with the Arabic sounds of the more earthbound Uqbar.

Lab. 27 (3) *Ficc*. 13

Topographia christiana see *Cosmas

Toulet, Paul Jean (1867-1920)

A French writer famous for his conversational wit and literary pyrotechnics. Toulet employed unusual syntactical structures, turns of phrase and analogies to convey complex ideas. His many works include *Le mariage de Don Quichotte* (1902). Borges refers to Toulet and his 'Contrerimes' (*Etern*. 115).

Lab. 64 (38) *Ficc*. 47

Toulon, rue de

In his 'Commentaries' Borges identifies the rue de Toulon with the Paseo Colón or the old *Paseo de Julio, a street by the port of *Buenos Aires known for its brothels and rowdy taverns (Aleph 173).

Lab. 110 (80) *Ficc*. 148

Tower, The

A collection of poems by W.B. *Yeats published in 1928. Lab. 102 (72): the lines 'So the Platonic Year / Whirls out new right and wrong', quoted as an epigraph to the story 'Theme of the Traitor and the Hero', come from section 2 of *Nineteen Hundred and Nineteen*, written in response to atrocities committed during 1919 by the *Black and Tans at Gort in Galway. The poem contrasts images of the past with the present in which 'the growing murderousness of the world' reappears. The passage evokes the concept of recurring history and the theme of men acting according to a 'prefigured' scheme, both central to the story. The term 'Platonic Year' refers to *Plato's theory enunciated in the *Timaeus* (39), concerning the revolution of the planets which will eventually return to their starting point (*Etern*. 92).

Lab. 102 (72) *Ficc*. 137

Trafalgar

A cape in Spain, south of Cadiz, the scene of Nelson's famous victory in the Napoleonic wars (21 October 1805).
Aleph 76 (120) *Aleph* 128

Trahison des clercs, La

'Betrayal of the intellectuals': the title of a French pamphlet by Julien Benda (1867-1956) published in 1927. Benda attacked nineteenth- and twentieth-century intellectuals who had failed to uphold their spiritual ideals, and had become involved instead in political and social causes. The expression has passed into common usage in France, though ironically it is often used to reproach those intellectuals who have retired from the problems of real life to their ivory towers.
Lab. 68 (42) *Ficc.* 53

Travancore (Travancor)

A state on the west coast of southern *India.
Aleph 33 (48) *Ficc.* 38

Treinta y tres

The thirty-three heroes of Uruguayan history. In 1825, under the leadership of Lavalleja, a band of Uruguayans conceived a plan to free their country from Brazilian rule. Secretly they crossed the River Uruguay and made a series of successful attacks on the vastly superior Brazilian forces. As a result the provisional government of an independent Provincia Oriental was formed and was joined to the United Provinces of the Rio de la Plata.
Brodie 40 (47) *Brodie* 103

Trèves (Treveris)

A city on the Rhine, founded by Augustus. More Roman ruins survive there than in any other German town. In the fourth century Trèves, now Trier, became an episcopal see.
Lab. 153 (122) *Aleph* 39

Trichinopolis (Trichinópoli)

A district of the Indian city of Madras. Aleph 33: Trichinopolis is known for its manufacture of cigars.
Aleph 33 (47) *Ficc.* 37

Triste-le-Roy

A name invented by Amanda *Molina Vedia. In a note for an American edition of 'Death and the Compass' Borges wrote: 'Triste-le Roy itself is a heightened and distorted version of the roomy and pleasant "Hotel las Delicias", which still survives in so many memories.' Distinguishing features of the imagined villa Triste-le-Roy, such as its portico, its niches with half-dressed nymphs and its patio with white diamond-shaped tiles, can be seen in an engraving of the hotel by Borges's sister Norah.

Lab. 112 (82) *Ficc.* 143

Triunvirato

An avenue in *Buenos Aires, in the vicinity of *Chacarita and Federico *Lacroze. See *Thames.

Brodie 24 (27) *Brodie* 27

Troy (Troya)

The city in north-west Asia Minor besieged by the Greeks in the *Iliad*. Its exact location, and even its existence, have long been debated. Recent archaeological evidence, however, has established the site. Lab. 70 (44): the allusion to 'those lost Troys' reflects the Spanish figurative meaning of the saying *aquí fue Troya* indicating either something good which has disappeared or the confusion and disorder following some particular event.

Lab. 70 (44) *Ficc.* 56

True History (Historia verdadera) see *Lucian of Samosata

'Truth whose mother is history' ('La verdad cuya madre es la historia') see *Don *Quixote*

Tsingtao (or Ch'ing Tao)

A Chinese port on the Yellow Sea.

Lab. 44 (19) *Ficc.* 97

Tule

More correctly, Toluy or Tuluy: the fourth and youngest son of *Genghis Khan, who succeeded him as ruler of Mongolia; the other regions of the Mongol Empire were divided among others of his sons.

Aleph 36 (52) *Ficc.* 42

Tupambaé

A battle which took place in 1904 in northern *Uruguay between the rebel forces of Aparicio *Saravia and the national army.
Aleph 67 (105) *Aleph* 72

Turdera

A rough district in *Lomas de Zamora, in *Buenos Aires Province.
Brodie 52 (63) *Brodie* 15

Turf Club (Club Hípico)

A riding club in the main park of *Buenos Aires (*Palermo).
Aleph 12 (16) *Aleph* 152

Turner, Joseph Mallord William (1775-1851)

A famous English landscape painter. Brodie 33 (37): Turner's distinctive use of light produces a sense of perspective and limitless space which gives an almost abstract impression.
Brodie 33 (37) *Brodie* 92

Tzinacán

A Quiché Maya leader mentioned in Bernal Díaz's *Historia verdadera de la conquista de Nueva España* (1632). According to Díaz, a chief by the name of Zinacán (the spelling 'Tz' adopted by Borges could be part of the Quiché graphic system) lived in Guatemala la Vieja together with another chief, Sacachul. Their houses were rich and beautiful, as became *caciques* (leaders), whose authority extended over the whole province.
Lab. 203 (169) *Aleph* 115

Ugolino della Gherardesca, Count (d. 1289)

A nobleman elected mayor of Pisa in 1284. A supporter alternately of the rival Guelph and Ghibelline factions, Ugolino was engaged to make a peace treaty with Florence but was accused of treason when he appeared to have conceded too much. In 1289 Archbishop *Ruggieri, whose alliance he had sought, had him imprisoned with his two sons and two grandchildren in a tower, where the whole family was left to die of starvation. The story is related in the *Divine Comedy. *Dante places Ugolino among the traitors in one of the most dramatic and pathetic episodes of the poem (*Inferno, Canto 33). He appears buried in ice, together with Archbishop Ruggieri who betrayed his friendship: both are sentenced to eternal damnation in the same circle. Lifting his mouth from

Ruggieri's skull which he is gnawing, Ugolino describes first the ominous dream they all had in the tower, the night before their prison door was nailed for ever, then his anguish as the children around him beg for food, and finally their death agonies and his macabre last hours when, blind with weakness, he cries out their names, feeling for their bodies in the dark. Ugolino's own story ends with the line: *'Poscia più che'l dolor, poté il digiuno'* ('Then fasting had more force than grief'). Borges, in 'El falso problema de Ugolino' (*Ens. dantescos*, 105-11), speculates on the possible ambiguity of this ending, questioning whether it means that Ugolino died not of grief but of hunger, or that he gave in to the torment of hunger and ate the flesh of his dead children. Borges suggests that this uncertainty, Ugolino's 'two possible agonies', is part of Dante's design, for ambiguity is the condition of art.

Lab. 201 (168) *Aleph* 141

'Ultra Auroram et Gangen'

Latin for 'beyond sunrise and the Ganges': an adaption of the line *'usque Auroram et Gangen'* ('as far as sunrise and the Ganges') from the opening lines of *Juvenal's tenth satire. The theme of the satire is that throughout the known world 'only a few know what is really good' and 'can see their way through the fog of deception'. Ambition for power and authority is based on the mistaken belief that they last, while in both the present and the past the lives of the great and powerful have shown that such privileges are fickle and short-lived. Only virtues are worth desiring. Aleph 82 (129): given that *India is frequently used by Borges as a metaphor for the universe, by replacing *'usque'* with *'ultra'* and extending the spatial allusion of the original verse the narrator adds further connotations of remoteness to the land in which the story is set, with implications of infinity.

Aleph 82 (129) *Aleph* 143

Ulysses (Ulises) (Greek: Odysseus)

A mythical hero, one of the Greek heroes at the siege of *Troy and the central character of the *Odyssey*. *Ulysses* is also the title of a novel by James *Joyce, first published in Paris in 1922 and, for reasons of censorship, in the USA and England only in 1937. Borges, who translated the last page (from Molly Bloom's monologue) for the magazine *Proa*, claimed to have been the first Spanish speaker to have 'ventured into Joyce's novel', of which he was not always appreciative. In an early collection of essays since withdrawn from publication (*Inq.*) he wrote that the novel, whose action stretches over the period of a single day, takes many days to read, adding that he was not counting the number of siestas this would induce. At the time Borges wrote 'The Approach to Almotasim' (1935), English readers had difficulty obtaining a copy and had to rely on a study by Joyce's friend Stuart Gilbert, entitled *James Joyce's Ulysses* (1930). In a discussion on the extreme system of causality which operates in literature, Borges mischievously cites as illustration '*el examen del libro expositivo de Gilbert, o en su defecto, de la vertiginosa novela*' ('the examination of Gilbert's explanatory work or, failing that, the vertiginous novel itself ', *Disc.* 91). Aleph 35 (51): *Ulysses* describes the wanderings of the main character, Leopold Bloom, with chapters arranged on the pattern of *Homer's *Odyssey*; but Joyce later removed these headings as too obvious, hoping that the connection would not be entirely missed provided Gilbert kept the Homeric titles in his book. Apart from discussing *The Episodes* under headings – Telemachus, Nestor, Proteus, Calypso and so on – Gilbert devotes a section of his introduction to parallels between *Ulysses* and the *Odyssey*. He points to similarities of style, such as the adaptation of voice to different speakers, a fusion of dialects, accuracy of description (neither work engaging in 'vain tautology'), and he observes that both works hellenise the semitic world.

Lab. 143 (113) *Aleph* 18, Aleph 35 (51) *Ficc.* 41

Unitarianism

A political ideology of the Southern Provinces (later Argentina) which inspired the Wars of Independence from Spain. Its main aim was to develop the supremacy of *Buenos Aires at the expense of the interior provinces, whose erstwhile function, to serve the decaying mining centres of Alto Peru, had led them to political conservatism and economic stagnation. The Unitarian leaders were cosmopolitan and free-thinking. Most of them were educated in Europe and drew inspiration from the latest philosophical and political ideas of their time, which they freely imported to Argentina without considering their adaptability to a different historical and geographical context. In their admiration for everything European, the Unitarians despised the *criollismo* of the *Federals, whose adherence to Hispanic traditionalism they regarded as retrograde, not to say barbaric. The more idealistic Unitarian leaders wished to unite the country under one banner. Developing an economic policy based on trade with Europe, they sought to Europeanise the country and its population, making Buenos Aires, as the gateway to Europe, the country's nerve centre and dominant seat of government. But unlike some Federalist leaders they proposed this policy in the interests of the nation as a whole, so that all the provinces would share in the wealth produced. Under the dictatorship of *Rosas, Unitarians were persecuted, exiled or assassinated, and though their opposition was silenced their policies were implemented by their arch-enemy Rosas, who brought the anarchical provinces under the rule of Buenos Aires. When in 1852 Rosas was defeated, the main remaining problem for the Unitarians was the status of the province of Buenos Aires. The Federation of Provinces did not wish to acknowledge the supremacy of Buenos Aires, and the Federalists of Buenos Aires did not wish to be integrated into the Federation and share the revenue of the port with other less favoured provinces. Fighting continued, but the supremacy of Unitarianism was firmly established in 1880 with the election of the Unitarian candidate, General Roca. Though existing governments may have been brought down by action from the provinces, Unitarianism, as a general policy, has not met any long-lasting challenge.

Universidad del Sur

The National University of Bahía Blanca, in the Southern Province of *Buenos Aires (inexplicably translated in the English version as the 'University of Córdoba').
 Brodie 112

University of Córdoba

The oldest university in Argentina, founded in 1613. Originally a Jesuit school, it later became a theological university with a reputation for conservative ideas. When the Jesuits were expelled from Latin America, the Dominicans took over the teaching. *Brodie* 112: the original actually refers to the *Universidad del Sur.
 Brodie 82 (100)

Unwin

A fictional character; in the context perhaps an allusion to Sir Raymond Unwin (1863-1940), the English architect who laid out the first English garden city.
 Aleph 73 (115) *Aleph* 123

Uppsala

A city in Sweden, north of Stockholm, the seat of the oldest Swedish university, founded in 1477.
 Lab. 27 (3) *Ficc.* 14

Uqbar

Arabic for 'the greatest': an imaginary land situated vaguely in Asia Minor and mysteriously referred to in only one copy of the *Anglo-American Cyclopaedia. See *Tlön.
 Lab. 27 (3) *Ficc.* 13

Ural-Altaic

A general term for a primary linguistic family of the eastern hemisphere. In its morphology there are few relational elements; it is an order of speech based on the use of suffixes attached to unmodified roots. For harmony the vowels of the suffixes are made to blend with the vowel of the root. The verb is not clearly differentiated from the noun. Some of these features are repeated in the southern language of the imaginary planet Tlön.
  Lab. 27 (3) *Ficc.* 14

Urdinarrain

A place in the province of *Entre Ríos, omitted in the English translation.
  Brodie 26

Urmann

From the German *ur*, 'primordial', 'earliest', and *Mann*: a fictitious character related to a saying of Martin *Buber. According to his commentator, Walter Kaufman, Buber was fond of the prefix *ur* because it opened words up to endless possibilities of regression, such as *Urgrossvater*, meaning 'great-grandfather' and *Ururgrossvater* meaning 'great-great-grandfather'. Borges too was fascinated by the theme of infinite regress.
  Lab. 132 (102) *Ficc.* 182

Urn Burial

A treatise by Sir Thomas *Browne (1658), written in the form of a discourse inspired by the discovery of ancient sepulchral urns in Norfolk. Following the discovery of this unsuspected 'subterranean world', Browne praises the custom of commending man's ashes to the anonymity of an urn 'not much unlike the Urns of our nativity', as opposed to the fallacy of monuments and the 'folly of posthumous memory'. The discourse is illustrated with a variety of classical examples and learned references. The writing is elegant, rich, highly rhythmical and poetic. Together with *Bioy Casares, Borges translated into Spanish chapter 5, which was published in the literary magazine *Sur* (January 1944, 15-26). Lab. 43 (18): the term Quevedian refers to the Latinate structure of Browne's sentences and the striking association of images and conceits which make *Urn Burial* an eminent example of baroque style.
  Lab. 43 (18) *Ficc.* 34

Urquiza, Justo José (1801-1870)

President of the Argentinian Confederation between 1854 and 1860. In 1836 Urquiza joined the *Federalists and was placed by Juan Manuel de *Rosas on the Uruguayan border. During the next few years he was engaged in several battles against the *Unitarians, under the command of the Uruguayan leader Fructuoso Rivera. In 1845, at *India Muerta, Urquiza finally defeated Rivera and broke with Rosas, whom he defeated at the battle of Caseros in 1852. Now President, he strove to bring *Buenos Aires, then governed by the staunch *porteño* autonomist Mitre, back into the Confederation. He defeated Mitre in 1859, but Mitre's forces retaliated in 1861 and a treaty was signed. Urquiza retired as Governor of *Entre Ríos, while Mitre, the first President of the Argentine Republic with Buenos Aires as capital, brought about the organisation Urquiza had desired. Aleph 69 (107): it was natural for the *gauchos* of *Entre Ríos to cheer Urquiza, the *caudillo* of the home province. See *Cagancha.

Aleph 69 (107) *Aleph* 75 Brodie 75 (92) *Brodie* 78

Ursprache

From German *ur*, 'promordial' and *Sprache*, 'language' – primaeval, original language: the term used in modern linguistics to indicate a hypothetical prototype of language constructed from the common characteristics of early known forms of speech.

Lab. 32 (8) *Ficc.* 20

Uruguay

The smallest country in South America, named after the river. The name, from Guarani, means either 'the river of shellfish' or 'the water where the Uru birds come from'. Uruguay gained statehood much later than Argentina. In Borges it often stands for a more colonial society, its *gaucho* and *criollo* heritage more intact. Aleph 60 (93): in the nineteenth and early twentieth centuries the frontiers between north-eastern Argentina, Uruguay and southern *Brazil were hot-beds of smuggling. Uruguayan raids into Brazil's province of *Rio Grande do Sul were the immediate provocation of the Paraguayan War (1865-8). See *Banda Oriental.

'Ut nihil non iisdem verbis redderetur auditum' see *Historia Naturalis*

Utrecht

A city in the central Netherlands renowned for its fourteenth-century

cathedral, university, sunken canals and gold and silver museum.
Lab. 40 (16) *Ficc.* 31

Valéry, Paul (1871-1945)

A French writer who entered the world of letters with the publication in
*La *Conque* of his poem 'Narcisse'. Later he published in the **NRF*. Like
*Mallarmé, from whom he derived many of his artistic views, Valéry
regarded poetry as the result of a long and patient intellectual process. In
an essay dedicated to Valéry, Borges referred to the intricacy and
sensitivity of his work by describing him as a 'personification of the
labyrinths of the spirit' (Other Inq. 73). Lab. 64 (38): Valéry's poem 'Le
*Cimetière marin' is an example of the rich imagery used to convey
complex ideas. Among the many themes of the poem is the *contest of
Achilles and the tortoise, the alleged theme of one of the works of Pierre
*Menard and a topic dear to Borges. Lab. 63 (37): Montpellier, where
Valéry resided for a long period and where Menard is said to have
published two of his works, is another possible connection between the
two writers. Lab. 70 (44): Menard's 'quadricular notebooks' and
'typographical symbols' may allude to Valéry's *Cahiers*, though these
were not published until after Borges wrote the story of Pierre Menard.
Some of the possible plots of stories considered by Valéry in his *Cahiers*
and *Oeuvres* resemble themes of stories by Borges (J.A.E. Loubère,
'Borges and the wicked thoughts of Paul Valéry', *Modern Fiction Studies*,
vol.19, 419-31)
Lab. 64 (38) *Ficc.* 47

Varela, Florencio (1807-1848)

An Argentine writer, poet and journalist who joined the cause of the
*Unitarians. In 1829, under the *Federalist dictatorship of *Rosas, he was
forced to flee together with other notable Unitarians to *Montevideo,
where he worked actively to bring down the Buenos Aires government.
He founded the newspaper *Comercio del Plata*, which became the most
powerful organ of the anti-Rosas party, and began writing a new history
of Argentina. Varela moved from youthful poetry to literary criticism. He
particularly admired the Neo-classical writers, but also included in his
newspaper extracts from Dumas and *Hugo, and encouraged the
development of *gaucho* poetry. He was stabbed to death, probably at the
instigation of Rosas.
Brodie 73 (90) *Brodie* 76

Varennes see *Louis XVI

Varus, Publius Quintilius (Varo) (d. 9 AD)

A Roman general whose three legions were wiped out by the Germans under Arminius in 9 AD, the worst defeat suffered by the Romans in Augustus' time. Varus committed suicide after the battle.
  Lab. 178 (146) *Aleph* 88

Vega Carpio, Lope de (1562-1635)

A Spanish playwright and poet of the Golden Age. Lope de Vega led an adventurous life: he sailed in the Armada, worked in the service of various noblemen, had many love affairs and repented of his earlier exploits, becoming a priest in 1614. He then wrote religious poetry until, seduced by an actress, he returned to a worldly life. He was a prolific dramatist whose 501 extant plays (he wrote over 1,500) form the nucleus of the Spanish national theatre. His plays are derived from various sources, but are set mainly within the Spanish historical and religious tradition. They uphold the monarch's role as defender of his people's honour, and also the people's right to be free and respected whatever their social position. (See *El mejor alcalde el rey*, 1602/3 and *Fuenteovejuna*, 1619.)
  Lab. 68 (42) *Ficc.* 53

Venetian Republic (Venecia, republica de)

An independent state with strong maritime and commercial interests which in the tenth century extended its political power to Dalmatia, Greece and beyond. Venice controlled key strategic outposts during the Crusades. It monopolised the overland trade with India and the East, but its mercantile importance declined with the discovery of the Cape route and the opening up of the New World. In 1797 it fell to *Napoleon and remained under foreign domination until 1866. In 1870 it became part of the new kingdom of Italy.
  Lab. 102 (72) *Ficc.* 137

Veracruz

A town on the Gulf of Mexico. Cortés landed there in 1519 and prepared for his march inland, destroying his boats in a dramatic gesture. It became one of the principal ports of call on the West Indies trade route.
  Aleph 15 (19) *Aleph* 156

Viaje del Parnaso

A long burlesque poem by *Cervantes written in 1614 after a work of the same title by the Italian Caporali. It consists of 3000 lines in eight cantos and contains autobiographical elements and flattering references to contemporary mediocre poets. It has seldom been reprinted. Fict. 66 (73) alludes either to Cervantes's known facility for writing or to his satirical remark in the *Viaje* that in Spain 'just about anyone was producing poetry'.

Fict. 66 (73) *Ficc*. 52, Lab. 67 (41) *Ficc*. 78

Vico, Giambattista (1668-1744)

An Italian philosopher and historian who propounded a cyclical theory of the history of mankind. In *Scienza Nuova* (1725), he envisages human societies as passing through periods of growth and decay: from the age of the beasts to the age of the Gods, from the age of heroes to that of men. Lab. 103 (73): in Vico's 'morphology' certain dominant constants of the human mind reappear both in the origin and in the regeneration of societies; they relate to religious customs and to the ambivalence between the animal and the angelic aspects of human nature. *Goethe, who was greatly influenced by Vico, visualised the process of man's spiritual evolution in the light of his prophetic insight. Lab. 148 (118): Vico set out his ideas on the 'Homeric question' in 'The Discovery of the True Homer' in the third book of *Scienza Nuova* (para. 803/90). Remembering *Aristotle's definition of *Homer's characters, Vico describes them as universal symbols, 'imaginative universals', to which the Greeks attached particulars proper to their specific 'genus': 'to Achilles the properties of heroic valour and all the feelings and customs arising from these natural properties'; 'to *Ulysses all the feelings and customs of heroic wisdom'. Homer himself, according to Vico, is but the symbol of different authors to whom, with time, people have attached different characteristics proper to the wandering poet: he was poor, he was blind and he moved from one town square to another singing his epics. We do not know for sure where Homer was born, but we accept that he wrote poems whose geographical settings are far apart; we are told that he never went to Egypt, yet we accept his description of the land and its customs; we do not know when he lived, and explain the differences between the *Iliad* and the *Odyssey* by saying that the first was written in his youth and the second in his maturity, although, in fact, centuries lie between the two works. 'The Greek people were...Homer,' concludes Vico. 'Lost in the crowds of Greek peoples', he 'is justified for having made men of Gods and Gods of men.'

Lab. 103 (73) *Ficc*. 139, Lab. 147 (116) *Aleph* 23

Victor Gollancz

A leading London publishing house founded in 1928 and named after its founder.

Aleph 32 (46) *Ficc*. 37

Victoria

Plaza de la Victoria was the original square and centre of the old city of *Buenos Aires. When Juan de Garay founded the city in 1580, it was here that he planted his 'tree of justice', a wooden pole symbolising punishment and authority. Today it forms part of Plaza de Mayo, the principal square of the city. Aleph 56 (84): the English translation is 'central square'.

Aleph 56

'Vindication of the Cabbala' ('Vindicación de la Cábala')

Borges is here quoting an essay of his own in *Discusión*. See *Cabbala.

Lab. 107 (77) *Ficc*. 145

Vindication of Eternity (Vindicación de la eternidad)

A fictitious title, an amalgamation of two actual works by Borges: *Historia de la eternidad* (1936) and the essay *'Vindication of the Cabbala'.

Lab. 118 (88) *Ficc*. 159, Lab. 129 (98) *Ficc*. 174

Virgen del Carmen

The patroness of the towns and villages in Southern *Buenos Aires Province; the cult of the Virgin Mary dates back to early colonial times. Brodie 70 (85): the English translation does not specify the title of the Virgin.

Brodie 71

Virgil (Virgilio) (70-19 BC)

The national poet of ancient Rome, author of the *Eclogues*, ten short pastoral poems in imitation of Theocritus; the *Georgics*, four long poems describing different aspects of rural life; and the epic *Aeneid*, revealing the divinity of Rome and the Julian family, supposedly descended from Aeneas, to which the Emperor Augustus belonged. Virgil's greatness, beyond his technical and narrative ability, lies in his sensitive insight, his image of cosmic suffering and his compassion towards human weaknesses: 'There are tears for misfortune and mortal sorrows touch the heart' (*Aeneid* 1. 462-3). A visionary note rings through Virgil's poetry, as he depicts an ideal society, stripped of treachery and corruption, returning to the innocence and simplicity of country life and the appreciation of old spiritual and religious values. Lab. 123 (93) and Aleph 72 (111) refer to the fourth Eclogue, famous for its prophetic tone. During the early centuries of Christianity the Sibylline allusion to the birth of a child bringing a new age – '*Iam nova progenies coelo demittitur alto*' ('A new-born child comes down from heaven above') – was believed to refer to the birth of Christ. The true identity of the child alluded to is still debated.

Lab. 123 (93) *Ficc.* 166, Aleph 72 (111) *Aleph* 79

Virgilius evangelizans see **Alexander *Ross**

Viterbo, Beatriz

A character in 'El Aleph', indifferent to the affection of her lover and unworthy of his respect and admiration. The name may be totally fictitious, or it may be meant to represent a woman known personally to Borges; he has both denied and acknowledged the autobiographical aspects of the story. When he wrote it he was in love with its dedicatee, Estela *Canto. The story is generally considered to be a humorous retelling of *Dante's mystical experience, inspired by the vision of Beatrice Portinari. It was first published in 1949, the year in which Borges wrote the introduction to a Spanish translation of the *Divine Comedy*. The treatment of the theme of revelation in the story may be an attempt to exorcise the haunting image of Dante. Borges admired Dante throughout his life and wrote several articles on him. The first was published in 1929, when Beatriz Viterbo is made to die. In one, 'El encuentro en un sueño', Borges remarks on the severity and harshness with which Beatrice speaks to Dante in his vision (*Purgatory*, Canto 32) and adds that, during her life also, she had treated him with dislike and contempt.

Aleph 11 (15) *Aleph* 151

Viviano, Juan Osvaldo

Former president of the *Sociedad de Bibliófilos Argentinos*.
Brodie 31 (33) *Brodie* 87

'Votre siège est fait' see *'Mon siège est fait'

Voyage autour de ma chambre see ***Savoyard**

Waite, Arthur Edward (1857-1942)

English mystical writer whose *Secret Docrine in Israel* (1913), later incorporated into *The Holy Kabbalah* (1930), is considered one of the most authoritative attempts to analyse the symbolism of the *Zohar (see G. Scholem, *Major Trends in Jewish Mysticism*, 1961).

Brodie 23 (26) *Brodie* 26

Wall Street

The headquarters of the main US banks and financial organisations and the site of the New York Stock Exhange.
Lab. 65 (39) *Ficc.* 49

Warnes

An avenue in central *Buenos Aires near Villa Crespo, a commercial district known at one time for its predominantly lower-middle-class Jewish population.
Lab. 167 (135) *Aleph* 63

'Was almost an impiety' ('Era una casi impiedad')

A quotation from the novel *Rebellion in the Backlands* (1902) by Euclides *Da Cunha. The paragraph from which it is taken describes the religious fervour and asceticism of the followers of *Antonio Conselheiro in *Canudos. The author comments that their lack of concern for material things 'carried far enough...led to the loss of high moral qualities...': 'To Antonio Conselheiro...strength of character was something like a form of vanity, it was almost an impiety', for 'it implied a forgetfulness of the marvellous longed-for beyond. His depressed moral sense was only capable of understanding the latter in contrast to sufferings endured' (trans. Samuel Putnam, University of Chicago, 1944, 150).
Lab. 128 (98) *Ficc.* 173

Watson, John H.

An oblique reference to Dr Watson, the chronicler in Conan Doyle's *Adventures of Sherlock Holmes* whose simplicity serves as a foil to the ingenuity of the master sleuth. The first Holmes story, *A Study in Scarlet* (1887), was presented as 'a reprint from the reminiscences of John H. Watson, M.D., late of the Army Medical Department', with illustrations by D.H. Friston. It begins with a brief sketch of Watson's early career. Conan Doyle was himself a doctor in general practice.
Aleph 31 (45) *Ficc.* 35

Weil, Gustave (1808-1889)

A German historian and orientalist, author of the best-known German translation of the *Thousand and One Nights*, published in four volumes in Stuttgart, 1837-41. Fict. 152 (167): this edition is illustrated with 2,000 drawings and ornamental vignettes by F. Gross.

Wheel (rueda)

A universal symbol. Lab. 150 (119): its circular form, without beginning or end, has been used as an emblem of eternity, 'monotony' and the recurrence of events. Lab. 144 (114): in some *Hindu religions, as well as being the weapon of the god Vishnu and the 'mandala' or axis of the earth and centre of energy, the wheel is also the 'kala chakra', symbol of the continuation of life through multiple individual manifestations, and of alternating patterns of destruction and rebirth, marked by the inward and outward breath of Brahma. Brahma is also refered to as 'Wheel'. Lab. 206 (172): a symbol of perfect totality, the wheel can allude to the Divinity present in its creation.

Lab. 144 (114) *Aleph* 20, Lab. 150 (119) *Aleph* 35, Lab. 206 (172) *Aleph* 120

'Where a malignant and a turban'd Turk ...'

A quotation from *Shakespeare's *Othello* (V:ii:356), from the concluding speech in which Othello, before stabbing himself, remembers his past deeds.

Lab. 67 (40) *Ficc.* 51

Whitman, Walt (1819-1892)

An American poet, author of *Leaves of Grass*, which was first published in 1855 and revised and enlarged in several subsequent editions. Borges, who translated and wrote an essay on Whitman, admired the 'effusive and orgiastic' quality of his poetry and his celebration of life (Other Inq. 66). He compared Whitman to Adam, saying that he looked at the world as if for the first time. Lab. 176 (144): in *Soergel's work there are several mentions of Whitman, and he has a separate entry.

Lab. 176 (144) *Aleph* 85

Wilde, Oscar (1854-1900)

An Irish poet and playwright, famous for his wit. Borges said that it is hard for us to imagine the universe without Wilde's epigrams, but that this does not make them less plausible (Other Inq. 81). Borges's long-standing interest in Wilde dates from the age of seven when he translated *The Happy Prince* into Spanish; his admiration is expressed in 'About Oscar Wilde', where he lists sayings by Wilde which have led him to the conclusion that Wilde 'is almost always right'. Some of the aphorisms mentioned are: that music reveals to us an unknown and perhaps real past; that 'all men kill the thing they love'; that to repent of an act is to modify the past; and that there is no man who is not, at each moment, what he has been or what he will be (Other Inq. 80).

Fict. 70 (77) *Ficc.* 82

Wilkins, John (1614-1672)

An English bishop who began his career as chaplain at the court of Charles I. Later he was a strong supporter of Cromwell, who appointed him Master of Trinity College, Cambridge. Deprived of this post at the Restoration, Wilkins nevertheless became bishop of Chester. He was interested in science and became one of the founders, and the first secretary, of the Royal Society. He wrote an unusual work on the possibility of life in the moon and a book entitled *An Essay towards a Real Character and a Philosophical Language* (1668). Lab. 63 (37): in the latter work Wilkins develops the possibility of a universal language based on the principle that reality can be divided into arbitrary categories whose members can be systematically renamed from words with the same roots. Borges speaks of the fascination that this project holds for him because of its totally arbitrary nature and, above all, its attempt to schematise and rationalise an otherwise chaotic and incomprehensible reality (Other Inq. 101). See *Descartes, *Leibniz.

Lab. 63 (37) *Ficc.* 46

'Words, words, words'

Hamlet's answer to Polonius' question, 'What do you read, my lord?' (*Hamlet* II:ii:193).

Brodie 88 (106) *Brodie* 121

Works and Days see *Hesiod

Writings see *De Quincey

Xul Solar (1887-1963)

The pseudonym of Alejandro Schultz, a friend of Borges in his youth. A linguist and painter, Xul illustrated some of Borges's early works: *El tamaño de mi esperanza* (1926), *El idioma de los argentinos* (1928) and *Un modelo para la muerte* (1946), written in collaboration with *Bioy Casares under the pseudonym B. Suarez Lynch. Xul Solar was known for his searching and original mind; he devised a language called 'Neocriollo' to which some aspects of the invented language of Tlön show marked similarities. Certain preoccupations of 'Pierre Menard' also seem to coincide with Xul's. Lab. 33 (8): there is no reference in the English

translation.
Ficc. 21

Yahoos

The fictional beast-like humans who live in the country of the Houyhnhnms (horses) in part 4 of *Swift's *Gulliver's Travels* (1726). Their brutality and total lack of self-restraint contrast with the 'behaviour orderly and rational' of the gentle horses who do not understand the meaning of lying and use the term 'Yahoo's evil' to denote illnesses. Brodie 92 (112): the Yahoos of 'Doctor Brodie's Report' share many of the characteristics of the Yahoos encountered by Gulliver: a savage appearance, an unpronounceable language (described by Swift as a 'roar'), a taste for corrupted flesh, the use of excrement to manifest their disposition towards others (though with *Brodie's Yahoos this indicates respect rather than contempt and anger), the deliberate choice of a deformed leader, and a wild and bellicose nature which often leads them into wars. The Yahoo Queen offering her favours to Brodie recalls the episode when Gulliver was embraced in a 'most foulsome manner' by a female Yahoo while swimming. Upon their return to 'civilisation' both Gulliver and Brodie experience difficulties in readjusting to their fellow men. Brodie draws the same parallel as Gulliver between his fellow men and these savages, but their reactions are mirror images of each other: Gulliver feels revulsion at the human image and at his own reflection, while the Scottish missionary, considering the similiarities between Yahoos and humans, seeks to 'redeem' that 'barbarous nation' in the eyes of the King whose protection for them he seeks. Borges's ambiguous conclusion is, like Swift's, that 'they stand for civilisation much as we ourselves do'.
Brodie 92 (112) *Brodie* 140

Yauk

In the *Koran, the name of an idol mentioned in chapter 71: 21 (Noah). The context reads: 'And Noah said: "Lord, my people disobey me and follow those whose wealth and offspring will only hasten their perdition. They have devised an outrageous plot, and said to each other: 'Do not renounce your gods. Do not forsake Wad or Sowa or Yaghuth or Ya'uq or Nasr.' They have led numerous men astray. You surely drive the wrongdoers to further error." And because of their sins they were overwhelmed by the Flood and cast into the Fire. They found none to help them beside Allah.'
Lab. 196 (162) *Aleph* 111

Yeats, William Butler (1865-1939)

An Irish poet, actively involved in *Ireland's nationalistic politics. In his poems and plays Yeats strove to create a specifically Irish literature, basing much of his work on themes taken from *Celtic mythology, episodes of the Irish insurrection and the lives of eminent patriotic figures like *Parnell. Yeats's poetry ranges from the popular and the love lyric to the more esoteric and conceptual texts of *The Wind among the Reeds* (1899) and the satirical invective of *Responsibilities* (1914). He experimented also with automatic writing. A personal 'system of symbolisms', as he described it, became more evident in his later poems 'Byzantium' and *The *Tower* (1928), in which sensual images alternate with historic allusions and irony. Here and in his last works Yeats opposes the power of the intellect to the failing physical strength of old age. Lab. 102: Yeats is presented as the prototype of the Irish poet, in opposition to the English Shakespeare, mentioned in the same context. The theme of betrayal and the ensuing desire to confess and make amends are well within the spirit of the lines spoken by Yeats on behalf of the Irish who repudiated Parnell: 'Come, fix upon me that accusing eye. / I thirst for accusation' ('Parnell's Funeral', *A Full Moon in March*). Equally the earlier lines from the same poem, 'Nor did we play a part / Upon a painted stage when we devoured his heart', recalls not only the theatrical setting of Fergus *Kilpatrick's execution, but also the role-playing theme which runs through 'Theme of the Traitor and the Hero'. The epigraph in Aleph 54 (81) is taken from the second part of the poem, 'A Woman Young and Old'. Its title is 'Before the World Was Made' and the full text reads: 'If I make the lashes dark / And the eyes more bright? And the lips more scarlet? Or ask if all be right / From mirror after mirrror, / No vanity's displayed: / I'm looking for the face I had / Before the world was made.'

Lab. 102 (72) *Ficc.* 137, Aleph 54 (81) *Aleph* 53

Yellow fever (Fiebre amarilla)

Yellow fever first appeared in *Buenos Aires in 1870, reaching epidemic proportions by the summer of 1871 and claiming altogether more than 13,000 victims. The port areas were at first the most affected; eventually as many as a hundred a day were dying throughout the city, which became deserted. Brodie 73 (90): Doctor Bernardo Juregui, who died 'practising his profession during the yellow-fever epidemic' may be a reference to the 'few courageous doctors and priests...at their posts' when 'Church services were suspended and government offices were closed' mentioned by R.B. Scobie (*Buenos Aires: From Plaza to Suburb*, 1974, 124). See *Chacarita, *Flores.

Brodie 73 (90) *Brodie* 77

Yemen

A kingdom in the south-west Arabian peninsula on the Red Sea, overrun in the seventh century by Islam and subsequently part of the Arab Caliphate. Between 716 and 756 Yemenite tribes vied with their Syrian rivals for the appointment of their leader as Arab governor in *Al-Andalus.

Lab. 183 (151) *Aleph* 96

Yiddish (Idisch)

The language spoken by the *Ashkenazi Jews, consisting mainly of a mixture of Hebrew or Aramaic and Old German. It is used mainly as a secular language in contrast to Hebrew, which until recently was considered sacred. See *Yidische Zaitung.

Lab. 169 (136) *Aleph* 65

Yidische Zaitung

The first daily Argentine Jewish newspaper, published from 1914 onwards. Its publication illustrates the strength of a movement prevalent in Argentina at the time when Borges wrote 'Death and the Compass', favouring secular Jewish culture expressed in *Yiddish.

Lab. 107 (78) *Ficc.* 144

Yrigoyen, Hipólito (1852-1933)

The leader of the Radical movement and twice President of Argentina, in 1916-22 and 1928-30. Yrigoyen, who came to power after the first Argentinian election to employ secret ballots, was also the first president who did not directly represent the interests of the landowning oligarchy.

Fict. 154 (169) *Ficc.* 190

Yu Tsun

One of the many leading characters in the Chinese novel *Hung Lu Meng* by Ts'ao Chan.

Lab. 44 (119) *Ficc.* 97

Yunnan

A province in south-east China, by the Yangtze River.

Lab. 47 (22) *Ficc.* 102

Zahir

Arabic for 'visible', 'manifest': one of the attributes of *Allah mentioned in the *Koran (57:3): 'He is the First and the Last, the Manifest (*zahir*), and the Hidden (*batim*).' The dichotomy between *zahir* and *batim* is reflected in the two ways of interpreting the Koran: whereas *zahir* is based upon a purely literal reading of the text, *batim* seeks more hidden or esoteric meanings.

Lab. 189 (156) *Aleph* 103

Zangwill, Israel (1864-1926)

An English novelist and poet, an early pioneer of Zionism. Aleph 74 (116) refers to Zangwill's *The Big Bow Mystery* (1891), a work important in the development of the detective story because it was the first 'to be based solidly and solely on the concept of the locked room' (E.F. Bleiler, *Three Victorian Detective Novels*, NY 1978, xv). A crime is committed in a place where all the exits are locked from the outside and there is no criminal inside; the solution is that the murderer is the person who discovers or pretends to discover the crime. *Poe's classic 'The Murders in the Rue Morgue' had already used a similar device.

Aleph 74 (116) *Aleph* 124

Zarathustra

In Greek, Zoroaster: a figure who probably lived in the sixth century BC in eastern *Persia. Very little is known about him. He was the consolidator of a religious doctrine now called Zoroastrianism, whose essential feature was dualism, expressed in a belief in two predominant spirits, Ormazd, the spirit of good and light, and Ahriman, the spirit of evil and darkness. The world was created out of the struggle between these two opposing powers; the conflict is reflected in man, who however is endowed with the freedom to choose between them. Zoroastrianism is a life-affirming religion, based on the ultimate triumph of good after the life on earth of a Saviour born of a virgin, for which it is thought to have influenced Apocalyptic Judaism and the New Testament. *Nietzsche, in his poem 'Thus spake Zarathustra', talks admiringly of 'that Dionysian monster, whose fundamental message is that manhood is a state to be surpassed'. Lab. 176 (144) refers to part 4 of the poem in which Zarathustra speaks of having overcome his last sin, pity. In a highly poetical rendering of an encounter with a soothsayer, who had come to seduce Zarathustra to feel pity for the *higher man* (italics in original), Zarathustra relates the various stages through which he overcame this temptation. Though pity for the suffering of the world hangs heavily upon a sensitive man, yet he must have courage to overcome it for 'courage is the best killer; courage kills even pity. But pity is the deepest abyss.' The English translation of

'Deutsches Requiem' slightly alters the correct emphasis given by Borges in the original. See *Parsis.

Lab. 176 (144) *Aleph* 85

Zeltnergasse

A well-known street in the centre of *Prague near the main square, Wenceslas Square. Kafka lived there with his family; the deep mark left on his mind by the years spent in the Zeltnergasse is recorded in his diary.

Lab. 118 (88) *Ficc.* 159

Zohar

Hebrew, meaning 'splendour', 'the book of splendour': a mystical thirteenth-century work written in Castile in the Aramaic dialect and thought to be by Moses de Leon. It is a prime example of the literary form of *Cabbalistic pseudepigraphy, its author pretending that it was the work of an apocryphal writer, hinting at mystical origins and permitting the persons in his dialogues a profusion of invented book titles and citations. Though considered the canonical book of the Cabbalists, the *Zohar* is not in any sense a systematic exposition of Cabbalistic doctrine but a work of mystical allegorisation in which the most seemingly insignificant verses of Scripture acquire unexpected depths of meaning. The style of the *Zohar* has been described by G. Scholem as 'tortuous and abstruse, lightened up occasionally by a magnificent clarity of symbolic expression'. Lab. 154 (123) refers to *Zohar* I, 240b, where the process of creation is explained as having taken place on two planes, one above and one below; the lower occurrence, the world of visible creation, corresponds to the higher world of the sephirot or Divine Emanations. This duality of creation is taken as a Cabbalistic explanation of the opening letter of Genesis, *Beth, the numerical value of which is two.

Lab. 154 (123) *Aleph* 40

Zorndorf

A village in north-east Germany, since 1945 in Poland. Lab. 173 (141): the Prussian victory referred to took place on 25 August 1758 during the war with Russia. See *Namur.

Lab. 173 (141) *Aleph* 81

Zotenberg

A nineteenth-century orientalist and translator of Arabic texts. His work, published in Paris in 1899, was considered one of the most important commentaries on the *Thousand and One Nights*, not only for its useful notes but because it put an end to conjectures about the source of Galland's unidentified tales (see Burton, 1885 edn., vol.6, 357). Lab. 189 (156): the assertion here attributed to him is of course apocryphal.

Lab. 189 (156) *Aleph* 103

Zuhair

An Arabic poet of the *Age of Innocence, or Jahilla (the period before Islam), considered one of the great poets of antiquity. His most famous poem is included in the Mu'allaqat. See *Mohalaca.

Lab. 185 (153) *Aleph* 98

Zumacos

Regulars in the Uruguayan army.

Aleph 73

Zunz

A fictional name, possibly a tribute to Leopold Zunz (1794-1886), one of the greatest Jewish scholars of the nineteenth century whose work on *Hasidism would have been familiar to Borges.

Lab. 164 (132) *Aleph* 59

Zur Linde

A fictional name creating a German atmosphere. The *Lindenbaum* (lime tree) which appears in many traditional and patriotic songs is emblematic of the German spirit.

Lab. 173 (141) *Aleph* 81

Biographical Summary

This select biography focusses on Borges's early years, before the publication of *Ficciones* and *El Aleph*. For more details see María Esther Vázquez, *Borges, sus días y su tiempo*, Javier Vergara, Buenos Aires, 1984. Where English titles are given in italics this indicates that the work has been translated into English.

1899 August 24: Jorge Luis Borges born to Jorge Guillermo Borges and Leonor Acevedo Haedo; paternal grandparents Francisco Borges Lafinur and Frances Haslam Arnet, maternal grandparents Leonor Suárez Haedo and Isidoro Acevedo Laprida. Brought up bilingually in Spanish and English through the influence of Frances Haslam.

1901 Family moves to a large house in Palermo.

1906 Writes *La visera fatal* (The Fatal Helmet), an old-fashioned romance in the style of Cervantes. Compiles an English handbook on Greek mythology.

1908 Translation of Oscar Wilde's *The Happy Prince* published in the daily newspaper *El País*; it is signed 'Jorge Borges' and assumed to have been by his father. Begins attendance at a state primary school dressed in an Eton collar and tie and wearing spectacles. Summer spent in Adrogué.

1914-18 Travels with his family to Europe, settling in Geneva where he attends the College of Geneva (founded by Calvin). Learns Latin and French and teaches himself German by translating Heine. Reads *Der Golem* (*The Golem*) by Gustav Meyrink. Establishes friendship with Maurice Abramowicz, who introduces him to Rimbaud and French symbolism.

1918 Graduates. Family moves to Lugano after the death of his maternal grandmother. Rediscovers his Argentine origins and reads gauchesque literature.

1919 Travels with his family to Spain, settling first in Barcelona and later in Majorca, where he composes poems in free verse in praise of the Russian Revolution, *Los salmos rojos* (The Red Psalms) or *Los ritmos rojos* (The Red Rhythms, both titles given by Borges who never allowed these early writings to be re-issued). *Los naipes del tahur* (The Sharper's Cards) a collection of short stories, also dates from 1919. Travels to Seville and Madrid, where he participates in the avant-garde literary movement called *Ultraism*. Reads the Spanish classics and translates German expressionist poetry into Spanish. Establishes friendship with the writers Guillermo de la Torre (later to become his brother-in-law), Cansino Assens and Gómez de la Serna, whom he ackowledges as major influences upon his work.

1921 Returns to Buenos Aires. Founds the short-lived 'mural magazine' *Prisma*. Publishes an 'Ultraist Manifesto'.

1922 Founds the literary magazine *Proa*, in collaboration with his father's philosopher friend Macedonio Fernandez.

1923 Publishes *Fervor de Buenos Aires* (Admiration of Buenos Aires), his first book of poems. Travels to Europe, returning in 1924.

1925 Publishes a second book of poems, *Luna de enfrente* (Moon Across the Way), and *Inquisiciones* (Inquisitions), a collection of essays which he later rejects, refusing permission for a re-issue. Meets the influential writer and publisher Victoria Ocampo.

1926 Publishes *El tamaño de mi esperanza* (The Dimension of my Hope), a second essay collection, which he later also repudiates.

1928 Publishes *El idioma de los argentinos* (The Language of the Argentines).

1929 Publishes a third poetry collection, *Cuaderno de San Martín* (San Martín Copybook), which wins the Second Municipal Prize.

1930 Publishes *Evaristo Carriego*, a monograph of a minor *porteño* poet. Meets Bioy Casares with whom he later collaborates under the joint pseudonym of H. Bustos Domecq.

1932 Publishes *Discusión* (Discussion), a third essay collection.

1935 Publishes *Historia universal de la infamia* (A Universal History of Infamy).

1936 Publishes *Historia de la eternidad* (A History of Eternity). Translates *Orlando*, and the following year *A Room of One's Own*, by Virginia Wolf.

1938 Contributes literary reviews to *El Hogar* (Home), a fashionable society magazine. Takes a minor clerical job as first assistant at the Miguel Cané branch of the Municipal Library in a poor district of Buenos Aires, where he stays for about 'nine years of solid unhappiness'. Deeply affected by the death of his father after a long illness. On Christmas Eve brushes his head against a freshly painted open window; his wound becomes poisonous and he suffers the agonies of septicemia for about a month. Writes his first short story, 'Pierre Menard, Author of the *Quixote*', to be followed by his best fiction. Eyesight begins to fail.

1940 Publishes *An Anthology of Fantastic Literature*, in collaboration with Bioy Casares and his wife Silvina Ocampo.

1941 Publishes a collection of 'fictions' *El jardín de senderos que se bifurcan* (The Garden of the Forking Paths), which fails to earn mention in that year's National Literature Prize.

1942 In protest his friends and colleagues from Spain and Latin America contribute to a special issue of *Sur*, 'Desagravio a Borges' (Amends to Borges).

Publishes the first work written in collaboration with Bioy Casares, the detective stories *Seis problemas para Don Isidro Parodi* (Six Problems for Isidro Parodi).

1943 Translates and writes a prologue to Kafka's *Metamorphosis* and other stories.

1944 Publishes *Ficciones* (Fictions), an expanded version of *El jardín de senderos que se bifurcan*. Awarded a new literary prize by SADE (Society of Argentine Writers).

1946 For signing anti-Peronist declarations is dismissed from his post as librarian. Named Inspector of Poultry and Rabbits in Municipal Markets. Resigns and begins his teaching career with lecture tours in Argentina and Uruguay.

1947 Publishes *El Aleph* (The Aleph), which with *Ficciones* is considered his best work.

1950 Named President of the anti-Peronist SADE.

1952 Publishes the essay collection *Otras inquisiciones* (*Other Inquisitions*).

1955 On Perón's fall from power appointed by the new government Director of the National Library. Becomes a member of the Argentine Academy of Letters.

1956 Place in world literature assured. EMECÉ begins publication of Complete Works (with the omissions noted above). Some translated into French and later into other languages. Given the Chair of English and American Literature at the University of Buenos Aires. Awarded an Honorary Doctorate at the University of Cuyo, in Mendoza, Argentina.

1958 Because of increasing blindness, not allowed to read or write. Composes poetry and short prose pieces which he memorises and later dictates.

1960 Publishes *El hacedor* (*Dreamtigers*), a miscellany of prose and poetry.

1961 Awarded the first Formentor prize in Majorca, shared with Samuel Beckett: the beginning of international fame. Publishes *Antología personal* (*Personal Anthology*). Invited to lecture by the University of Texas. Travels for six months to the USA accompanied by his mother.

1962 Designated by the French government Commander of Arts and Letters. English and American editions of *Fictions* and *Labyrinths*.

1963 Travels to Europe accompanied by his mother.

1964 *L'Herne* dedicates an entire volume to Borges, with contributions by leading writers and critics.

1967 September 21: marries Elsa Astete Millán, a friend from his youth. Invited by Harvard University to give the Charles Eliot Norton lectures.

1968 After a short stay in Buenos Aires, travels to Chile and then to Europe and Israel, where he meets the Cabbalist scholar Gershom Scholem.

1969 Invited to lecture by the University of Oklahoma. Publishes *Elogio a la sombra* (*In Praise of Darkness*). Translates Walt Whitman's *Leaves of Grass*.

1970 Publishes new story collection *El informe de Brodie* (*Doctor Brodie's Report*). Divorces. Returns to his mother's home.

1971 Receives honorary doctorate from Oxford University. Invited by the ICA in London to give four lectures. Publishes short story 'El congreso' (The Congress).

1972 Publishes *El oro de los tigres* (*The Gold of the Tigers*). Many honorary doctorates awarded.

1973 Resigns as Director of the National Library of Buenos Aires.

1975 Publishes last short-story collection *El libro de arena* (*The Book of Sand*), the poems *La rosa profunda* (The Unending Rose) and *Prólogos*, a collection of prologues written between 1923 and 1974. His mother Doña Leonor Acevedo de Borges dies aged 99.

1976 Publishes poetry collection *La moneda de hierro* (The Iron Coin).

1981 Publishes a further book of poems *La cifra* (The Cypher).

1983 Decorated with the Order of the Légion d'Honneur.

1986 Shortly after his marriage to María Kodama, on June 14, in Geneva, Borges dies.